Why Is English Like That?

Historical Answers to Hard ELT Questions

Norbert Schmitt
Richard Marsden

University of Nottingham

Michigan Teacher Training

THE UNIVERSITY OF MICHIGAN PRESS

Dedication

This book is dedicated to Kenneth Schaefer, whose enthusiasm for English and its history inspired it.

Copyright© by the University of Michigan 2006
Copyright© Vocabulary Test [pp. 106–110] Norbert Schmitt 2000
All rights reserved
ISBN 0-472-03134-1
(978-0-472-03134-4)
Published in the United States of America
The University of Michigan Press
Manufactured in the United States of America

♾ Printed on acid-free paper

2017   2016   2015   6   5   4

Acknowledgments

Grateful acknowledgment is given to the following authors, publishers, and individuals for permission to reprint their materials or previously published materials.

Blackwell Publishing for "Doublets in Modern English" from *A History of English Words* by G. Hughes. Copyright © 2000. Reprinted with permission of Blackwell Publishing Ltd.

Cambridge University Press for material from *Cambridge Encyclopedia of the English Language* by David Crystal. Copyright © 1999. Reprinted with the permission of Cambridge University Press.

Cambridge University Press for material from *English as a Global Language, 2nd Edition,* by David Crystal. Copyright © 2003. Reprinted with the permission of Cambridge University Press.

Cambridge University Press for material from *Learning Vocabulary in Another Language* by I. S. P. Nation. Copyright © 2001. Reprinted with the permission of Cambridge University Press.

Cambridge University Press for material from *Vocabulary in Language Teaching* by Norbert Schmitt. Copyright © 2000. Reprinted with the permission of Cambridge University Press.

HarperCollins UK for material from *The Gift of Tongues* by M. Schlauch. Copyright © 1943.

Hodder Education for material from *An Introduction to Applied Linguistics,* edited by Norbert Schmitt. Copyright © 2002 Arnold. Reproduced by permission of Edward Arnold.

Tom McArthur for "McArthur's Circle of World English" from "The English Languages?" in *English Today.* Copyright © 1987.

Penguin Group (UK) for "English Use around the World" from *The English Language* by David Crystal, maps by Philip Patinall (Penguin Books, 1988). Copyright © David Crystal, 1998. Reprinted by permission of Penguin Group (UK).

Thomson Learning for permission to reproduce material from *Teaching & Learning Vocabulary* by I.S.P. Nation, copyright © 1990 Heinle, a division of Thomson Learning. All rights reserved.

Every effort has been made to contact the copyright holders for permission to reprint borrowed material. We regret any oversights that may have occurred and will rectify them in future printings of this book.

Preface

Perhaps you have found yourself confronted by awkward questions from your students such as:

- Why is *night* spelled with *gh*?
- Why do some people say that we can't end sentences with a preposition?
- Why does English have so many synonyms like *intelligent, clever, astute,* and *bright*?

You may have found yourself at a loss for satisfactory responses, and you may have had to provide vague answers, such as "That's just the way it is." Luckily, there are historical answers to these questions. This book will give you confidence in responding to students by showing you how the English we use today has developed from the English of past times.

The book is designed to give you a brief and accessible account of the history of English without assuming any prior knowledge of the subject. It will outline the historical events that shaped English; explain how its grammar, vocabulary, spelling, and pronunciation developed over time; and highlight the quirks and exceptions in English that can be explained on a historical basis. We believe students long for good explanations for these quirks and exceptions and appreciate it if you can give them concrete reasons for their existence. Pedagogically, the explanations are not guaranteed to help your students learn English any faster, but at a minimum, we feel that they can help alleviate their frustration with some of the seemingly unreasonable aspects of the language and, as a result, maintain their motivation and interest. At best, the explanations may help your students to a more informed understanding of the English system and may actually facilitate their learning.

To help you incorporate some of this knowledge into your classroom activities, the book contains reproducible exercises. Some of these, such as the ones on vocabulary, can be used as actual teaching exercises where the students can learn new words and practice old ones. Similarly, the grammar exercises focus directly on irregular verb and noun forms your students need to know.

Other exercises, such as those on the place of English in the world today, are designed to increase your students' interest in language and linguistics in general.

The book is written with English language teachers in mind, and the exercises are thus designed to be used with ESL/EFL students. However, we feel that they may also be used fruitfully with teachers in training (both L1 and L2), as well as with advanced ESL learners as part of a content-based instruction course.

We have tried to avoid the excessive use of referencing and linguistic jargon, but the rendering of the sound system of English poses special problems. The main difficulty lies in the fact that the Roman alphabet is not very well matched to the sounds of English, especially vowels. An example is the vowel *a*, which is pronounced differently in each of these words: *father, hat,* and *plate.* A phonemic alphabet, such as those used in dictionaries to indicate pronunciation, avoids this problem by rendering sounds into symbols on a one-to-one basis. When necessary, therefore, we use a phonemic alphabet based on learner dictionaries to illustrate the development of the pronunciation of English over the ages. For your convenience, a guide to the alphabet we use is given on p. x. However, to make the book as accessible and as nontechnical as possible, we often use rhymes to indicate pronunciation; for example, until about 1700 *swan* rhymed with *man,* not *con.*

Finally, we find the history of English a continually fascinating area and hope that we have presented the information in this book in a manner that both you and your students will find stimulating and engaging.

Norbert Schmitt
Richard Marsden
2006

Contents

Guide to the Phonetic Symbols
Used in This Book

Note that symbols between slashes indicate a sound; for example, /b/ indicates the sound that the letter *b* represents.

CONSONANTS

Sound	Examples
/p/	pair, cup
/b/	bad, crab
/t/	tall, hit
/d/	dark, head
/k/	cab, lack
/g/	good, tag
/f/	fine, wife
/v/	very, above
/θ/	thing, both
/ð/	this, father
/s/	saw, house
/z/	zap, goes
/ʃ/	shape, push
/ʒ/	pleasure, beige
/h/	her, ahead
/x/	loch
/tʃ/	cherry, match
/ʤ/	judge, injury
/m/	man, team
/n/	nail, tan
/ŋ/	ring, singer
/l/	let, tall
/r/	right, scary
/w/	wet, away
/j/	you, soya

VOWELS

Sounds	Examples
/ɪ/	bit, pin
/ɛ/	bet, pen
/æ/	bat, ran
/ɒ/	pot, often
/ʌ/	shut, enough
/ʊ/	book, put
/ə/	about, dogma
/i/	pretty
/i:/	bean, see
/u/	influence
/u:/	soon, clue
/ɑ:/	father, barn
/ɔ:/	caught, law
/ɜ:/	bird, fur

DIPHTHONGS/GLIDES

Sounds	Examples
/aɪ/	right, buy
/ɛɪ/	wait, rain
/ɔɪ/	toy, voice
/əʊ/	go, although
/aʊ/	mouse, allow
/ʊə/	poor
/ɛə/	hair
/ɪə/	hear

1

WHY ENGLISH?

Why Are We Teaching English and Not Some Other Language?

- How important is English in the world today?
- Why did English become a major world language?
- Is English any "better" than other languages?

The Importance of English in the World Today

There are approximately 4,000–6,000 languages in the world today, so why is this book written in English, and why is it written specifically for teachers of English as a Second/Foreign Language (ESL/EFL)? One good answer to those questions is that English is simply the most influential language in the world today. But just how far does this influence extend?

English is closer to being a world language than any other language in history has ever been. English is estimated to have had only 4 million speakers in 1500, 6 million in 1600, 8.5 million in 1700, between 20 and 40 million in 1800, and between 116 and 123 million in 1900.[1] By 1999, it is estimated that there were about 322 million native speakers of English. But this number is not extremely impressive when Chinese was estimated to be at 885 million.[2] What points to the importance of English is the number of speakers learning and using it as a second language, which is at least 400 million. In China alone, there are probably as many people learning it as a second language as there are people living in the United States (around 290 million). In Europe, one agency reported that 42 percent of European citizens claimed to have a conversational understanding of English in 1995,[3] while a study of European television viewers found that 70 percent felt able to understand television news or read a newspaper in English.[4] Globally, perhaps one-third of the world's population is regularly exposed to English.[5] Some estimates have about 1 billion people using it every day. These

1

numbers are huge, and so it is unsurprising that English is fast becoming the standard language of communications and technology.

A number of items suggesting the importance of English in the world today are listed below. In many cases, the most current information available dates from the 1990s, or even the 1980s. Moreover, most of the information is impossible to determine precisely, and so the figures are only estimates. Still, one message comes through very clearly: English is involved in a large part of the communication taking place in the world every day.

- English is the principal language of intercontinental telephone communication.[6]
- Perhaps as much as 75 percent of mail around the world is written in English.[7]
- About half of the world's newspapers are published in English.[8]
- Twenty-eight percent of the books published annually are in English.[9]
- The majority of academic journals with international readership are in English.[10]
- The majority, and perhaps even more than two-thirds, of international scientists write in English. For example, nearly two-thirds of the publications produced by French scientists were in English in the early 1980s. Likewise, English was the major working language for German academics surveyed in the early 1990s. In 13 out of 20 disciplines, at least 40 percent claimed to work in English, and for psychology, biology, chemistry, and physics, the figures ranged from 81 to 98 percent. One can only suspect that these figures are even higher today.[11]
- Ninety percent of Internet hosts were based in English-speaking countries in the mid-1990s.[12]
- Close to 80 percent of the world's computer data available on the Internet was stored in English in the 1990s, which is not surprising considering that English-speaking countries took the lead in developing the Internet. However, as other countries rapidly increase their use of the Internet, the use of non-English languages is rising. Still, English sites on the Internet continue to attract a disproportionately high percentage of hits.[13]
- Forty percent of the people online on the Internet speak English (228 million people), though this may eventually drop to around 30 percent.[14] The next highest language is Chinese at 9.8 percent (55.5 million people).[15]
- The most influential software company, Microsoft, is based in an English-speaking country: the United States.

- Most of the largest advertising agencies are based in the United States.[16]
- Eighty-five percent of world institutions use English as their language, or as one of their languages;[17] for example, it is the official language of the Olympics and the World Council of Churches.
- The official international language for both aviation and maritime use is English.
- English is the dominant language of international trade, with about 40 percent of the business deals made in English.[18]
- The most influential movies and modern music come from English-speaking countries.
- In 1994, 80 percent of all feature films that were shown in cinemas worldwide were in English.[19]
- About 85 percent of the global movie market was controlled by the United States in 1995.[20]
- The fact that large numbers of people are learning English as a second language is reflected by the large number of people taking the TOEFL® Test (about 689,000 people in 215 countries)[21] and University of Cambridge Local Examinations Syndicate (UCLES) tests (more than 1 million people in more than 130 countries)[22] every year.

Clearly, these points do not mean that English is important for everyone in the world; actually about two-thirds of the world's population do not use it. But it is unmistakable that English is the language of a large part of the world's knowledge, especially in areas of science and technology.

It has often been suggested that English is now becoming (or some say has already become), the world language. Whether or not one is quite ready to accept this, there does seem to be a need for some sort of international language. Business, science, and academia are now global in nature. In the age of instant international communications and quick air travel, speakers of different languages now come together on a regular basis and need to communicate. Numerous multinational organizations (e.g., the United Nations [with more than 190 nations] at a global level and the European Union [25 nations] at a regional level) and multinational businesses (such as Sony and Volkswagen) need a *lingua franca* (common language) to function. Translating between languages is possible in these organizations and businesses, but it rapidly becomes cumbersome as the number of languages increases, so having a lingua franca is the most efficient and expedient solution to the multilingual communication problem.

English clearly serves the role of a lingua franca in a wide variety of cases, but is it fair to label it *the* world language? It depends on how we define the term. According to David Crystal, to be a truly global language, the language would have to have a special role in every country.[23] That special role could be the simple fact that the language is the mother tongue of the majority of the people in a country, as English is in the United Kingdom or Australia. It could be as an official language of a country, as English is in Singapore, Nigeria, and India. The role could also be as a language that has lost its official status but that still plays an important role in the community, such as in Kenya and Tanzania. Table 1 shows the 75 territories where English has special status according to these criteria and gives the estimated English usage. Note that this table is to some extent a reflection of historical/political structures and does not always accurately reflect the realities of how English is used in the modern world. For example, English is used much more extensively in Scandinavian countries not on the list than in some countries on the list such as Bhutan and Rwanda. Still, with this caveat in mind, the list is a powerful indication of the reach of English in today's world.

Not shown in the table, but equally important, are the countries where English is increasingly being taught as a foreign language (e.g., Brazil, China, Indonesia, and Russia), where there are very large populations with the potential to become English speakers. English is the most frequently taught second language around the world, in more than 100 countries, and in cases where more than one second language is taught, it is usually the dominant one.[24] Obviously, adding these "non-special-role" second language learners and users to the list would greatly increase the total number of English speakers illustrated at the end of the table.

TABLE 1
TERRITORIES WHERE ENGLISH HOLDS A SPECIAL ROLE

Territory	Population (2001)	Usage estimate
American Samoa	67,000	L1 2,000
		L2 65,000
Antigua & Barbuda (c)[a]	68,000	L1 66,000
		L2 2,000
Aruba	70,000	L1 9,000
		L2 35,000
Australia	18,972,000	L1 14,987,000
		L2 3,500,000
Bahamas (c)	298,000	L1 260,000
		L2 28,000
Bangladesh	131,270,000	L2 3,500,000
Barbados (c)	275,000	L1 262,000
		L2 13,000
Belize (c)	256,000	L1 190,000
		L2 56,000
Bermuda	63,000	L1 63,000
Botswana	1,586,000	L2 630,000
British Virgin Islands (c)	20,800	L1 20,000
Brunei	344,000	L1 10,000
		L2 134,000
Cameroon (c)	15,900,000	L2 7,700,000
Canada	31,600,000	L1 20,000,000
		L2 7,000,000
Cayman Islands (c)	36,000	L1 36,000
Cook Islands	21,000	L1 1,000
		L2 3,000
Dominica (c)	70,000	L1 3,000
		L2 60,000
Fiji	850,000	L1 6,000
		L2 170,000
Gambia (c)	1,411,000	L2 40,000
Ghana (c)	19,894,000	L2 1,400,000
Gibraltar	31,000	L1 28,000
		L2 2,000
Grenada (c)	100,000	L1 100,000

TABLE 1 (CONTINUED)
TERRITORIES WHERE ENGLISH HOLDS A SPECIAL ROLE

Territory	Population (2001)	Usage estimate
Guam	160,000	L1 58,000
		L2 100,000
Guyana (c)	700,000	L1 650,000
		L2 30,000
Hong Kong	7,210,000	L1 150,000
		L2 2,200,000
India	1,029,991,000	L1 350,000
		L2 200,000,000
Ireland	3,850,000	L1 3,750,000
		L2 100,000
Jamaica (c)	2,665,000	L1 2,600,000
		L2 50,000
Kenya	30,766,000	L2 2,700,000
Kiribati	94,000	L2 23,000
Lesotho	2,177,000	L2 500,000
Liberia (c)	3,226,000	L1 600,000
		L2 2,500,000
Malawi	10,548,000	L2 540,000
Malaysia	22,230,000	L1 380,000
		L2 7,000,000
Malta	395,000	L1 13,000
		L2 95,000
Marshall Islands	70,000	L2 60,000
Mauritius	1,190,000	L1 2,000
		L2 200,000
Micronesia	135,000	L1 4,000
		L2 60,000
Montserrat (c)	4,000	L1 4,000
Namibia	1,800,000	L1 14,000
		L2 300,000
Nauru	12,000	L1 900
		L2 10,700
Nepal	25,300,000	L2 7,000,000
New Zealand	3,864,000	L1 3,700,000
		L2 150,000

TABLE 1 (CONTINUED)
TERRITORIES WHERE ENGLISH HOLDS A SPECIAL ROLE

Territory	Population (2001)	Usage estimate
Nigeria (c)	126,636,000	L2 60,000,000
Northern Marianas (c)	75,000	L1 5,000
		L2 65,000
Pakistan	145,000,000	L2 17,000,000
Palau	19,000	L1 500
		L2 18,000
Papua New Guinea (c)	5,000,000	L1 150,000
		L2 3,000,000
Philippines	83,000,000	L1 20,000
		L2 40,000,000
Puerto Rico	3,937,000	L1 100,000
		L2 1,840,000
Rwanda	7,313,000	L2 20,000
St. Kitts & Nevis (c)	43,000	L1 43,000
St. Lucia (c)	158,000	L1 31,000
		L2 40,000
St. Vincent & Grenadines (c)	116,000	L1 114,000
Samoa	180,000	L1 1,000
		L2 93,000
Seychelles	80,000	L1 3,000
		L2 30,000
Sierra Leone (c)	5,427,000	L1 500,000
		L2 4,400,000
Singapore	4,300,000	L1 350,000
		L2 2,000,000
Solomon Islands (c)	480,000	L1 10,000
		L2 165,000
South Africa	43,586,000	L1 3,700,000
		L2 11,000,000
Sri Lanka	19,400,000	L1 10,000
		L2 1,900,000
Suriname (c)	434,000	L1 260,000
		L2 150,000
Swaziland	1,104,000	L2 50,000
Tanzania	36,232,000	L2 4,000,000

TABLE 1 (CONTINUED)
TERRITORIES WHERE ENGLISH HOLDS A SPECIAL ROLE

Territory	Population (2001)	Usage estimate
Tonga	104,000	L2 30,000
Trinidad & Tobago (c)	1,170,000	L1 1,145,000
Tuvalu	11,000	L2 800
Uganda	23,986,000	L2 2,500,000
United Kingdom (UK)	59,648,000	L1 58,190,000
		L2 1,500,000
UK Islands (Channel Island, Man)	228,000	L1 227,000
United States	278,059,000	L1 215,424,000
		L2 25,600,000
U.S. Virgin Islands (c)	122,000	L1 98,000
		L2 15,000
Vanuatu (c)	193,000	L1 60,000
		L2 120,000
Zambia	9,770,000	L1 110,000
		L2 1,800,000
Zimbabwe	11,365,000	L1 250,000
		L2 5,300,000
Other Dependencies[b]	35,000	L1 20,000
		L2 15,000
Total	2,236,730,800	L1 329,140,800
		L2 430,614,500

Notes:

a. (c) = In addition to speakers of Standard English, these countries contain significant numbers of speakers of creole and pidgin varieties of English (see Chapter 7).

b. The category Other Dependencies consists of territories administered by Australia (Norfolk Is., Christmas Is., Cocos Is.), New Zealand (Niue, Tokelau), and the United Kingdom (Anguilla, Falkland Is., Pitcairn Is., Turks & Caicos Is.).

Source: From *English as a Global Language* (pp. 62–65), by D. Crystal, 2003, New York: Cambridge University Press. Copyright 2003 by Cambridge University Press. Reprinted with permission.

Overall, then, the number of people using English is impressive, but whether these figures are convincing enough to label English as the world language will always be debatable. In the end, it probably does not matter much whether English carries this label or not because the simple fact is that whenever a common language is required, English is usually the language of choice (or one of several) to serve this need, making it the principal lingua franca of the world.

How English Became a Global Language

One can ask how English achieved its prominent place. It almost surely was not because English was intrinsically better than any other language. Languages are all suited to the communication requirements of the people who use them. The languages of the Eskimo peoples may not have many words to describe computer terminology, but they can differentiate between several distinct kinds of snow. Rather, a language usually rises in prestige and power in response to external factors. Languages are closely and unmistakably tied to the people who speak them, and when those people rise in power and begin spreading their influence, their language becomes involved in the process. A small powerful group can impose its regional dialect on a much larger population until the dialect becomes a considerable language, and that language in turn may be spread into new territories. Conversely, if a group of people is conquered or enslaved, its language may die out completely. The Celtic languages in southern Europe suffered this fate (though they survived in various northern areas, including Britain). It has been said that "language is a dialect with a army and a navy." A good example is how the Romans made Latin the most influential language of its time in the Near East and Europe, and how after the decline of the Romans, the Christian church helped Latin retain its influence for another thousand years in Europe. Something similar happened with English. Britain's naval and financial power allowed the British to become masters of both the Industrial Revolution and the largest empire the world has ever known. Another English-speaking giant, the United States, succeeded Britain. But it was not only military and industrial strength that bolstered the position of English. During this time, the most influential financial and investment centers (especially after Germany's defeat in 1918) were English speaking: New York and London. Likewise, English has been spread worldwide by popular Western culture, much of it in English—for example, Hollywood movies and pop music. Thus, English rose to prominence on the strength of centuries of unbroken dominance over large parts of the world by its speakers.

English's Strengths and Weaknesses as a Language

English rose to prominence on the back of its speakers' military, industrial, financial, and cultural strength, but this does not mean that English has no strengths of its own as a language. One of its principal assets must be its large and varied vocabulary. It has a much larger vocabulary than that of German, Italian, French, or Spanish, with estimates that there are anywhere from 200,000 words in common usage to a total stretching into the millions.[25] One important reason for this is the unashamed willingness of English to borrow vocabulary from any language that holds out a word that might prove useful. This free borrowing of foreign loanwords has been a prominent feature of English ever since Anglo-Saxon times.

Another asset is its inflectional simplicity. A student learning English does not have to be concerned with the complicated inflectional agreements that other languages, like German, require (so that the adjective *kalt*, "cold," changes according to the gender of the noun it describes: *kalder Wein, kalte Milch, kaltes Bier*). In almost all instances, other methods of organization, predominantly word order and the use of prepositions, have replaced the hard-to-memorize word endings that some languages use to identify gender, number, and grammatical relationship (and that English itself once added, as we shall see). A related strength is that English uses natural gender for its nouns; that is, nouns naming living creatures are masculine or feminine according to the sex of the individual, whereas all other nouns are neuter. This may seem unremarkable until one examines other languages: In German, the word for *sun* is feminine (*Sunne*), that for *moon* masculine (*Mond*), and those for *girl* and *young lady* neuter (*Mädchen, Fräulein*), while in French, the word for *sun* is masculine (*soleil*) and that for *moon* feminine (*lune*). To be sure, English syntax has its own particular difficulties, and in the end, English grammar is probably not any easier to learn than that of inflected languages like German. At least English does not force memorization of arbitrary gender classifications.

English uses more distinctive sounds than most languages. Hawaiian uses only 12 different sounds, whereas Chipewyan (a native language of Western Canada) uses 45. Taken together, languages use between 25–30 sounds on average, and so English with its more than 40 sounds is well above average.[26] This phonetic richness is an advantage because it allows the diversity needed to give sound to the vast number of words in English. In fact there are plenty of sounds to spare. For example, *plom* is not a word, but it could be; the sound and letter combinations are "legal," but it just happens not to be used. It is waiting for someone to give it a meaning and to start using it. The diversity of the English sound system also provides variety and richness to English poetry and prose. Of course, phonetic diversity is a double-edged sword: Although it gives English plenty of phonetic capacity, it also gives students more sound combinations to master.

Every language has its difficulties for second language learners, and one of these in English is its spelling system. An ideal system would have one character for each sound. Unfortunately, English has many characters for some sounds, and many sounds for some characters. In fact, Feigenbaum states that there are 251 written representations for 44 sounds in English![27] An example of this is the consonant *g*. When followed by *h* at the beginning of a word like *ghost*, it retains its /g/ sound, while at the end of a word like *rough* it sounds like /f/. Inconsistencies like these make English a headache to spell, not only for international students, but for native speakers as well. Most of the inconsistencies have historical explanations, and although understanding these may not make the spelling any easier to learn, at least knowing there are logical reasons for the inconsistencies may help to make them less infuriating.

All living languages change; the only ones that do not are no longer spoken. The same external factors that affect the prestige of a language may also affect its structure. English has gone through a great deal of change in its 1,500-year lifetime. Historians traditionally describe the history of the English language in terms of four main periods. Opinion about the precise dating of these periods varies; our divisions are these: **Old English 450–1100, Middle English 1100–1500, Early Modern English 1500-1700, and Modern English 1700–Present Day.** Linguistic change is slow and of course Old English did not magically become Middle English in 1100. Rather, these datings are connected with important events in the life of the English nation that had a major impact on its language, and they enable us to make sense of certain sets of related changes. They are boundaries of convenience, splitting a continually evolving language into parts small enough to analyze. Old English began with the invasion of Britain by Angles, Saxons, and other Germanic tribes in the 5th century. Their language was first written in the Latin alphabet in the 7th century after the conversion of its speakers to Christianity, and it developed under various influences, including those from settlers speaking a Scandinavian language, until the Norman Conquest of 1066. This instigated major changes in English society and its language, and the subsequent Middle English period saw radical grammatical simplification and the absorption of a large amount of French vocabulary. The beginning of the Early Modern English period coincided with the Renaissance, which further enriched the vocabulary of English, and the establishment of printing in England brought the possibility of standardization, especially of spelling. The Modern English period began about 1700 and was characterized by a combination of language consciousness and confidence that culminated in the production of the first great dictionaries; the establishment of American independence foreshadowed the rise of national varieties of English.

Chapter 2 gives a brief overview of the historical journey of English, and the succeeding chapters focus on how the historical environment affected specific elements of the language. In Chapter 3, we examine grammar, in Chapter 4 vocabulary, and then in Chapters 5 and 6 the sound and writing systems of English. In Chapter 7, we look at how English is somewhat different in various countries, and finally, in Chapter 8, we ask what the future of English might hold. We feel confident that, upon completion of the book, you will be a much more knowledgeable teacher of English and will be better prepared to answer some of the tricky questions about the English language that may have previously seemed to have no logical answers.

FURTHER READING

Two books that describe the place of English in the world today and that suggest how it might develop in the future.

- Crystal, D. (2003). *English as a global language*. Cambridge: Cambridge University Press.
- Graddol, D. (1997). *The future of English*. London: The British Council.

A lively reference book with a vast variety of short, interesting entries.

- Crystal, D. (2003). *The Cambridge encyclopedia of the English language* (2nd ed.). Cambridge: Cambridge University Press.

Classroom Activity: 1.1

The Importance of English in Today's World

Statements about English as it is used in the world today follow. Decide whether they are True (T) or False (F). The first one has been done for you.

1. __T__ English is the language of international air traffic control.

2. ____ About 40 percent of the world's scientists write in English.

3. ____ Approximately 75 percent of the world's mail is written in English.

4. ____ About 80 percent of the world's computer information is stored in English.

5. ____ English has the largest number of native speakers of any language.

6. ____ There are about 1,000 different English newspapers in India.

7. ____ About half of the world's newspapers are in English.

8. ____ The European Free Trade Commission conducts its business in English.

9. ____ English is the most common language on the Internet.

10. ____ English is the official national language of the United Kingdom and the United States.

11. ____ English is an official language of the United Nations.

Classroom Activity: 1.2

How Does English Compare to Other Languages?

Statements comparing English to other languages follow. Check the box that best shows English's position.

1. How large is English's vocabulary compared to other languages?

   ☐ smaller than average   ☐ about average   ☐ bigger than average

2. How many inflections (suffixes like walk*ed*, walk*ing*, walk*s*) does English have compared to other languages?

   ☐ fewer than average   ☐ about average   ☐ more than average

3. How many sounds does English have compared to other languages?

   ☐ fewer than average   ☐ about average   ☐ more than average

4. In some languages, the relationship between a word's spelling and its pronunciation is very close. In other languages, it is not. How well does the spelling system of English match the sounds in English?

   ☐ relatively difficult to know spelling from the pronunciation   ☐ about average   ☐ relatively easy to know spelling from the pronunciation

5. All languages change, but sometimes this change is resisted by governments, schools, etc. How free is English? Can it easily change to take on new ways of expressing ideas compared to other languages?

   ☐ change is quite controlled   ☐ about average   ☐ relatively free to change

6. Where does English rank in number of speakers compared to other languages?

   native speakers: ☐ #1 ☐ #2 ☐ #3 ☐ #4 ☐ #5
   non-native speakers: ☐ #1 ☐ #2 ☐ #3 ☐ #4 ☐ #5

Classroom Activity: 1.3

English Use around the World

This chart shows countries in which English holds a special place because of historical, political, or social reasons. The first column is for the estimated percentage of native English speakers in the country. The second column is for the estimated percentage of people who speak English as a second language. Try to guess the percentages for each country and fill in the blanks with the figures from the list.

	Percentage of native English speakers	Percentage of second language speakers
Australia	79%	18%
Bahamas	87%	
Canada		
Hong Kong		
India		19%
Ireland		
Malaysia		
New Zealand	96%	
Philippines	<1%	
South Africa		
United Kingdom		3%
United States		

<1%	4%	22%	77%
<1%	8%	25%	79%
2%	9%	31%	87%
2%	9%	31%	96%
3%	18%	48%	97%
3%	19%	63%	97%

2

A BRIEF HISTORY OF THE ENGLISH LANGUAGE

A Language Evolves in a Changing World

- Where did English come from in the first place?
- How old is English?
- How did wars, new ways of thinking, and the printing press change English?
- How have English grammar, vocabulary, spelling, and pronunciation changed over time?

Languages change continually. If that were not the case, there would be no history of them at all. Their form would be fixed for all time and, indeed, the whole world might well be speaking a single language. In fact, we know that there may be as many as 6,000 languages spoken in the world today.[1] Furthermore, we can see clearly, in the case of those with a written record going back many hundreds of years, how much they have changed during that time. There seems little reason to doubt that our prehistoric ancestors spoke very differently from us, but what causes language change and diversity? In some respects, languages seem to change naturally and spontaneously (see Chapter 5 on sounds), but a key factor also is the influence of the national and social history of the speakers. In other words, the historical events that affect people also affect the languages they speak. This chapter gives a brief overview of the events in history that affected the people who spoke English, and how those events in turn changed the language itself. This historical framework will give you a picture of how English has developed through the centuries and will provide the background necessary for the more detailed discussions of English grammar, vocabulary, pronunciation, and spelling in later chapters.

Before English

Where did English come from? Before answering this question, it is important to ask where does *language* come from? We know that language is the main distinguishing feature that sets mankind apart from all other living species on earth, although experiments with apes suggest they may have some basic facility with it as well.[2] There is no known human community in existence without language. It is our birthright, as instinctively natural for us as flying is for birds. We do not need to be taught; as children we absorb our first language naturally from mere exposure. Unfortunately, however, it is difficult to say anything with certainty about how the first language(s) developed.

We know that man's ancestors split from those of the chimpanzee (our closest biological relative) somewhere between 4 million and 8 million years ago. Evidence from fossil bones indicates that early hominoids spread out from Africa at least 1 million years ago and dispersed around the world.[3] Probably one of the most important reasons for mankind's success was the ability to use speech. This verbal tool greatly increased the chances for survival. It made group organization more efficient, assisted collective hunting, and facilitated the handing down of knowledge to younger generations. Estimates of when man started speaking range from 35,000 to 100,000 years ago.[4] The exact mechanism of how the first language developed is impossible to determine, but this has not stopped people from speculating with several interesting (and amusing) theories through the ages.[5] One, the bow-wow theory, suggests that words may have first been formed mimicing natural sounds, such as *bow-wow* for dog or *whoosh* for a puff of wind. Another, the pooh-pooh theory, postulates that emotional interjections, such as *pooh-pooh* or *bah*, could have formed the first words. Still another, the yo-he-ho theory, suggests that groups of people working together may have developed rhythmic word chants in order to coordinate their efforts. The la-la theory postulates that words may have originated in the baby talk of mothers or the utterances of children playing. Early man may have also used his face and lips to point, vocalizing different sounds to indicate distance. Perhaps more plausible than these theories is the idea that early communication was a mixture of gestures and sounds, with gestures probably predominating. As his manual dexterity improved, man learned how to do more things with his hands. This may have prompted a greater reliance on sounds to communicate ideas.

Whatever the cause and timing, language became established. Some linguists suggest there was a single mother tongue from which all known languages have evolved, called *Proto-World*.[6] If there was a Proto-World language, it eventually began splitting into many different language families, as groups of speakers dispersed and became isolated. The oldest families on which there is general agreement date from 7,000 years ago. Of these, some, like the Sino-Tibetan family, contain numerous languages still being spoken today. Others, whose speakers are aboriginal tropical people, are quickly nearing extinction. Still others, like Basque, contain only a single language member. The best known and most studied family is *Indo-European*, the family from which most present European languages, including English, is derived.

The Indo-European people probably originated around the Black and Caspian seas. Perhaps as early as 3,500 BC they undertook a series of migrations westward and eastward, perhaps as a result of overpopulation and the need to find new land to settle.[7] With them went their language, or more likely, various mutually intelligible dialects of a common language ("Indo-European"). As they spread westward, one branch advanced south down the Balkans into what we now know as Greece and Turkey. Another continued westward and then south, reaching areas we now know as France, Italy, and the Iberian Peninsula. A more northerly branch settled Germany and Scandinavia. Meanwhile, an eastern migration worked its way through Iran and ended up in India. It is not difficult to imagine that, as the Indo-Europeans spread over larger and larger areas and the various migratory branches lost contact with the others, their dialects also diverged more and more. If dialects are isolated from each other for somewhere in the region of 1,500 years, they can develop into distinct

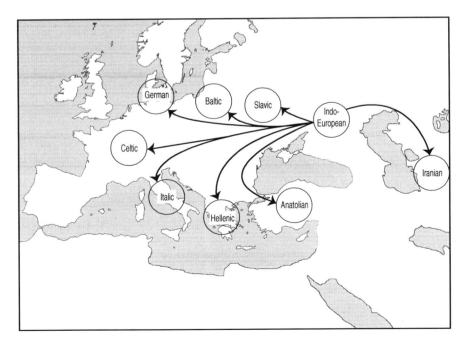

FIGURE 1   The Spread of Indo-European Languages

languages.[8] Eventually Indo-European splintered into a number of language groups; some of the more important of these are shown in Figure 1. The Indo-European language groups went on to develop into languages that are now the mother tongues of more than one-quarter of the world's people.

The dispersal of the different Indo-European languages took place a very long time ago, and the sense that they belonged to the same family was lost. Not until the 18th century did scholars begin gaining an awareness that most European languages were related in some way. They already accepted that all of the Romance languages had their common descent from Latin, but they did not see the connection with other languages. The breakthrough occurred in 1786 when Sir William Jones linked classical Sanskrit from India to the European Latin, Greek, Germanic, and Celtic languages, showing that they all had sprung from a common source. The sentence in Table 2 given in various Indo-European languages clearly shows the relationship between them. If the versions were spoken, the similarities would be even more striking.

TABLE 2
THE RELATIONSHIP BETWEEN INDO-EUROPEAN LANGUAGES

Germanic Group	
English:	Yes, mother, I have three.
German:	Ja, Mutter, ich habe drei.
Dutch:	Ja moeder, ik heb drie.
Flemish:	Ja moeder, ik heb drie.
Swedish:	Ja, moder, jag har tre.
Danish:	Ja, mor, jeg har tre.
Norwegian:	Ja, mor, jeg har tre.
Icelandic:	Já, móðir, ek hef þrjá.
Italic Group	
French:	Oui, mère, j'en ai trois.
Spanish:	Sí, madre, (yo) tengo tres.
Portuguese:	Sim, mãe, tenho tres.
Italian:	Si, madre, ce n'ho tre.
Rumanian:	Da, mama mea, eu am trei.
Balto-Slavic Group	
Czech:	Ano, matko, mam tři.
Polish:	Tak, matko, mam trzy.
Russian:	Da, mat[j], u men[j]á tri.
Bulgarian:	Da, maika, imom tri.

Source: From *The Gift of Tongues* (pp. 50–58), by M. Schlauch, 1943, London: Allen and Unwin. Copyright 1943 by Allen and Unwin.

Old English (c. 450–1100)

Britain before the Germanic Invasions

It is altogether incorrect to think of English as the first and only language to ever have been used in England. After all, English as a language is only slightly more than 1,500 years old, and the British Isles have been populated for at least 50,000 years.[9] The first inhabitants, collectively known as Iberians, worked bronze, erected Stonehenge, and traded with merchants from as far away as the Levant. The second group to set foot in Britain was the Celts, perhaps as early as the 7th century BC. They displaced the Iberians and by 150 BC the Celts of southern Britain had their own gold coinage, and later they sent reinforcements to their continental Gallic cousins who were fighting Julius Caesar. This brought Roman attention to their offshore island. In 54 BC, Caesar tried but failed to invade Britain and make it into a Roman province, but his successor Claudius had better luck. In 43 AD, his legions landed in Kent and within a few years controlled most of the south and west of the country, though the north took longer to subdue. The occupation lasted for four centuries and, despite sporadic resistance from the Celts, a certain amount of cross-cultural cooperation took place, to the extent that we can talk of a Romano-Celtic society. But by 410 the overstretched Roman Empire had become fatally weakened by attacks on Rome itself (by continental Germanic tribes), and the legions pulled out of Britain, leaving an impressive array of fine buildings and a legacy of settlement enshrined in place-names (such as those ending today in -*chester*, which indicates a place where a Roman fort once stood). Britain reverted to its original condition as a collection of Celtic kingdoms, under perpetual threat both from each other and from outside raiders, who included Irish from the west, Picts from the far north, and Saxons from the Continent.

The Arrival of the "English"

By 370 AD, Germanic tribes from today's Denmark and coastal Germany were already well acquainted with the southeast coast of Britain, and there was probably some small-scale Germanic settlement. In the following century, the Germanic tribes began sailing toward Britain in unprecedented numbers. Overpopulation may have been the reason for these migrations, as the Germanic people favored scarce coastal and river valley areas. Rising population would have inevitably forced them to look elsewhere for new land. Whatever the case, according to the account of the English monk and scholar Bede (d. 735), relying on an even earlier historian called Gildas, the main settlements were triggered by the request of a British king called Vortigern for military aid from the continental tribes (often referred to simply as "Saxons") to fight off Picts and Scots from the north in exchange for some land. The mercenaries duly performed this task successfully but then turned the tables on their British hosts. Britain was clearly a rich source of both plunder and agricultural land, and so they encouraged more and more of their continental compatriots to join them. A process of conquest lasting 100 years began, in which the Germanic mercenaries became masters of large parts of Britain, pushing the native Celts to the peripheries, mostly in the west and north.

According to Bede, the invaders came from the three most powerful of the Germanic tribes. The Jutes, led by two brothers called Hengist and Horsa, came from Jutland, the northern part of modern Denmark. They arrived first (in 449, according to Bede) and settled in Kent and other parts of the south. Somewhat later came the Angles from the south of Denmark who settled large parts of the north, the east midlands, and the area now known as East Anglia. The Saxons came from a homeland in the north of modern Germany, between the Elbe and Rhine rivers, and settled in the south (see Figure 2). Archaeology broadly confirms Bede's account but adds other Germanic tribes also, including Frisians and Franks. By as early as the 7th century, the people of all these tribes were being

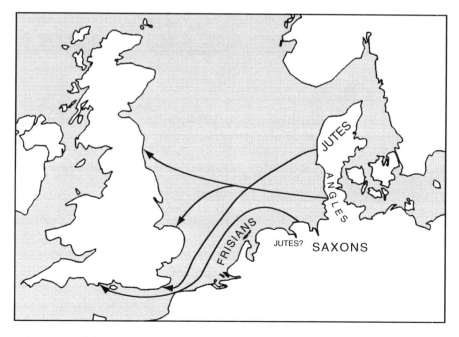

FIGURE 2   Bede's Account of the Germanic Invasions

referred to collectively by the name of one of them, Angles (though today we call them "Anglo-Saxons"), and their country became known as *Englalond* ("the land of the Angles"). Each tribe spoke a variety of the same West Germanic language, and it seems to have been known almost from the start as *Englisc*—English.

The settlers organized themselves into a number of independent (and often warring) kingdoms, there being seven at first: those of Northumbria, Mercia, the West Saxons (Wessex), the East Saxons, the South Saxons, East Anglia, and Kent. Settlement areas are commemorated to this day in county and district names such as East Anglia, Sussex (the home of the South Saxons), and Essex (East Saxons) (see Figure 3). Northumbria was dominant in the 7th century, Mercia in the 8th, and Wessex from the second half of the 9th onward, under King Alfred the Great (d. 899).

But beginning in 787, the greatest threat was again from outside. A new series of attacks and incursions began, again by Germanic peoples but this time from farther north, the area we now call Scandinavia. The attackers were mainly Danes but also included Norwegians, and they were known collectively as Vikings. To begin with, the attacks were sporadic and disorganized—guerilla raids for plunder, in which the monasteries were particularly tempting targets because they tended to be situated on islands

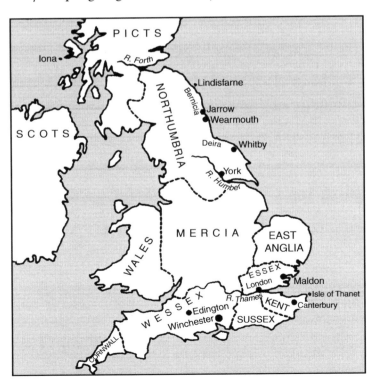

FIGURE 3   Map of the Seven Anglo-Saxon Kingdoms

or isolated coasts. But inland areas became increasingly threatened, too, especially with the arrival of a huge Danish army in 865. The Danes were now intent on settlement, and they soon controlled most of England, except Wessex. Even this was on the brink of defeat in 878, but at the last moment King Alfred rallied the people and won a victory over the Danes at Edington. An agreement was reached that the Danes would be allowed to occupy a large area of England, all the land to the east of the old Roman road (Watling Street) running between London and Chester (see Figure 4). Because Danish laws were to be in effect here, the area became known as the Danelaw.

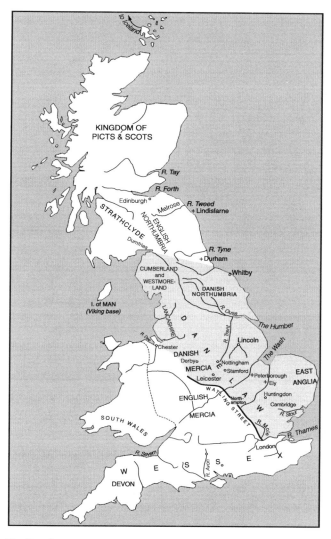

FIGURE 4   The Danelaw

There was peaceful integration between the settlers in the Danelaw and the native population, and eventually Alfred and his heirs would bring most of the area back under English control, but the threat of new invasions always remained. From about 925, another series of Viking attacks from across the North Sea began. In the 990s, these culminated in invasions led by two kings, Olaf Tryggvason of Norway and Svein Forkbeard of Denmark, and there was no Alfred this time to save the day. Svein ruled England briefly (1013–14), and his son Cnut (or Canute) became king from 1016 until 1035, while simultaneously controlling Denmark and much of the rest of Scandinavia. English kings ruled again from 1042, in the persons of Edward and then Harold, but by now there was a new enemy with a claim to the throne—William of Normandy, whose successful invasion in 1066 would impose, for a time, a French culture on England.

A key cultural landmark in the Old English period had been the bringing of Christianity to the pagan Anglo-Saxons. This was accomplished first by the mission of St. Augustine, who arrived in Kent from Rome with 40 monks in 597, and then by the efforts of Celtic missionaries originating in Ireland, who began their work in the north in the 620s. By the end of the 7th century, all of England was effectively Christianized. Nevertheless, echoes of the old pagan ways remained; the names of four weekdays, for instance, commemorate pagan gods— Tiw in *Tuesday*, Woden in *Wednesday*, Thor in *Thursday*, and Frig in *Friday*—and *Easter* is the name of an old pagan festival. With Christianity came literacy, and Christian monks for the first time used the Latin alphabet to write down the English language in the early 7th century. Thus the tradition of English literature began, though the language of the church and of learning was still Latin. England in the later 7th and 8th centuries became renowned throughout Europe for its Christian scholarship. This "golden age" faded after the attacks of the Vikings began in the late 8th century, but after King Alfred's successful containment of the Danes 100 years later, Anglo-Saxon learning prospered again—and now writings in Old English had at least equal status with those in Latin (though this remained the official language of the church). English came into its own as a viable and expressive language, suitable for any purpose. The later 10th and earlier 11th centuries were a high point for English, with its status as a national language assured. But this would soon be challenged on the battlefield of Hastings.

The Effect of Historical Events on Old English

The historical events outlined affected Old English in various ways, some of which are highlighted here. More detailed discussion will be provided in the following chapters.

• As the native Britons were pushed westward and northward by the Germanic invaders, their Celtic languages became marginalized, although Welsh is still spoken in parts of Wales today and Cornish was used in Cornwall until the 18th century. There was almost no influence of Celtic on the Germanic language of the invaders (which became Old English), just a handful of borrowed words.

• At the heart of the grammar of Old English was a complex system of distinct word endings (inflections) to mark the grammatical relationship between the different elements in sentences. For example, "the angel" could be *se engel, þone engel,* or *þam engle* in Old English, depending on whether the noun functioned in a sentence as the subject (*The angel was here*), direct object (*I saw the angel*), or indirect object (*I prayed to the angel*). Over time, the distinction between many of the inflections was lost and they became redundant, so that word order became more and more vital in conveying meaning. Scandinavian settlers, speaking a different but closely related West Germanic language, Old Norse, may have influenced these changes.

• The vocabulary of Old English was basically Germanic, but the introduction of Christianity prompted the borrowing of many Latin words (such as *altar, hymn, candle,* and *priest*). From the 9th century, Old Norse also had a great impact on Old English vocabulary (*law, fellow, kindle, sky*), and to some extent on grammar. Some 40 percent of the vocabulary of the modern language is Old English in origin.

• Christian monks introduced the Latin alphabet for the writing of Old English. Because the latter had more sounds than Latin, several new letters were introduced (þ, ð, ƿ, æ). Some letters still had to be used to represent more than one sound, but the correspondence between spelling and pronunciation in Old English is very close.

• We can distinguish four main dialects in Old English: Northumbrian (spoken north of the River Humber), Mercian (in the midlands), West Saxon (in the south and southwest), and Kentish (in the southeast). In the 10th and 11th centuries, the political and cultural dominance of Wessex allowed a sort of standard Old English to develop, based on the West Saxon dialect. It is the variety used by the writers of most of the documents and literary manuscripts that survive from the Anglo-Saxon period.

Middle English (c. 1100–1500)

The Norman French Conquer England

William of Normandy defeated the last Anglo-Saxon king, Harold, at the battle of Hastings in 1066 and initiated a period of Norman French dominance over England that would have a profound effect on the English language. The Normans ("northmen") descended from Scandinavians who had occupied northern France in the 9th century. William, known as "the Conqueror," believed he had a claim to the English throne. He was crowned on Christmas Day, 1066, though it took him four more years of campaigning to secure the whole of England. Normans now occupied positions of power. Most of the English nobles had been killed either with Harold at Hastings or in the uprisings that followed; the ones that survived were replaced. This policy extended to the church also, and its hierarchal ranks were filled with imported Norman officials and monks. French was now the language of prestige, and it replaced English as the medium for governmental and legal affairs. In the monasteries, where English had held a privileged place alongside Latin during the Anglo-Saxon period, Latin dominated again, and it would be used increasingly in legal documents, too. Thus, after the Conquest, there were two status languages in England, and neither was English.

But the English language proved resilient in the face of this apparent setback. Within about 300 years it would again become the official language of the kingdom. There are many reasons for this: There is no evidence that English was suppressed after the Conquest, and generations of English people continued to be born to English-speaking parents and they never spoke anything but English themselves. Written works in English were still produced throughout the period of French dominance (e.g., the *Anglo-Saxon Chronicle* was continued until 1154, there was much copying of religious literature, and poets still composed in their native tongue). However, English was no longer a national language: National documents were in French or Latin. The use of English was now local and parochial, and because there was no longer a standard form (the standard of Wessex) exerting its control over the written language, each dialect area began to go its own way in terms of the spelling and grammar, and even vocabulary.

French was never spoken regularly by more than a minority of a few thousand speakers who held all the power, and they still had to be able to communicate with the majority who spoke English. French lords often took English wives, and their children were usually cared for by English nursemaids and servants. Almost from the start, these children were exposed to English.

Conversely, many Englishmen aspiring to a higher position learned French. These factors lead to a good deal of bilingualism in England.

Although the upper classes continued to speak French among themselves and to enjoy their own courtly literature in French, there was a steady distancing between them and France. First, the political ascendancy of Paris at this time had led to the linguistic ascendancy of its Central French dialect. The Norman dialect that William and his nobles spoke (to which we give the name Anglo-Norman) began to attract ridicule. Then, in 1204, King John lost Normandy to the French crown. Both politically and economically, France and England began to draw apart, and the king and nobles (though many still had great French estates, mainly in the south) looked on England as their first concern. There was now a greater commitment to England and a growing sense of national identity. When John's son, Henry III, encouraged even more of his French friends to settle in England and gave them English estates, a reaction against all things French set in. Nationhood was more and more associated with language—the English language.

Throughout the 13th century, the upper classes began to use English with steadily increasing frequency. The emergence of tutor books designed to teach French to aristocratic children who no longer learned it as a first language exemplified the decline of French. In 1258 official documents in the king's name were issued for the first time in English, and by the time that Edward I came to the throne in 1272—the first English-speaking king of England since the Conquest—government officials were again mostly English. Then the new century brought two events that sealed the fate of French in England: the Hundred Years War (really a succession of wars about the possession of French territories, 1337–1453) and the Black Plague (at its worst in 1348–1350). War with France predictably made French unpopular, and in the end French victories stripped England of all her French possessions except Calais. Without a stake in France, French no longer had any practical purpose. The Black Plague killed between one-third and one-half of the population in Europe, including perhaps 2 million people in England. Labor suddenly became a scarce commodity, and so the lower classes were able to break (to some extent) the stranglehold of feudalism and gain economic clout. There was a rapid growth, too, in urbanization, with mass migration from the countryside to the towns, primarily London. In these urban centers an influential middle class of skilled people and merchants became prominent. The language of these newly empowered citizens was English. They sent their sons to the grammar schools, and by the end of the 14th century, the language of teaching in these schools was English, not French. By 1362, English had become the official language of legal proceedings and the language of Parliament.

But what was "English" at this time? As the language began to take on national functions again, the lack of a written standard to act as a model, as the Wessex standard had done for the Anglo-Saxons, became apparent. The English of the manuscripts of the time reflected the dialect and foibles of each particular writer or copyist, and so there was wide and confusing variation. Four main regional dialects may be distinguished—those of the north of England, the west midlands, the east midlands, and the south—but within these there was much further local variety. However, London's political influence was being felt throughout the country, and it was only natural that its dialect would eventually become the standard. It was essentially an East Midlands dialect, but owing to London's cosmopolitan character as a center of trade and commerce, it drew on dialects from everywhere in England. Linguistically, it was midway between the conservative southern dialects and the more flexible northern ones. The most popular poet of the time, Chaucer, composed in it, and this may have helped to increase its influence. The emergence of a new standard took time, however, and bewildering variety continued to characterize documents and literary manuscripts for many years.

By 1500, everybody spoke English in England, and the status of the language for all purposes was assured. The native tongue may have ousted French, but it was left deeply affected by it. Thousands of French words had entered English and indeed would enhance its capacity for eloquence and range of expression. There was a French legacy also in terms of orthography and spelling, for French-trained scribes had introduced many changes. In the meantime, a process of morphological (i.e., structural) simplification that was already under way before the Conquest had been completed, and changes in syntax, some of them influenced by the language of Scandinavian settlers in the north, had taken effect. English was considerably altered. In some ways it was now a simpler language, but many inconsistencies developed, specifically in spelling, and some of these would become permanent.

The Effect of Historical Events on Middle English

The Middle English period was one of great change and variation in the language. There were probably more changes of greater consequence during this period than in any other in English history. They radically affected grammar, vocabulary, spelling, and pronunciation.

- With the anchor of the Old English standard based on the Wessex dialect gone, written Middle English was characterized by wide and confusing variations, many arising from the free use of regional dialects, none of which had more status than the others at that time.

• English continued the pre-Conquest process of change from a language dependent on inflections to one dependent on word order and prepositions.

• A large number of French loanwords were absorbed. Between 1250 and 1400, more French words were borrowed than any time before or after. Modern English has more than 10,000 such borrowings, the majority taken during the Middle English period. Scandinavian also continued to contribute loanwords, most notably the pronouns *they, them,* and *their,* whereas Latin supplied hundreds of words in areas such as religion and law.

• With no standard language to act as a model for most of the period, spelling was free and phonetic, with scribes using their own regional dialect and their own spelling conventions. Thus we find *watir* and *watter* (water); *treese* and *tres* (trees); *nakid, nakud,* and *nakyd* (naked); and so on. At the extreme, the word *through* may have had as many as 500 variant spellings during the period— *throgh, þorow, dorwgh, thurhgh, þurch,* and *trghug* among them.[10]

• The French-trained scribes trying to transcribe English imposed their own writing conventions. Most of the changes they made are still with us today; for example, Old English *hw* was changed to *wh* (as in *what*) and the character *ash* (*æ*) was replaced by *a*.

• New sounds appeared, including the French *oi* (pronounced then /ɔɪ/, rather than in the modern French way), as in *toil* and *enjoy*; almost all of today's English words with this sound were borrowed from French. Many Old English words with a short vowel sound before *mb, nd, ld, rd,* and *rþ* lengthened that vowel (which later would be altered further); examples are *blind, climb, child,* and *gold*.

• A new standard language eventually was established, based on the East Midland dialect, and encouraged by the political and economic dominance of London, where the dialect was used. The activities of the Royal Chancery (a department of what would later become the Civil Service) had an important effect, with its official documents reaching every corner of England; its clerks were trained in a relatively uniform "Chancery style" of English, which influenced regional scribes to adopt forms that were largely independent of their own regional dialects. However, wide inconsistency in spelling remained.

Early Modern English (c. 1500–1700)

English History in the Early Modern English Period

The Early Modern English period was the first in which English was not greatly affected by invasions and war. Invasion by Angles and Saxons had established the language in the first place in the 5th century, and Scandinavian invasions later affected it significantly. The Norman Conquest sparked many of the radical changes of the Middle English period and gave an entirely new complexion to the vocabulary of English. This was the period when English finally began to acquire the form familiar to us today, but it took time, and there was continued instability in many respects throughout the period.

One of the most important developments of the period was printing, and William Caxton set up the first press in England in 1475, at Westminster. The advent of printing provided the means for an explosion of written communication and the impetus for the more rapid development of a standardized English language. By 1640, more than 20,000 titles in English had appeared. But standardization did not happen immediately, and there was little agreement at first among the printers about choice of words (where alternatives were available), punctuation, and, above all, spelling. Caxton's earliest books showed as much inconsistency in their spellings as handwritten manuscripts had done. Often a printer would change a spelling because he had run out of a certain letter in his font of type and substituted another, or he would add a letter in order to "justify" a line of type (i.e., make its length equal to the others). The early printers showed little concern for consistency in such matters, and standardization was not completely attained until about 1700. In the end, despite much talk of reform by a succession of scholars and writers, especially during the 16th century, printers tended to show great conservatism in their selection of spellings, so that in many cases it was those of Middle English that were chosen and became permanent features of the language.

By 1500, the effects of the Renaissance, a revival of the values of the classical world that had begun in Italy in the 14th century, had spread to England. It was a movement of great intellectual energy and excitement and of new scientific discoveries. Its humanist ideals, which put mankind (rather than God) firmly at the center of the universe, had a democratizing effect on learning. The impulse to read and learn extended beyond the cultured elite to ordinary people; they, too, wanted access to the classics and to books on a variety of subjects, from history to geometry, to rhetoric to navigation. The Renaissance was also an age of exploration, one with an outward-looking worldview. Colonial conquest and trade took English to North America and the Caribbean and to parts of Africa and Asia. The intellectual ferment of the times was fully reflected in the new influx of words into the English language, from Latin most of all, but from many other languages as well. Among the writers of the Early Modern English period, William Shakespeare (1564–1616) dominated, and his English illustrated the times: New words tumbled out (some to disappear as quickly as they came), alternative grammatical structures existed side by side, and there was a heady sense of linguistic freedom in his work.

It can be said that English came of age during this period. In the later years of the 15th century, there was still some doubt among some commentators about the ability of the language to compete with the perceived elegance and expressiveness of French. But during the Early Modern period, English triumphed in all areas of discourse—official and literary, as well as private. It was now inevitable that the more thoughtful users of the language (teachers prominent among them) should begin to take a more objective view of it. The second half of the 16th century thus saw a rush of books *about* English. They had in common a desire to bring order to what was perceived as the unsettling variety and even chaos of the language—in grammar, vocabulary, and spelling (for, as we have seen, printing had not yet brought consistency). The first real English dictionary (containing definitions, not simply lists) is usually credited to Robert Cawdrey, who published his *Table Alphabeticall* of "hard usuall English words" from foreign languages in 1604 (see p. 161).

The only real competitor to English for serious written discourse was Latin, not French. Latin was the international language of learning in western Europe for many centuries, the language of the great humanist scholars such as Erasmus (d. 1536), Copernicus (d. 1543), and Galileo (d. 1642). The tradition of Latin in England was strong and would not disappear overnight. It was the language of the grammar schools ("grammar" was Latin grammar) and would remain the language of instruction in the universities until the 18th century. However, English slowly displaced Latin as the language of academic writing. For example, Isaac Newton's revolutionary *Principia* (1689), in which he set out the fundamental laws of physics, was written (as the title indicates) in Latin, but his later works, such as his *Opticks* (1704), were mostly in English.

The Reformation, too, was a stimulus to the abandonment of Latin. The Protestant ideal, which the movement promoted, was for the Christian to have direct access to Scripture, with no mediation by priest or interpreter. Essential, therefore, were versions of the Bible in the vernacular languages, rather than Latin, the language of the Vulgate Bible, which had been in use among Christians for a thousand years. The simple but eloquent English of William Tyndale's Bible (left incomplete at his death in 1536) and its successors (most notably the King James Version of 1611), along with the Book of Common

Prayer (1549), had a significant effect on raising the status of the English language.

One of the most important changes English underwent during the Early Modern period, with far-reaching effects, concerns pronunciation. Between about 1450 and 1650, a radical transformation of the long vowels of English—the Great Vowel Shift—took place. The whole series of English long vowels underwent a systematic change in their pronunciations; without this shift, *moon*, for example, would sound something like *moan* today, and *green* like *grain*. The effects of such changes are still with us. Even as printers were fixing spelling conventions for the English language, its sounds were moving. This is one of the major reasons why there is often such a gap between the way a word is pronounced today and the way it is spelled. To a large extent, English ended up with a modern pronunciation tied to 14th- or 15th-century spelling.

The Effect of Historical Events on Early Modern English

English had become largely standardized by the end of the Early Modern English period, but this process took time, and there was still a considerable amount of variation during the earlier part of the period.

• As the new learning of the Renaissance took hold and new ideas flooded in, new words were needed to describe and express them. It is calculated that some 27,000 entered the language (both borrowed and created from existing resources) between 1500 and 1660, with the peak of borrowing in the period 1580–1620.[11] As many as one-third of these borrowings were from Latin, many others from French, and the rest came from a dozen other languages. However, about one-third of the new words did not survive into Modern English.

• The morphology of Early Modern English continued to simplify, until today's pattern was almost reached. For example, many irregular verbs took on regular past forms during this period (thus *helped* replaced *halp* as the past of *help*). Likewise, Early Modern English syntax was approaching today's norms, especially with the rising popularity of expressions using *do*. The singular second-person pronouns *thou* and *thee* were used alongside *you*.

• Spelling became largely standardized during this period. Attempts to rationalize spelling in the second half of the 16th century (by omitting "silent" letters, for example) came to nothing, and so many old forms were preserved.

- A scholarly fashion for "etymological" respelling meant letters were inserted in some words to make their Latin origin visible, as in *doubt* (Latin *dubitum,* but borrowed as French *doute*); the *b* was never pronounced.

- The Great Vowel Shift brought a systematic change in the values of all the long vowels of English. Its timing, after many spellings tied to the older pronunciation had been fixed, created further potential for mismatch between sound and spelling in some words.

- As Early Modern English became more standardized, a natural tendency developed for non-standard dialects to become discredited and eventually stigmatized. This tendency became much more pronounced in the 18th century.

Modern English (c. 1700–Present Day)

English History in the Modern English Period

The England of the middle part of the 17th century was disrupted by regicide (the execution of Charles I), civil war, and a period of "republican" government led by Oliver Cromwell. The eventual restoration of the monarchy in 1660 was largely a reaction against the political and social turmoil of the preceding 30 years. What was restored was not only the monarchy itself but also a sense of caution and a yearning for the old values. At the same time, England began to play an eager part in the Europe-wide movement of the Enlightenment, whose enthusiastic participants (practically all the great men of the age) shared a self-confident belief in progress through reason and science. They looked back to the classical world of Greece and Rome as the supreme incarnation of civilization and order, and they believed that progress in all areas of intellectual and social endeavor would come through a reassertion of that world's values.

The Enlightenment's faith in science and rational thought meant that men believed that there were natural laws for all things and that these laws could be derived from logic. Language was no different. Latin was held up as the language least corrupted by man's use, and so when grammars of English were written, most had the implicit intention of purifying English by reference to Latin models. This was a time of *prescription,* not *description,* and these men took it upon themselves to decide correct usage and condemn what seemed to them improper. Scores of books on grammar appeared between 1750 and

1800, but the most influential was one called *A Short Introduction to English Grammar* (1762) by the scholar, clergyman, and professor of poetry at Oxford, Robert Lowth. He believed that English could be reduced to a set of inflexible grammatical rules, and that "correct" use of the language depended on following them. Lowth's confidence allowed him to criticize even some eminent writers for their use of English. Among his prohibitions were the ones against using double negatives (*I haven't got no bananas*) and the contraction *ain't* (for *am not* or *is not*), and he laid down the rules for the use of *shall* and *will*. Proficient speakers of English today will be aware that the rules about *shall* and *will* are mostly disregarded in all areas of discourse but that the others are commonly broken only in some regional varieties of English. (See Chapter 3 for more details.)

We now judge the prescriptive grammarians to have made several serious mistakes in producing their grammars. First, they ignored the fact that language is a living thing, always changing and adapting to the new needs of its speakers. Trying to describe an English that is "set in stone" was never going to reflect its real usage in the world. Second, they tried to base the description of English on the grammar of Latin, which is inappropriate. Latin is a very different kind of language, based on a complex inflectional system, and trying to describe English in terms of Latin grammar was like trying to fit a square peg into a round hole. The grammarians were forced to fabricate a number of rules for English that made little sense, in order to follow the Latin model. Third, the grammarians sometimes applied questionable logic in their analysis of language. For example, Lowth reasoned that, just as in mathematics two negatives equal a positive, the same logic should apply to language (as it did in Latin). This resulted in the rule against double negatives. From a different but equally valid logical standpoint, we might argue that multiple negatives *emphasize* the negative quality being expressed, rather than reverse it.

A number of 18th-century scholars were aware of these shortcomings, among them the radical politician and writer William Cobbett (1763–1835), who published a highly popular *English Grammar* in 1817, in which he poked fun at language "snobs." However, books such as Lowth's *Short Introduction* were eagerly bought and were published in many editions. The prescriptive grammatical "rules" caught on. They are still with us and continue to cause headaches for English language teachers and students alike. The idea of "proper" English developed during this time, based on the notion that that there must be right (and consequently also wrong) ways to write and to speak the language.

It was the desire to record what was proper and acceptable that stimulated Samuel Johnson to publish in 1755 *A Dictionary of the English Language*, which soon became the standard reference work. By about 1700, printers had reached a consensus about English spellings, and it was these that Johnson enshrined in his *Dictionary*. Its appearance thus did more to fix standard spelling and usage than any other single event in the history of English. In many ways, Johnson was an innovator, giving a guide to contemporary pronunciation (he declared in his preface that he aimed to "fix" it), along with etymologies, definitions, and examples of usage—though these were taken only from literary sources, those that Johnson judged to be the finest. He was only interested in recording what he called "polite" usage, not the language of everyday communication on the streets of London. Nevertheless, his methodology was sound, even though occasionally his personal political prejudices were clear in his definitions. The result was a dictionary that would remain the unchallenged standard until Noah Webster published an American rival, his *An American Dictionary of the English Language*, in 1828, and the first parts of the multi-volume *Oxford English Dictionary* appeared in 1888. These three works established the great authority of dictionaries, to which today most people still unquestioningly defer.

The 1800s brought the continued expansion and consolidation of a global British Empire, and with it, the further spread of English. America had already gone its own way after the Declaration of Independence in 1776 and was busy creating a distinctive American English, encouraged by Noah Webster. But large parts of the world continued to come under the influence of British English. This English was that of the personnel of the colonial service who administered the Empire. They were drawn largely from the upper classes, ensuring that the English used in the Empire (and learned assiduously by its non-British inhabitants) would be based on the London standard. But, in time, national varieties emerged, which is one of the most noticeable features of the second half of the Modern English period. English is today spoken as a first language in such diverse places as Australia, New Zealand, India, South Africa, Ireland, and Canada. All the countries that speak English as an L1 are recognized as having their own national varieties and often several dialects within that variety.

In addition to the countries where English is the native language, there are many countries where it holds a position as a second or compromise official language, as explained in Chapter 1 (see Figure 5). Some countries, like India or Nigeria, contain so many indigenous languages that some compromise language must be chosen for common communication. Political reasons often exclude a native language, making English a logical alternative choice. In other countries, such as Singapore, economic reasons promote the learning of English as a second language. Countries like the Philippines have kept some English as part of their colonial heritage. In addition to countries where it is present

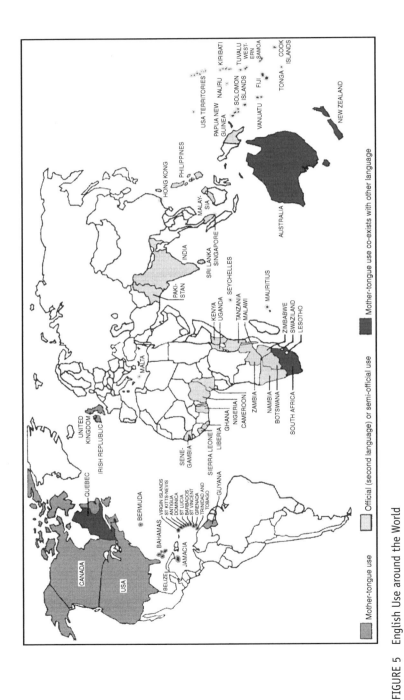

FIGURE 5   English Use around the World

Source: From *The English Language* (pp. 8–9), by D. Crystal, 1988, London: Penguin. Copyright 1988 by Penguin. Reprinted with permission.

for official or historical reasons, the fact that English is becoming the "global language" further encourages its study in schools around the world.

The Effect of Historical Events on Modern English

By the beginning of the Modern English period, the variations and instabilities of the previous period had largely disappeared (mostly in the first half of the 17th century) and the language essentially became the one we recognize today. The Enlightenment's emphasis on logic and reason and its reverence for the classical languages had both positive and negative effects on English: Very useful dictionary resources were created, but so were prescriptive grammars.

• Spelling has been the most stable aspect of Modern English, with Samuel Johnson's spellings preserved, bar a few exceptions (such as words with *-ick*, which we now spell with *-ic*, as in *music*). However, some marked differences developed between British and American usage—as in *colour/color*, *levelled/leveled*, and *centre/center*.

• In morphology, the only remaining variations in the standard language are plural *(e)s* and possessive apostrophe *s* on nouns (the apostrophe being settled as late as the 19th century), and third-person singular *s* on verbs. *You* is the only standard second-person pronoun and varies only for the possessive (*your, yours*); the other personal pronouns have remained remarkably unchanged since the Middle English period. The object-pronoun *whom* has survived, but only just, into the 21st century (*The man whom you saw*).

• Prescriptive grammar rules characterize the period and continue to be influential, even arbitrary ones such as that against ending sentences with prepositions, although newer grammar books are more tolerant of variation and do a much better job of describing spoken (not simply written) grammar.

• In terms of changes in syntax, one of the most obvious innovations has been the acceptance of *to get* in expressions of obligation, as in *I have got to do it*, and as a passive marker, as in *He got hurt in the fight*. These constructions were in use in English by the end of the 17th century but did not appear regularly in writing until the end of the 19th century, after which they were accepted quickly. At that time, inverted questions such as *What say you?* were still possible, but by the 20th century the use of *do*, as in *What do you say?* had become the norm.

• English's lexicon continues to increase, with borrowing from a wide variety of languages (including those of the Empire), and compounding (a characteristic of Old English) continues to be a productive source of new words—*fingerprint, hitchhike, software*. New words have also been created by "functional shift"— verbs from nouns (*to impact, to date, to telephone*) and nouns from verbs (*skid, spin*). The largest single area for new words has been science and technology, but here the native resources of English are clearly not sufficient, so most of the new specialist terms are based on Greek or Latin—words such as *biology, spectroscopy, genetics, chlorine, stethoscope,* and *stratosphere.*

• In terms of the way English is spoken, by the early 20th century Received Pronunciation (RP) was dominant in educated and official discourse in Britain (but not America). It was based on the pronunciation of the ruling classes and became a marker of social status and reliability (see pp. 139–140). In the later 20th century, however, its grip loosened and regional accents became more acceptable.

• As English has become more international, there has been an increasing acceptance of different varieties and dialects of the language. Concurrently, there has been a debate about what role a "Standard English" might have in such a global environment and what form that Standard English might take.

FURTHER READING

Three standard texts on the history of English.
- Barber, C. (1993). *The English language: A historical introduction.* Cambridge: Cambridge University Press.
- Baugh, A. C., & Cable, T. (2002). *A history of the English language* (5th ed.). London: Routledge.
- Pyles, T., & Algeo, J. (1993). *The origins and development of the English language.* Fort Worth, TX: Harcourt Brace Jovanovich.

An accessible introduction with exercises.
- Culpepper, J. (2005). *History of English.* London: Routledge.

Three popular books on the history of English.
- Bragg, M. (2003). *The adventure of English.* London: Hodder & Stoughton.
- Bryson, B. (1990). *The mother tongue.* New York: Avon Books.
- Crystal, D. (1988). *The English language.* London: Penguin.

A book that shows the dialectal variation of English throughout its development.

- Crystal, D. (2004). *The stories of English*. Woodstock, NY: Overlook Press.

An excellent reference source for many aspects of the English language, including its historical development.

- McArthur, T. (Ed.). (1992). *The Oxford companion to the English language*. Oxford: Oxford University Press.

Classroom Activity: 2.1

The Development of English

English has changed a lot since its beginnings around 450 AD. Below are four examples of the language taken from different stages in its development. The Bible was translated into English during each of these stages, and in this activity we compare one passage from it to see how English changed over time. Examine the four examples and discuss these questions:

1. How did grammar, vocabulary, and spelling change as English developed?

2. How are the older examples of English different from Modern English?

3. How comprehensible are the older examples of English?

OLD ENGLISH (c. 450–1100)

Witodlice maria stōd þarūte æt ðǣre byrgyne and wēop. ðā cwæþ iesus tō þām wife; wif hwi wepst ðū. hwone secst þū. hēo wende þæt hit se wyrtweard wǣre and cwæð tō hym. lēof gif þū hine name sege mē hwǣr þū hine lǣdest. and ic hine nime.

[*Literal translation: Truly Mary stood there-out at the grave and wept. Then said Jesus to the woman, Woman, why weepest thou? Whom seekest thou? She thought that it the plant-guardian were, and said to him, Sir, if thou him took, tell me where thou him laid, and I him take.*]

MIDDLE ENGLISH (c. 1100–1500)

Forsoth Marie stood at þe grave without wepynge.Thanne Jesus seid to þe wyf: Wyf, whi wepist thou? Whom sekist thou? She gessinge þat he were the gardner, seid to hym, Sire if thou hast takun him vp seʒe to me where thou hast layd him, and I schal take him a weʒ.

EARLY MODERN ENGLISH (C. 1500–1700)

And Mary stode without att the sepulcre wepynge. Then Jesus sayde vnto the woman: Woman, why weepest thou? Whom dost thou seek? She supposynge that he were the gardner, sayde unto hym: Sir if thou have borne him hence tell me where thou hast layde him, and I will take hym awaye.

MODERN ENGLISH (C. 1700–PRESENT DAY)

Now Mary stood outside the sepulchre weeping. Then Jesus said to the woman: "Woman, why do you weep? Who are you seeking?" She, assuming him to be the gardener, said to him: "Sir, if you have carried him away, tell me where you have laid him, and I will take him away."

3

ENGLISH GRAMMAR

Why Are There So Many Irregular Forms in English Grammar?

- *How can we describe English grammar?*
- *What are some limitations of books on English grammar?*
- *Why do some nouns not use plural -s (deer, children, lice)?*
- *Where do the irregular verbs in English come from (drink/drank/drunk)?*
- *What is the source of rules like "No double negatives" and "No split infinitives"?*
- *Is English grammar still changing today?*

What Is Grammar?

No other aspect of language is likely to cause more anxiety in both native speakers and non-native learners of English than grammar. There seem to be social and even moral implications in the use of "good" or "bad" grammar. But what exactly *is* grammar, good or bad, and where do the rules for English come from?

Grammar is an essential aspect of all languages. It is a set of conventions and procedures that allow for the smooth operation of the communication process. In essence, grammar is the term we use to represent the organizing system of a language. And of course such a system is needed. Take the following contrived sentence as a case in point:

> After two boy yesterday discover the body of a man, the police witnesses asked to contact they urgently.

This sentence has enough grammatical problems to significantly affect communication—the primary purpose of language in the first place. As an ELT teacher, you are probably very familiar with this kind of ungrammatical sentence, and if a student wrote it, you might provide feedback based on the following "rules" of standard English:

- English adds a special marker, normally *-s*, to show that a noun is plural: *boys*, not *boy*.
- When an action described is in the past, English uses a form of the verb (the past tense) different from that used to express the present time (the present tense): *discovered*, not *discover*.
- In statements in English, the subject of a verb is usually put immediately before it and the object afterward: *the police asked witnesses*.
- In English, different forms of the pronouns are used according to function; the object form after a verb is *them*, not *they*.

Having rules like this is certainly not a bad thing, especially for learners of the language. These particular rules make good sense and are used in most varieties of English around the world, but a few other rules are more contentious—such as the notorious one about not splitting the infinitive (e.g., *to really know*). Grammar rules are an aspect of what we shall call "traditional grammar." The traditions are in fact surprisingly modern, in relation to the 1,500 years of the history of English. Most were invented by the prescriptive grammarians of the 18th and 19th centuries (see Chapter 2), and it is interesting that the most contentious of them involve aspects of the language that are not crucial to meaning. They are often matters of style that have been given prestige through their use by influential writers.

One major problem with traditional grammar is that its rules were laid down exclusively in relation to written English, especially the sort of literary English used by those considered to be the "best" writers. This meant the writers who were steeped in the classical tradition, for whom good style and good grammar usually meant Latinate style and Latinate grammar. Less formal written English and the spoken language were left out. Inasmuch as such language does not follow traditional rules, it was (and still is to some extent) deemed to be incorrect, or is "ungrammatical."

As we shall see, ideas of correct grammar are in fact always changing; until the 18th century, for example, the double negative construction that today is not permissible in Standard English was perfectly acceptable. Grammar even varies between contemporary language communities; American English does a few things differently from British English, for instance, although the differences are slight and do not normally interfere with communication (see Chapter 6).

The word *grammar* was taken into English from French in the 14th century and derives from a Latin (and ultimately Greek) expression meaning "the craft of letters." The term in the Middle Ages was invariably used in connection with Greek and Latin, both of them languages of great morphological and syntactical complexity. Grammar schools were originally schools where Latin was taught. In the earliest attempts to write grammars of English, Latin was invariably the model against which the newer language was compared, so it is not surprising that our traditional grammatical terms and systems of analysis are Latinate. Ideas of "correct" English have often been derived (illogically) from such comparisons: If Latin does not allow a double negative construction, then English should not either.

Two main aspects of grammar can be distinguished:

- *Morphology* (from Greek words meaning "form" and "word") deals with the structure of words—how their forms vary to modify meaning (especially by the addition of different inflections or endings).
- *Syntax* (from Greek words meaning "together" and "arrange") deals with the structure of sentences—how words are arranged to give overall meaning to a spoken or written utterance.

This chapter explores these aspects and shows how many of the tricky elements of English developed (e.g., third-person *-s* in present tense verbs, and irregular verbs such as *drink, drank, drunk*). It will also show how the grammar of English has been, and continues to be, in a constant state of change. First, however, we look at the different approaches to describing English grammar.

Describing Grammar

English grammar seems quite complex to the newcomer. Of course native speakers acquire it automatically and are able to use it without thought, but being able to analyze and describe it is an entirely different matter. ELT teachers know from experience the challenge of trying to elucidate grammatical complexities in the classroom. Likewise, researchers in applied linguistics strain to capture the complete grammar system in a single reference book; for example, *The Cambridge Grammar of Spoken and Written English* has around 950 pages and still struggles to describe every detail of the language. In fact, it is probably impossible to describe completely and accurately the full grammar of English, and this inevitably means that only certain elements are highlighted in any particular situation so that these elements can be small enough for students (and teachers!) to understand. This reminds us of a story from India about the five blind men of Hindustan who went out to learn about an elephant. They all felt different parts of the elephant's body and came to very different conclusions about what such an animal is like. The man who felt the trunk thought an elephant was like a snake, the one who felt a leg thought an elephant was like a tree, the one who felt the ear thought an elephant was like a fan, and so on.[1] Similarly, our view of grammar depends on which elements we happen to focus on.

Various approaches to grammar can be taken. DeCarrico and Larsen-Freeman[2] summarize a number of them as follows.

• *Prescriptive grammar.* This type of grammar asserts which forms are correct and which are incorrect. It thus tells us how we ought to speak and what we ought not to say. It tends to bring value judgments into play, referring to forms from standard varieties of English as correct or "good" English and forms from non-standard varieties as incorrect or "bad" English. Many of the problematic rules of English come from this approach to grammar.

• *Descriptive grammar.* This is a more linguistically sound approach in which the rules of English are described from the way people actually use the language. Modern applied linguists can analyze large language databases (*corpora*) of 100 million words or more and understand the way grammar features are being used in the real world, not only by speakers of standard varieties but also by speakers of non-standard varieties. This approach reports actual grammar usage but makes no value judgments about that usage.

• *Pedagogical grammar.* This type of grammar caters to the needs of second language learners and teachers. Although it may prescribe some general rules, it is typically mainly descriptive in nature, drawing on a wide range of insights from both formal and functional approaches, as well as other applied linguistics disciplines such as discourse analysis and pragmatics.

• *Formal grammar.* This is a model of grammar that focuses on the forms (rules) themselves and how they operate within the overall system. Many people have this model in mind when they think of *traditional grammar*.

• *Functional grammar.* Whereas formal grammar focuses on forms, functional grammar goes beyond this and also considers appropriate language use. It looks at the relationships between linguistic forms and their practical functions. For instance, the linguistic form *How are you doing?* normally functions as an informal greeting to friends rather than an actual question. This focus on both form and function is sometimes also referred to as **discourse grammar.**

• *Lexicogrammar.* This is a model of language that recognizes that grammar and vocabulary are not really two different systems but one integrated whole. It attempts to explain how meaning is constructed by the interrelationship between lexis and grammar, highlighting, for instance, multi-word units such as *to make a long story short* that have a single meaning or function (in this example, reaching a conclusion). These multi-word units are extremely common in language, but more traditional formal grammars have a difficult time explaining them.

These approaches to grammar have had various degrees of influence over the years, with the more descriptive and integrative perspectives currently being favored. At a more personal level, however, your own approach to grammar has probably been influenced by a number of factors, including the school environment you were brought up in, the one you teach in, the attitudes at the teacher training program you attended or are attending, the place of grammar in your school syllabus, and the attitudes of your culture toward the issue of correctness versus flexibility. You are also likely to be influenced by the grammar reference book you use. Whether this is a formal or functional grammar book, either with or without prescriptive tendencies, it will surely color the way you present grammar to your students.

But regardless of what kind of grammar book you use, it is important to be aware of its limitations. Many teachers look at grammars as an unerring source of "true knowledge" about language, but this faith may be misplaced. Although modern corpus-based descriptive grammars are very good, they have all had to make compromises. The first is purely practical: Grammars need to be a manageable size, even though this means many language matters are inadequately covered or not included at all. Even 1,000-page grammars do not provide the complete coverage their authors would like. The net result is that grammars always represent to some degree an idealized version of the language. A second issue concerns what form of English is included in the grammar. Given the range of English varieties around the world (see Chapter 6), it is impossible to take into account every detail of every variety in a single book. Therefore, most grammars focus on Standard English, typically British or American. Thus the book that teachers use may not accurately describe the variety of English they are involved with—e.g., Pakistani English or Kenyan English. Third, even though corpus-based grammars are a significant improvement on made-up data, they still only relate to the corpus they were based on. No corpus can fully represent a language, and so any grammar based on a corpus reflects the limitations of its parent corpus. Another problem relates to the ever-changing nature of English grammar. Although the core features seem to be relatively stable, some elements are in a state of flux (see pp. 72–74). The changes are not as rapid as those affecting vocabulary, yet grammar books, like dictionaries, are always in the state of becoming out of date.

APPLICATIONS TO TEACHING

The important point of this discussion is that there are many ways of dealing with English grammar. It is a large and complex subject, and reference books approach it in various ways. Each approach has its advantages but also its limitations, and none can automatically be considered the best in all circumstances. In other words, there is no one "correct" approach to grammar.

This view may be a bit of a shock to teachers who have always seen grammar as a constant. If there is no correct approach to grammar and if grammar books are not to be seen as infallible guides, where does this leave teachers? One way is to go back to the beginning and carefully consider what grammar is. If it is indeed the organizing system of a language, we must take into account all of the elements that affect it and its facility in affecting communication. Although most people associate grammar with formal rules about the structure of words and sentences, *form* in fact makes up only part of the system of English; there are also the elements of *meaning* and *appropriacy*. Grammar helps determine the meaning of words by controlling their correct placement in a sentence, and the importance of the appropriacy of language will be apparent when we think how often students err by using syntactically correct sentences in inappropriate ways once they are outside the classroom. Considering grammar in a more holistic way, with an equal emphasis on all three essential elements, can lead to more balanced teaching. Celce-Murcia and Larsen-Freeman illustrate this with a pie chart that shows the three aspects of grammar (Figure 6) and reminds teachers that "learners need to achieve a certain degree of formal accuracy, but they also need to use the structures meaningfully and appropriately as well."[3]

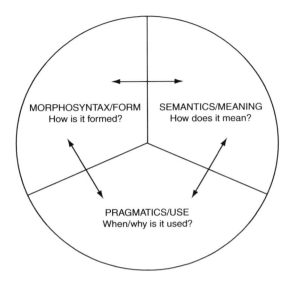

FIGURE 6   Three Aspects of Grammar

Source: From "Grammar" (p. 23), by J. DeCarrico and D. Larsen-Freeman, in N. Schmitt (Ed.), *An Introduction to Applied Linguistics*, 2002, London: Arnold. Copyright 2002 by Arnold. Reprinted with permission.[4]

Irregularities in Morphology

We now examine how the English grammar system developed over time, only although we will not attempt to offer a detailed description of every grammatical feature. Rather, we will focus on those forms that seem to be exceptional or in some way irregular or that simply do not seem to make much sense. Many of these have a historical explanation. Knowing the background will not necessarily make the forms less irritating, but they will perhaps be seen to be somewhat more logical. We will start with elements of morphology.

We have seen already that Modern English is an *inflected* language. Inflections— i.e., endings—are added to many words to modify their basic meaning: *-s* to make a noun plural (*boy* → *boys*), *-ed* to mark a verb in the past tense (*discover* → *discovered*), and so on. But modification sometimes involves a change to the words themselves. This can happen to a few nouns (the plural of *man* is *men*, not *mans*), most pronouns (*she* for the feminine subject of a verb but *her* for the object), and many verbs (the past form of *come* is *came*, not *comed*). All these changes in the forms of words are morphological changes. In this section, we deal with morphology under the headings of the various word classes or parts of speech.

Articles

Articles—the definite article *the* and the indefinite article *a* (or *an*)—are among the hardest grammatical features for second language students to learn, with respect to how and when they are used. They are used in so many different ways that it is difficult for teachers to explain them all. Morphologically, however, they are very simple, because their *forms* are invariable: always *the* and always *a* (except where a noun beginning with a vowel follows, when *n* is added). Learners of French, on the other hand, must distinguish between masculine, feminine, and plural forms of the definite article *(le, la, les)*, and those tackling German have an even more complex task *(der, die, das, den, etc.)*. Articles in Old English were at the same sort of level of complexity as modern German, varying their forms according to three separate criteria—gender (masculine, neuter, or feminine), number (singular or plural), and case (nominative, accusative, genitive, or dative). The concept of *case* will be explained briefly, but it is interesting first just to view all the possible variations of the Old English word for *the* in Table 3:

TABLE 3
THE DEFINITE ARTICLE IN OLD ENGLISH

	Singular			Plural
	Masculine	Neuter	Feminine	All Genders
Nominative	se	þæt	sēo	þā
Accusative	þone	þæt	þā	þā
Genitive	þæs	þæs	þǣre	þāra
Dative	þǣm	þǣm	þǣre	þǣm

Case is a way of classifying nouns and the articles that go with them (as well as other parts of speech) according to their function in relation to other words in a sentence. Nouns function in four main ways in Modern English, as well as in Old and Middle English:

as the **subject** of a verb (i.e., the person or thing performing the action of the verb): "*the child* shouted"

as the **direct object** of a verb (i.e., the person or thing directly acted on by the verb): "the child shouted *the word*"

in **possessive relationship** with another noun: "the *teacher's* child"

as the **indirect object** of a verb (i.e., the person or thing indirectly affected
by the action of the verb): "the child shouted the word to *the man*"
(and note that a preposition, here *to*, almost invariably intervenes
between the verb and the noun)

In traditional grammar, these functions are known as cases, and Latinate
names are given to them:

nominative = the subject case
accusative = the direct object case
genitive = the possessive case
dative = the indirect object case

Thus, in Old English, the definite article could theoretically have up to 24
different forms—four singular and four plural cases for each of three genders.
In practice, as Table 3 showed, there was much repetition, and only about 12
different forms actually occurred. Nouns had different inflections covering the
same range of grammatical criteria, and identifying these case endings, and
the form of the definite article, is often vital for the understanding of an Old
English sentence.

It might be challenging to explain all these case functions to your students,
but fortunately for them, as we have noted, their use is more or less redundant
in Modern English (but not in German and many other languages). The articles
are invariable, and inflections on nouns have been reduced to only four, as we
show in the following section.

Nouns

The morphology of nouns in Modern English is relatively simple, with only
four possible forms:

singular	friend
plural	friends
possessive singular	friend's
possessive plural	friends'

This is much less complex than the Old English noun system, which (as
noted previously) had numerous inflections, as Table 4 illustrates.

TABLE 4
THE FORMS OF OLD ENGLISH NOUNS

	Masc. *stān* "stone"	Neut. *scip* "ship"	Fem. *lār* "teaching"	Masc. *oxa* "ox"
Singular				
Nominative	stān	scip	lār	oxa
Accusative	stān	scip	lāre	oxan
Genitive	stānes	scipes	lāre	oxan
Dative	stāne	scipe	lāre	oxan
Plural				
Nominative	stānas	scipu	lāra	oxan
Accusative	stānas	scipu	lāra	oxan
Genitive	stāna	scipa	lāra	oxena
Dative	stānum	scipum	lārum	oxum

The Middle English period brought the acceleration of a process already under way before the Norman Conquest—the "falling together" or "leveling" of inflections, owing in large part to the fact that word endings were unstressed and so were hardly distinguished in speech. Thus, final *u*, *-a*, and *-e* fell together as *-e*.

As far as the plural is concerned, the ending of Old English nouns like *stān*, which formed their plurals in *-as*, was eventually adopted in the reduced form *-es* for nearly all nouns, probably because it was distinctive (despite the convergence with possessive *-es*). The *-e* of the full syllable was eventually lost in pronunciation and then in spelling, except in words ending in *x*, *s*, *sh*, and *ch* (*boxes, buses, peaches, bushes*). When a Modern English noun already ends in *-e*, this is retained (*case/cases*); if the preceding consonant is *f*, this may change to *v* to reflect a slightly changed pronunciation (*knife/knives*). Another orthographic change in *-s* plurals occurs in words ending in *y*, which becomes *ie* (*spy/spies*). However, there are exceptions to the plural *-s* rule of Modern English, and these are often because of the survival of traces of the Old English inflection system, as can be seen with *oxen*. Let us look at these exceptions in more detail.

Zero-Plurals

Two nouns, *sheep* and *deer*, remain unchanged in the plural form, and so are said to have **zero plural:** *He saw the sheep* is thus ambiguous—there may have been only one sheep or several. Both of these nouns belonged to a class of Old English noun that had no inflection in the plural, and for no clear reason, they never attracted the *-s* inflection in the way that others like them did. Many other nouns in Modern English, especially those referring to hunted animals, game birds, or fish, can be used with either *s*-plural or zero-plural: "he shot fifty *buffalos/buffalo*," "*herrings/herring* are in short supply."

N-Plurals

Several nouns that make their plural with the *-en* suffix in Modern English belonged to the class of Old English nouns illustrated previously by *oxa*. Their basic forms ended in *-a* or *-e*, and most of their inflections were made by adding *-n*. Thus, *oxa* had plural *oxan*, which became Modern English *oxen*. Curiously, a number of new *-n* plurals were created during the Middle English period by analogy with nouns like *oxen*, though these nouns did not originally inflect in this way. *Children*, the plural of *child*, is a case in point; the Old English plural had been *cildru*, without an *n* (but *cildru* does explain the *r* in *children*). Similarly, a new plural for *brother* was made in the form of *brethren* (which included a vowel change also); the Old English plural had been *broþru*. Eventually, an *s*-plural for *brother* became the norm (*brothers*), but the *n*-plural survived as well and is used in Modern English mainly to describe male members of religious communities.

Mutated Plurals

A few Modern English nouns change the vowel or diphthong of their stem to make their plural forms and are therefore said to undergo **mutation**:

foot	→	feet	man	→	men
goose	→	geese	louse	→	lice
tooth	→	teeth	mouse	→	mice

These belonged to a small group of Old English nouns that, at an earlier stage of the development of the West Germanic languages, had been subject to mutation of their stem whenever they carried inflections containing *-i*. (In altering its shape in anticipation of saying the *i*, the mouth caused the preceding vowel to alter also.) These mutations remained in place even after the *i*-inflection was lost. Most of the mutated plural forms have been preserved in Modern English, but some were dropped. It is interesting to note that *book* was originally this type of noun in Old English, with plural *bēc* (pronounced be:tʃ); improbable though this may sound, if its mutated plural had been kept, we would probably be saying *two beech* today, not *two books.*

It is often puzzling in Modern English to see very similar words with dissimilar plurals. Why, for instance, is our plural of *house* not *hice*, on the pattern of *mouse/mice*? It is because the two words came from Old English nouns with different inflection patterns: *Hūs* was a neuter noun and never carried the endings that caused mutation in masculine *mūs*. Indeed, *hūs* was like *ship* in Table 4 on p. 51, which stayed unchanged in the nominative and accusative plural. *Hūs* was eventually drawn into the normalization process that gave most nouns the *-s* plural inflection, while the inflection pattern of *mūs* meant it would end up keeping its mutated plural form *mice*.

The Plurals of Foreign Nouns

Many foreign nouns borrowed into English come from languages in which the system of forming the plural is different. Although there is a tendency for such words to become anglicized in time (using normal *-s*), there may be much confusion while this process takes place. Many cases involve words of Latin or Greek origin, which causes obvious problems in an age when few people have knowledge of the classical languages. There is no regular pattern to the treatment of these foreign words in Modern English; some singular forms are given new English plurals, whereas some plural forms are treated as singular and then given new plurals. In general, the form in which the words are most commonly encountered seems to be adopted eventually as the singular form, whether it originally was or not. Here are the main types of foreign borrowings, divided according to the original languages. Most were borrowed in the 16th or 17th centuries.

- *Greek borrowings*
-on with plural -a
Examples are *automation, criterion,* and *phenomenon.* The standard Greek plural of each has *-a* in place of *-on*, but alternative plurals with *-s* are now heard for the first two: *automatons* and *criterions.* But there is a further complication. Though it is still considered incorrect, it is not unusual to hear people treat the Greek plural forms *criteria* and *phenomena* as singulars, so that they may say (and even write) "a criteria" and "a phenomena." It is likely that this trend will continue, and new plurals *criterias* and *phenomenas* will no doubt be formed—though whether *criterions* or *criterias* eventually wins out is anyone's guess.

• *Latin borrowings*
-us with plural -i
Examples are *alumnus, cactus, crocus,* and *locus.* The plurals *cactuses* and *crocuses* are well established and are rapidly superseding *cacti* and *croci,* but *alumni* and *loci* are holding their own, probably because these words are used far less than the others.

-us with plurals -ora/-era
Examples are *corpus* and *genus.* The first developed an anglicized alternative plural *corpuses,* alongside *corpora,* during the later 20th century, but, in the second case, *genera* (confined largely to technical use) seems to have held its ground.

-a with plural -ae
Examples are *alga, antenna, formula,* and *vertebra.* Plurals in *-s* are frequent; thus *antennas* rather than *antennae.* In the case of *alga,* its plural form *algae* has always been encountered much more often than the singular, and for this reason it is often mistakenly assumed to be itself the singular form; thus we may hear "an algae."

-um with plural -a
This group contains some contentious words, notably *datum, medium, bacterium,* and *stratum,* whose plurals in *-a* are now more often treated as singulars. In the case of *datum,* this singular form is relatively rare in English and is thus unfamiliar, and the better-known plural form *data* is often used as an uncountable (grammatically singular) noun: "The data is being processed." The plural *media* is taking longer to become established as a singular than *data,* no doubt because it does so obviously refer to a plurality of things: newspapers, radio, and television together. It is not unusual to read newspaper articles in which the writer treats *media* as singular in one sentence and plural in the next. The singular *medium* is still used frequently to convey the sense of a means or channel or vehicle for something: "Texting is a new medium of communication." When the word is used to describe a communicator with spirits, the new plural *mediums* is always used. *Bacterium,* like *datum,* is a singular form that is rarely used in general discourse, and plural *bacteria* is often mistaken for singular: "a bacteria." The same has happened with *strata,* singular *stratum,* and an alternative plural *stratas* is now sometimes heard. Two other nouns in this group are *curriculum* and *stadium.* Plurals *curriculums* and *stadiums* are now heard as often as *curricula* and *stadia.*

A long-established example of the singular approach to such words is *agenda.* This was also originally a plural form, from singular *agendum,* but in the years since it was borrowed in the 17th century it has become totally naturalized as a singular; the plural is now invariably *agendas*. We could compare the curious case of *news*. This looks like a plural form and indeed was in the Early Modern English period when *these news* would be heard; but since then it has come to be used exclusively as a singular noun: *this news*.

-ex/-ix with plural -ices

Examples are *appendix, codex, index,* and *matrix*. Latin plural forms are found almost interchangeably with anglicized inflection, thus, both *appendices* and *appendixes*.

-is with plural -es

Examples are *analysis, axis, basis, crisis, diagnosis, hypothesis, parenthesis,* and *thesis*. The original Latin plurals are always retained for these nouns (*analyses, bases,* etc.), no doubt because an anglicized inflection—*analysises, basises*— would be almost unpronounceable.

- *French borrowings*

-eau with plural -eaux

Examples are *bureau* and *tableau*. Both the original French plural forms (which are pronounced exactly as the singular) and the anglicized *-s* forms are found in Modern English, for example, *bureaux* and *bureaus*.

- *Italian borrowings*

-o with plural -i

Two commonly used Italian words occur almost invariably in the plural, *graffiti* and *paparazzi*, so that their original singular forms are unfamiliar to most English speakers. The first is a 19th-century borrowing, describing pictures or words inscribed on, for instance, a wall. *A graffito* is the original singular form, but *a graffiti* is often heard and found in print today; it seems also that *graffiti* may be turning, like *data*, into an uncountable noun. *Paparazzo*, which describes a freelance photographer who specializes in sensational pictures of famous people, was unknown before the later 20th century. It derives from the name of a character in the Fellini film, *La Dolce Vita*. As with *graffito*, the plural form is frequently heard in singular use: "a paparazzi." We have not yet come across plural *graffitis* and *paparazzis*, but no doubt they will eventually appear.

Other more famous Italian plurals have long since lost their plural sense for English speakers, among them are *macaroni* and *spaghetti*. These are now universally treated as uncountable nouns: *The spaghetti is delicious.*

Two other Italian words of this type, *tempo* and *virtuoso*, well known in the singular, have traditionally been given their original plural forms: *tempi* and *virtuosi*, but forms in *-s* have become acceptable also (*tempos* and *virtuosos*).

Adjectives

Comparatives and Superlatives

Adjectives are words that describe some characteristic of a noun or pronoun, and in their basic (or absolute) use they have only one form in Modern English: "a *small* car," "two *small* cars," "the cars are *small*." In Old English, adjectives varied their forms by adding inflections, but these had been lost by the 14th century. However, most adjectives do inflect in Modern English when they are being used in what are traditionally known as the **comparative degree** (indicating more of the quality expressed by the adjective) and the **superlative degree** (indicating the most amount of the quality). There are two ways to express these degrees:

1. By adding inflections to the absolute form of the adjective: *-er* for the comparative degree and *-est* for the superlative (or simply *-r* and *-st* when the adjective already ends in *e*): "My car is *smaller* than yours, but that one is the *smallest*."
2. By leaving the adjective unchanged but preceding it with *more* and *most*: "My car is *more powerful* than yours, but that one is *the most powerful*."

The rules as to which method to use are complex and variable, though in general, short words are used with the inflections (*kind-er, dark-est*) and longer words with *more* and *most* (*more famous, most interesting*). But there are many exceptions (*commonest*, as well as *most common*), and students can only learn by being alert to current usage. In the earlier stages of English, comparative and superlative forms were used much more freely. Examples such as *perfecter, difficultest*, and *famousest* will be found in Early Modern English texts. If an author wanted to provide emphasis, forms like *more lovelier* and *most unkindest* could be used—and such double expressions will be heard today in some non-standard dialects (and among small children), though they are frowned upon in Standard English.

Some very common adjectives form their comparative and superlative irregularly:

good	→ better	→ best	little	→ lesser	→ least
well	→ better	→ best	much	→ more	→ most
bad	→ worse	→ worst	far	→ farther	→ farthest

All these irregular forms were in place in Old English and have reached the modern language intact. The forms *worser*, *badder*, and *baddest* were also commonly found until the 18th century and are still used in some non-standard varieties. The forms *further/furthest* are alternatives to *farther/farthest*. They seem to be used interchangeably when the context is a simple reference to distance: *This way is farther/further by at least a mile*, but *further* is usually preferred in abstract and figurative use: *This book is of no further use.*

Adverbs

Adverbs form a varied class of words, conveying information about manner, degree, extent, direction, time, or place. They do not only modify verbs! In Latin *verbo* meant "word" in general, so that *ad-verbum* could describe any word that modifies another word. They may be used with a verb ("he ran *quickly*"), an adjective ("*quite* happy"), or another adverb ("*very* quickly"). They can also modify a sentence ("*surely* he'll understand," "*then* he arrived by car"). Sentence modification may be performed also by an adverbial phrase or clause, as in: "*After the flood*, devastation reigned," or "It finished *with the sound of a bass drum.*"

Most adverbs of manner in Modern English have the suffix *-ly*. This derives from Old English *lice* (meaning "like"), which went through several changes before it was eventually reduced to *-ly*. Many adverbs in Modern English derive directly from their Old English versions: *boldly*, *deeply*, *fully*, *openly*, *rightly*. Others come from the great period of adverb formation in English in the later 16th century, when many adjectives were simply converted to adverbs with zero inflection. These included many so-called "booster" adverbs, such as *ample*, *extreme*, *detestable*, *dreadful*, *exceeding*, *grievous*, *intolerable*, *terrible*, and *vehement*. But others were supplied with *-ly* from the start (*horribly*, *terribly*, *violently*), and use of the inflection gradually gained ground. During the 18th century, the pressure for normalization ensured that the suffix became the rule. We still use this suffix regularly today to make new adverbs from adjectives.

Adverbs are also formed by adding other suffixes. One of the most popular in Early Modern English was *-wise*, as in *leastwise, likewise,* and *lengthwise*. This was again of Old English origin, being the word *wisa*, "manner" or "fashion." Similarly, adverbs implying direction may be made by adding the Old English suffix *-ward(s)*, as in *skyward, downward*.

Pronouns

The word class in which Modern English has retained the most complexity from earlier periods of the language is pronouns. They are usefully classified as ***first person*** (singular *I*, plural *we*), ***second person*** (singular and plural *you*), and ***third person*** (singular *he, she, it,* plural *they*). For each person in the pronoun system, in both singular and plural, we have up to four separate forms, depending on the context, and in the third-person singular we distinguish for gender also (i.e., *he, she,* or *it*). Also, two different possessive forms are used—dependent ("this is *my* book") and independent ("this book is *mine*").

	Singular			Plural		
	1st pers.	2nd pers.	3rd pers.	1st pers.	2nd pers.	3rd pers.
Subject	I	you (thou)	he, she, it	we	you	they
Object	me	you (thee)	him, her, it	us	you	them
Dependent possession	my	your (thy)	his, her, its	our	your	their
Independent possession	mine	yours (thine)	his, hers, its	ours	yours	theirs

In the second person, *you* is now used in all normal circumstances however many people are being addressed. But most users of English are still familiar with a special set of second-person pronouns specifically for use when only one person is addressed *(thou, thee, thy, thine)*. These can be found in the works of Early Modern English writers such as Shakespeare and in some older versions of the Bible. They ceased to be current on a regular basis by the early 1700s but are used to this day by members of certain religious groups, such as the Society of Friends (the Quakers), as well as in some regional dialects of British English.

Me and *I*

Pronouns sometimes cause confusion even for native speakers, and one of the fuzziest areas is the use of *me* and *I*. Prescriptive grammar dictates that subject (nominative) forms should be used in sentences such as "It is I." However, real language use often pays little heed to prescriptive grammar and its arbitrary rules, and when we consult a descriptive grammar,[5] we find that the object (accusative) form is most commonly used today (*It's me*), except in the case of *it + be +* pronoun *+ who*, where *I* is the preferred form (*It was I who was wrong*). Particularly confusing are instances where *me* and *I* exist in coordinated noun phrases (i.e., phrases where they are connected to another noun by *and*: for example, "James and I," "the team and me"). In these cases, it is probably best to forget the prescriptive rules altogether and focus more on distinctions between spoken and written discourse, because this factor seems to determine most strongly which forms are used. In general, "James and I" is preferred in written texts, whereas "James and I" and "me and James" seem to be about equally common in conversation. However, when the coordinated phrase is detached from the main sentence (most common in spoken contexts), the accusative forms are commonly used (*You and me, we're two of a kind, Me and my friend Bob, we'd been to a game*).

Problematical also is the use of these pronouns when they are not subjects but objects. No one would disagree about the form of this sentence, where *you* and *me* are the appropriate object forms of the pronoun: *He likes you and he likes me*; for the last phrase, we would never say, *he likes I*. Yet if the sentence is condensed, so that the verb is used only once, with two object pronouns, the following is commonly heard: *He likes you and I*. This is a result of hypercorrection, the anxiety of people to speak "correct" English. They know that "you and me" in some contexts is considered wrong and do not realize that it is only so judged when the pronouns are used as subjects.

Who, Which, or *That?*

Traditionally, the relative pronoun *who* is used after animate nouns, but *which* or *that* after inanimate ones: "the man *who* came back" but "the house *which/that* fell." In the latter case, *that* is preferred in American written style and *which* in Britain. However, *that* is increasingly heard in both varieties in relation to animate and inanimate nouns: "the man *that* came back." The relative pronoun *who* also has an inflected form, *whom*, which derives from Old English. It is the object form (accusative): *The man whom I saw*. After about 1500, *who* was mostly used in all situations, but in the 18th century prescriptive grammarians promoted the use of *whom* again. It is still liked by some speakers of British English, but you will often hear it misused by those anxious to show their command of "good" English: "It doesn't matter *whom* you are" is wrong because the pronoun here is a subject, not object.

Verbs

Morphologically, verbs fall into two main categories: **regular** and **irregular.** We shall deal with them in turn. Students will need to know how to use a few important descriptive terms. *Tense* indicates the time period (present, future, or past) in which the action or state expressed by the verb occurs. For example, using the verb *to see*: *I see* (the present tense), *I will see* (the future tense), *I saw* (the past tense). We can refine our expression of the past tense by saying *I have seen* or *I had seen*, and the modified form of the verb, *seen*, is known as the **past participle.** (This distinguishes it from the **present participle,** which is the term used to describe *-ing* form of verbs, as in *I am seeing*.) As we note, in most regular verbs the simple past form and the past participle are identical (e.g., *I loved, I have loved*).

Regular Verbs

The majority of verbs make their past tense and past participle predictably by adding *-(e)d*: *walk → walked*. These are known as **regular** verbs. Newly acquired verbs are invariably given this ending in Modern English: *fax → faxed, party → partied*. A small group of verbs forming their past forms regularly with *-ed* have developed an alternative with *-t* in British English: *burned/burnt, learned/learnt, smelled/smelt, spelled/spelt, spilled/spilt, spoiled/spoilt*. In American English, the *-t* forms are rarely used. In the case of *build*, whose past tense and past participle used to be *builded*, the form today is exclusively *built* in all varieties.

Irregular Verbs

A sizeable minority of verbs make their past tense by changing their form in unpredictable ways, as in *shine → shone*; they do not take the *-ed* inflection. These are known as **irregular verbs** and are characteristic of Germanic languages. There are some 200 of them in Modern English but Old English had many more; some of these went out of use altogether and some subsequently became regular (see p. 62). We can arrange the irregular verbs of Modern English in three main categories, according to the way in which their past and past participle forms have developed from Old English forms. (The more detailed descriptions in grammar books can break irregular verbs into as many as seven categories.[7])

• More than 70 verbs retain a vowel change in the past and in the past participle (sometimes the same vowel in both but usually not) and in the latter case also add *-(e)n*. Irregular verbs that add *-(e)n* are the closest to the original Old English inflection system:

blow	→	blew	→	blown
see	→	saw	→	seen
take	→	took	→	taken
tear	→	tore	→	torn

A few verbs, originally irregular, have become regular (using *-ed*) but retain an alternative *-n* form for the past participle: thus *mow* gives *mowed* or *mown* and *swell* gives *swollen* or *swelled*. In a few cases, the *-n* form in such verbs has been retained only for specialized use: Irregular Old English *meltan* "melt" (with past *mealt* and past participle *multon*) became regular *melted*, but the irregular past participle survives as the adjective describing "melted" metal, *molten*.

• About 30 verbs have similarly preserved different forms for the past and the past participle but do not retain *-(e)n* on the latter:

drink	→	drank	→	drunk
sing	→	sang	→	sung
swim	→	swam	→	swum

In the case of *drink*, the original past participle with *-en* does survive, however, as an alternative (perhaps rather more literary) adjectival form: *a drunken man*.

• In another 50 or so verbs, past and past participle forms have fallen together into a single form:

find	→	found	→	found
sit	→	sat	→	sat
spin	→	spun	→	spun
stand	→	stood	→	stood
strike	→	struck	→	struck

In the case of *strike*, the single form *struck* has been adopted in Modern English for both past and past participle, but an *-n* form of the latter, *stricken*, has survived also; it is reserved for cases where someone or something has been hit by illness or disaster. In a few of these verbs, even the infinitive has the same form as the past:

burst	→	burst	→	burst
let	→	let	→	let

In non-standard varieties of Modern English, much variation will be heard in the irregular verbs. In particular, there is a tendency to simplify further in verbs of the first two categories on p. 61 and to use a single form in all circumstances: *He's drank too much, I seen him yesterday.* These forms are considered to be poor usage in standard varieties of English.

IRREGULAR TO REGULAR
Many verbs that originally had irregular forms in Old English subsequently took on new, regular forms. Some are still in the middle of this change today, having both irregular and regular forms that are used pretty well interchangeably, as, for example, *shine: shone/shined, shone/shined.* Another example of such morphological instability in our time is *slay,* with past *slew* and past participle *slain* but with the regular past *slayed* also being heard.

REGULAR TO IRREGULAR
In a few cases the reverse process occurred and originally regular verbs became irregular in their past forms, presumably by analogy with existing irregular verbs. Examples are *dig, spit,* and *stick,* whose irregular past forms *dug, spat,* and *stuck* arose only in the 16th century, before which time *digged, spitted,* and *sticked* were used. *Spit* today has an alternative (unchanged) past form *spit.* Another example is *dove,* a past form of *dive* apparently made by analogy with forms such as *weave/wove. Dove* is commonly used in American English, but British English retains *dived,* though *dove* is recorded in a few dialects.

Some Special Irregular Verbs

A few very common irregular verbs have present forms as well as past forms that are often unpredictable. Examples include *be, go, have, do,* and the modal verbs.

BE
The verb *to be* is both the most used and the most complex verb in Modern English in terms of its morphology, with seven distinct forms: *be, is, am, are, was, were,* and *been.*[8] This complexity is a headache for both students and teachers, but at least it is very much the exception in the English verb system. Other Indo-European languages (including French and German) have a similar complexity in their versions of *to be.*

To be is unique in Modern English in having distinct forms for singular and plural in the past tense: *was* and *were.* However, in non-standard dialects, *we was, you was, I were, she were,* etc., are commonly heard. These are considered poor usage according to today's Standard English norms, yet *you was* is quite logical in singular usage (distinguished from plural *you were*). It was acceptable in Early Modern English and at least up until the end of the 18th century. By then, however, the prescriptive grammarians were condemning it on the grounds that *you* is, strictly speaking, a plural pronoun, and insisting on the use of the far less logical *you were* in the singular as well as plural sense. The Americans held out for a while, with Noah Webster defending *you was* in singular use, but eventually the prescriptivists won, and America also ended up adopting the current form.[9]

MODAL VERBS

Modal verbs are so called because in a broad sense they express **mood,** especially the ideas of necessity, possibility, or desire. Among the most important of them, given here in their present- and past-tense forms, are *shall/should, will/would, can/could, may/might,* and *must/must.* In Old English times, *must* had a separate present-tense form, but that became lost and the same form is now used for present and past. Modal verbs have no *-s* forms in the third-person singular: *it will, she may,* etc.; nor do they have an infinitive ("to can"). *Shall* is now relatively rare and is mainly used to express personal volition ("I *shall* go the extra mile") or in questions acting as offers or suggestions ("*Shall* we wait for them?"). It is interesting to note that the earlier form of *could* did not contain an *l* (*coude*). It was added only in the 17th century, by analogy with *should* and *would,* but was never pronounced, as it had been originally in *should* and *would.* (See more about such spelling changes in Chapter 6 and more about modals in the next section.)

Irregularities in Syntax

Syntax is concerned with the order of words and the relationships between those words in sentences. In terms of comprehension, word order in Modern English is often more important than morphology, as we saw in the example at the beginning of the chapter. We may understand a sentence with a few inflectional errors, but if the word order is muddled, sense may disappear.

But what is a "sentence"? Traditionally it is defined as a self-contained unit of meaning, and more specifically, it must have at least a subject and a verb; the part of the sentence that contains the verb (which in turn may have an object) is usually known as the **predicate.** In fact, analysis of any discourse, especially a spoken one, will show that sentences do not always follow these rules. Consider the following: *All right?—Not really.—Oh dear!—Easy come, easy go.—Absolutely!* Each of these units is complete and will be meaningful in context; yet all but one have no verb, and none has a subject (unless we count *all* in the first example). Prescriptive grammarians might say that these utterances—proverbial statements, catch phrases, and exclamations—are ungrammatical, though they are a vital part of spoken discourse. The fact of the matter is that English does not have a single grammatical model that covers every case of usage. The grammar that most people are familiar with applies to more formal written discourse, and so in this section we highlight a few aspects of written syntax—basic word order, elements of verb use, negation, and so on—in which a historical explanation can lead to a better understanding of today's usage. Spoken discourse has its own set of grammatical conventions, some of which are quite different from written grammar. For more information on these spoken conventions, see the grammar reference books in the Further Reading section.

Word Order

The most crucial aspect of syntax is word order. English is a Subject-Verb-Object (S-V-O) language, but this was not always the case. In Old English, there were other ways of marking word function within a sentence than simply word order—and this is still the case with German and many other modern languages. In Old English, as discussed, the definite article (*the*) or demonstrative adjectives (*this, these, those*) that went with nouns, and often the nouns themselves, were marked for grammatical function. Thus subjects and objects were clearly differentiated. Take the following two sentences:

1. Se hund   biteþ   þone catt
   the dog   *bites*   *the cat*
2. Þone catt   biteþ   se hund
   the cat   *bites*   *the dog*

If you read the modern versions word by word, it appears that the Old English sentences say very different things: In the first sentence, the cat is the victim, in the second sentence, the dog. But in Old English, the meaning of the two sentences is in fact exactly the same; that is, it's bad news for the cat! This is because the subject is marked by the subject form of the word for *the, se,* as used before masculine nouns such as *hund,* and the object is marked by the object form of the word for *the, þone,* as used before a masculine noun, *catt* in this case (see Table 3 on p. 49). So *se hund* <u>must</u> be the subject, and *þone catt* <u>must</u> be the object, whatever their position in the sentence.

We can actually get something of the flavor of this inflectional system even in Modern English, for we still vary the form of pronouns according to grammatical function: "The dog bites *him*" (object pronoun), not "The dog bites *he*." But in Old English, the system was far more pervasive.

Thus, in Old English, word order was far less important than it is today; different elements in a sentence were marked by inflection to show their grammatical function, and so word order in itself was not necessarily an indicator of meaning. But when, during the Middle English period, this inflection system was drastically reduced (with the adoption of a single form for the definite article, *þe* [later spelled *the*], and the loss of all but possessive and plural endings on nouns), word order became absolutely crucial to meaning. S-V-O had already been the most common arrangement in Old English; now it became the *only* permissible arrangement. In the Modern English version of the first sentence, the cat *has* to be the victim, and in the second sentence it *has* to be the dog, because both the cat and the dog follow the verb.

Adjectives

The rule in Modern English is that adjectives (and other modifiers) come before the nouns that they qualify: *a red box, a powerful politician*. This was the case in Old English too, but in Early Modern English, probably under the influence of French, the reverse order was sometimes found (especially in the context of government or law), and a few set expressions from this period survive, such as *proof positive*. Dealing with the order of a succession of adjectives is a difficult aspect of Modern English for learners. Why is *those two, splendid, old, electric trains* acceptable, but not *those electric, splendid, old, two trains?* There seems to be some hierarchy of specification that is seldom stated but that proficient users intuitively know. John Sinclair suggests that modifiers are generally ordered according to the following categories, although the order can be changed to highlight particular elements.[10]

Determiner	Numerative	Adjective (evaluative)	Adjective (objective)	Classifier	Thing
those	*two*	*splendid*	*old*	*electric*	*trains*
that		*big noisy*	*brown*	*cuckoo*	*clock*

Prepositions

When, during the Middle English period, English lost most of its inflections, prepositions became especially important as function words in the syntax of sentences. Old English had comparatively few prepositions, and each had a far wider range of meaning than their present equivalents. Thus *æt (at)* could have the Modern English senses of "in, from, to, next to, with," as well as "at," and *on* could mean "in, into, onto, to, at, against, during, among, amid, for, as, with, according to," as well as "on." The *a-* element of modern prepositions such as *among* and *amid* is a reduction of Old English *on*: The words started life as prepositional phrases, *on gemang,* "in among," and *on midde,* "in the middle of."

The basic meaning of Old English *of* was "from," a usage that survives in certain expressions such as, *What do you want of [i.e., from] me?* and in the American way of giving the time: *It's a quarter of six,* i.e., a quarter of an hour from or before 6 o'clock, where British English prefers *to.* In Old English, *of* was also used as an adverb; for that usage in Modern English, a spelling change is made: *off* (e.g., "he rode *off*").

Old English *wiþ* (i.e., *with*) meant basically "toward," "against" or "from," a meaning retained in the Modern English verb prefix *with-*; thus, *withstand* means "stand *against*," and *withold* means "keep *from*"—meanings that seem to contradict our usual modern understanding of the preposition.

In Early Modern English, many prepositions still had a far wider range of meanings than they do today. Now they are quite restricted in use, with consequent difficulties for learners. One reason for the changes is that many new prepositions and specialized prepositional phrases came into use in later Middle English and Early Modern English, meaning that the scope for each word became smaller. For example, several earlier functions of *by* were taken over by *near, in accordance with, about, concerning, by reason of,* and *owing to; for* came to be replaced often by *because of* or *as regards;* and prepositional *but* became almost wholly replaced by *unless, except,* or *bar* (though it survives in the phrase *all but you*).

The following quotations from Shakespeare give some idea of the sorts of changes that have occurred since the 17th century; the preposition required in Modern English in each context is given in brackets:

We are such stuff as dreams are made *on (The Tempest)* [of]

Read *on* this book *(Hamlet)* [in]

In this time of the night *(Othello)* [at]

Take *of* me my daughter *(Much Ado about Nothing)* [from]

How say you *of* the French lord? *(The Merchant of Venice)* [about]

Say you choose him / More *after* our commandment *(Coriolanus)* [according to]

The placing of a preposition at the end of a sentence (sometimes called a stranded or dangling preposition) has been frowned on by prescriptivist grammarians since the 17th century. Examples are *Here is the man I spoke to* and *That's something I wasn't aware of.* The rule against stranded prepositions in English was based on Latin usage, which does not allow it. In fact, stranding has been in normal idiomatic use in English since Anglo-Saxon times, so the rule is best ignored. The alternatives, such as *Here is the man to whom I spoke* and *That's something of which I was not aware,* seem stilted to most users. When Winston Churchill was corrected after using a stranded preposition, he reacted with a remark that nicely emphasized the point: *That is the sort of English up with which I will not put.* Only in academic contexts is the construction preposition + *wh-*word somewhat more common than the stranded construction.[11] Most grammar books overlook the fact that it is common practice in the spoken language to use stranded constructions but to omit the preposition altogether:

> That would be the very last place that Marion and I would want to go [to].
> What about the place we were going to stay [at].[12]

Verbs

Third-Person *-s*

We have seen that Old English was a highly inflected language and that most of the inflections became lost, resulting in a more rigid word order and increased use of function words, such as prepositions. Only in the pronoun system has English retained something of the original complexity. Annoyingly for students, however, an echo of it survives also in one of the most problematic forms—the third-person singular present tense *-s* in verbs. The *-s* is a reminder of a period when each of the three persons of the verb was marked by its own special inflection. For the third-person singular, this had been *-eþ*, that is, *-eth*, in Old English, but during the Middle English period the alternative *-s* (taken from northern dialects of English) had begun to rival it. During the Early Modern English period, the two were used side by side (*loves* and *loveth*), until by about 1700 *-s* had become the dominant form. Exactly why the inflection remained at all is not clear; it serves no useful function, for the pronouns or nouns used with the verb give all the information required, and this in itself makes it extremely difficult for learners to acquire the inflection. So great are the complexities of this single feature of verbs that one grammar book dedicates almost an entire chapter to it.[13] At least teachers can be thankful that it is the only such needless inflection to have slipped through during the evolution process of verbs.

Split Infinitives

One of the most notorious rules of Modern English has been the one that states that the infinitive must not be split—that is, no words must intervene between *to* and the following verb. Based on this directive, the famous opening voice-over for the 1960s television series *Star Trek* "... to boldly go where no man has gone before" is "wrong"—only *boldly to go* or *to go boldly* would be acceptable. In fact, this is one of the more pointless rules of English (established by the 18th-century prescriptive grammarians) and is now largely ignored. At least as early as the 13th century, other words were regularly intervening between *to* and its verb, and admired writers in English at all periods since have been splitting infinitives. There are indeed cases where not to do so may result in ambiguity, especially in writing, where special phrasing cannot be used to give clarification. If you write, *He failed completely to convince them*, it is not clear whether the adverb *completely* goes with *failed* (i.e., his failure was complete) or *to convince* (i.e., he did convince them, but only in part). If you mean the latter, this can only be made clear by putting *completely* immediately before *convince*, and thus splitting the infinitive: *He failed to completely convince them.*[14]

The Modals *Will, Shall, Can,* and *May*

In traditional grammar, the use of *will* and *shall* was strictly delineated: To express future tense, *shall* must be used with the first person, both singular and plural (*I/we shall arrive tomorrow*), and *will* with the other persons (*you/(s)he/it/they will arrive tomorrow*). To express intention or insistence, on the other hand, *will* must be used with the first person (*I/we will do it*) and *shall* with the others (*you/(s)he/it/they shall do it*). These rules were first codified in the 17th century by John Wallis, a professor of geometry at the University of Oxford who published a grammar of English in 1653—written in Latin (*Grammatica linguae anglicanae*). A cautionary tale used to be told to pupils in the more traditional British schools about a man seen in a lake, waving his arms frantically while other people look on. A passerby is inclined to help, but when he hears the man shouting, "I *will* drown and nobody *shall* save me!" he changes his mind. He thinks the man means, "I intend to drown and nobody is permitted to save me." If the man had shouted, "I *shall* drown and nobody *will* save me" (i.e., "I am about to drown and nobody is willing to save me"), rescue might have been forthcoming!

In fact, the distinction between *will* and *shall* was never widely adopted outside standard southern British English and never caught on in America.

Today it is hardly made by users of any variety of English. In American English, *will* is used almost to the exclusion of *shall* in all instances. Even in British English, sentences such as "He *shall* come tomorrow" or "I know you *shall* do it" (to express the simple future) would sound distinctly odd, even to the most conservative users. However, *shall* is still frequently used in legal documents: "In the event of breakdown, the manufacturer *shall* be liable under this guarantee"; and there is a curious tendency among today's university students to use *shall* in introductions to essays: "This essay *shall* be about the language of love in Shakespeare's plays." A formal expression of intention seems to be the objective. The origin of the modal *can/could* is in the Old English verb *cunnan*, "be acquainted with," "know how to," "be able to." It had no connection with the idea of being allowed to do something, which was always the province of *may*. Its use to express permission seems not to have begun before the 19th century, after which the clear distinction between *can* and *may* was soon all but lost, to the dismay of prescriptive grammarians. Older speakers of British English will remember being rebuked for asking, *Can I have some more cake?* rather than *May I have some more cake?* However *can* is now in fact the norm, with the use of *may* being especially rare in the sense of giving or asking for permission, except perhaps when used with children:[15] *You may do your language work if you want to.*

Contraction of Forms of *to be*

Contraction of forms of *to be* when used with pronouns is frequent in less formal writing and reflects speech habits; for example, *it is→it's*. In earlier English, it was the *i* of the pronoun that was dropped, producing *'tis*, but this was replaced after the 17th century. *It was* was contracted to *'twas*, but this too died out in written English, though it will still be heard in rapid speech. Similarly, *it'll* stands for *it will* or *it shall*; again there was an earlier form, with ellipsis of the vowel of the pronoun, *'twill*. The older contractions are sometimes used today when speakers want to give their utterance an "antique" character for comical or ironical effect.

For the first-person singular, there was the contraction *an't* for *am not*, and this developed a variant *ain't* in the 18th century. As those familiar with 18th-century plays will know, this was perfectly acceptable usage among the upper classes at one time, though today it not part of Standard English. It is common in conversation (more so in American English than in British English), but not in written discourse, other than in quoted speech in fiction.[16] In many circles its use is seen as stigmatizing, even as a sort of benchmark for uneducated speech. In British pronunciation, the *a* in *an't* came to be sounded long rather than short (see Chapter 5), and thus the contraction began to sound very much like *aren't* (the regular contraction of *are + not*). This explains today's "ungrammatical" but accepted colloquial use of *aren't* in the first-person singular, as well as plural: "I'm right, *aren't* I?" To avoid this, we would have to say "am I not?"

Negation

In Old English, the negative particle was *ne*, and it always came before the verb: *ic ne cume*, literally "I not come" (i.e., *I am not coming*), *ic neom frēo*, "I not am free." In the latter example, *neom* is a contraction of *ne eom*; such contraction was frequent in Old English (as in *nis* for *ne is*, "isn't"). The Modern English negative adverb *not*, often *nat* in Middle English, evolved as a reduced form of Old English *nāht* or *nānwiht* (an adverb meaning "not at all"); the full word has survived as the noun *naught* or *nought*, which is used in Modern English both to mean a zero and as a rather literary variation on "nothing": "It came to nought." American English prefers the spelling *naught*. In Early Modern English, the position of *not* was after the verb: "I know not," but already the periphrastic (i.e., roundabout) construction that is obligatory today, using *do*, was evolving: *I do not know*. The negative particle always follows an auxiliary verb: *You must not talk; We shall not succeed.*

In earlier Middle English, a double construction with both *ne* and *nat* was still frequent, but the use of the preceding *ne* then began to die out. However, the practice of double negation continued in Early Modern English, as in Shakespeare's *I cannot go no further* (*As You Like It*). It then became less frequent in the written language and was one of the "faults" frowned upon by the prescriptive grammarians of the 18th century. They formulated the logical rule, which they knew from Latin, that two negatives make a positive so that to say "I won't have none of it" means "I will have some of it." Of course, this logic is only true from one point of view; most people instinctively see double negation as a mark of negative *emphasis*, rather than a convoluted way to express a positive idea. In fact, many languages around the world use double negation (e.g., French and Russian), and so it cannot be inherently illogical.[17] However, the rule still holds firm in standard varieties of English, though many non-standard varieties ignore it, and here multiple negatives will sometimes be heard: *I don't need nothing from nobody.*

APPLICATIONS TO TEACHING

In the last two sections, we have explained some of the irregular forms and rules that second language students often ask teachers about. Sometimes the reason behind these troublesome forms is purely historical accident, as with third-person *-s*. No one knows why it remains in English after virtually every other inflection disappeared. Other problematic rules are the result of ill-advised language engineering; prescriptive grammarians decided the way English *should* be spoken, often with no real consideration of the way it was *actually* being spoken. In many cases this resulted in the confusing situation of rules that posited a language very different from language in the real world. The rules for split infinitives and the use of *shall* and *will* are examples of such misguided prescription.

Perhaps as damaging as the actual rules themselves was the establishment of the idea that there exists a single correct English grammar. This attitude is pervasive among both students and language teaching professionals. Students want to know the "correct" answer, teachers want a single "correct" form that they can teach with confidence, and language assessors want grammatical forms that they test according to the criterion of correctness. Grammatical variability makes things more difficult for everyone. In reality, language is a living thing, always changing and always adapting to new ideas and needs. It is complex and varied, and when it comes to grammar, it is particularly difficult to pigeonhole into neat categories. The authors of the *Longman Grammar of Spoken and Written English* (LGSWE) found variation throughout the English grammar system. After spending more than six years analyzing and describing English, they should be as aware as anyone of the true nature of English grammar. They conclude:

> It would...be wrong to assume that standard English is fixed, with little or no variability. In fact, one of the major goals of the *LGSWE* is to describe the patterns of variation that exist within standard English, and to account for those patterns in terms of contextual factors. For example, standard English uses two relative pronouns with inanimate head nouns—*that* and *which*:
>
> *I could give you figures that would shock you.*
> *This chapter is devoted to a discussion of various flow processes which occur in open systems.*

In most sentences, either of these two forms would be grammatical, although there are a number of contextual factors that favor the use of one or the other. Thus, the existence of a standard variety has not leveled out variability of this type. In particular, the notion that the standard insists on "uniformity"— allowing just one variant of each grammatical feature—is a serious fallacy, arising from a misleading application to language of the notion of "standard" and "standardization" taken from other walks of life.[18]

The point to take from all of this is that grammar is far from an absolute set of rules set in stone. Of course, some grammatical elements are relatively consistent and may well be best taught as rules. However, other elements may be quite flexible, with the most appropriate form depending largely on context. In these cases, it is probably best to think of the grammatical elements as regularities rather than rules—that is, having a regular form in most cases but also varying somewhat depending on the situation. Teachers can become better grammar instructors if they recognize the flexibility of the English grammar system, particularly if they become conversant with the contextual elements that affect variation. One of the most potent contextual factors is whether discourse is spoken or written. Because of the importance of this dichotomy, we suggest that teachers consult reference sources that highlight the different grammatical tendencies of spoken and written discourse rather than those sources that essentially treat English grammar in a "one size fits all" manner. There are recommendations for such sources in the Further Reading section.

Modern Changes in Grammar

One of the key themes of this book is that English has constantly changed through its history and continues to change. This will not surprise anyone when it comes to English vocabulary—slang changes and comes in and out of fashion with sometimes amazing speed. However, most people tend to think of English grammar as something fixed.

Although it is true that grammar is relatively stable overall, some elements are in flux. Here are three instances of this.

1. In the formation of the past tense and past participles of verbs we have seen that there has frequently been instability, and this continues. For the past tense of *dive* and *sneak*, Americans more often than not use *dove* and *snuck*,

but they have the choice of *sneaked* and *dived* also. The latter forms are those that you are more likely to hear from British users, who may indeed find *dove* and *snuck* rather odd, but neither of the alternatives is incorrect. In the case of the verb *slay*, the irregular past *slew* is still the most commonly used, but *slayed* is also heard today. Several originally regular verbs, especially those whose basic form ends in *t*, have long had an alternative contracted form for the past tense: thus *knit* and *knitted*, *quit* and *quitted*, *lit* and *lighted*. In the first, the *-ed* form seems to be gaining ground at the moment (perhaps because of potential confusion with the present-tense form, *knit*), but *lit* is preferred over *lighted* by most users. The use of *gotten* in place of *got* as a past participle, characteristically American, is currently being heard often in Britain as well and seems likely to increase in popularity.

2. The grammatical characteristics of some words are changing. Let us take the example of *datum/data*. We noted earlier in the chapter that *datum* is falling out of use and that *data* is taking over the function of both singular and plural, in effect becoming an uncountable noun. Let us look at the specific figures that show this. *Data* occurs 139 times per million words in the British National Corpus, while *datum* only occurs 0.4 times per million. Some of this difference may be because the plural form is more useful than the singular form, but nonetheless, *datum* is clearly now a very low-frequency word in English. As for the issue of *data* developing into an uncountable noun, there are 689 cases of *data are* in the British National Corpus and 585 cases of *data is*, which is not a very large difference in corpus terms. It seems that, in fact, both forms are currently correct. However, over the long term, it is likely that *data* will continue to move toward being an uncountable noun. Within decades, *data are* may fall completely out of use.

3. The function of some words is changing. For example, *like* has a number of common uses that you are probably familiar with. It is a common verb for expressing what someone prefers (*"Do you like London?"*). It is also a preposition that means "similar to," and often occurs with verbs of sensation such as *look*, *sound*, *feel*, *taste*, and *seem* (*"Some people say ostrich meat tastes like beef"*). *Like* has functions similar to that of an adjective (*"They are women of like mind"*), and as an adjective-forming suffix (*"Soaring above the island, almost ghost-like, was a Lockheed Electra 10E airplane"*). *Like* is also being used more and more in colloquial speech as a conjunction (though this is traditionally considered to be bad grammar): *He said it like he meant it*, rather than *He said it as though he meant it*. However, in addition to these and other uses, the authors of the *Cambridge Grammar of Spoken and Written English* discovered that there has been a recent large increase in the use of *like* as a marker of direct speech in informal spoken English. This usage is especially frequent where the report

involves a personal reaction or response and is commonly used by young people:

> So this bloke, he was drunk, came up to me and I'm *like*, "Go away, I don't want to dance."

> And my mum's *like* non-stop three or four times, "Come and tell your grandma about your holiday."[20]

In this chapter we have seen how the grammar of English has changed in the past, but these examples serve to illustrate that it continues to change, even as we speak it. In the next chapter, we look at another component of English where change has been remarkable—vocabulary.

FURTHER READING

Two popular teacher's reference books on grammar.
- Leech, G., & Svartvik, J. (2002). *A communicative grammar of English.* London: Longman.
- Swan, M. (1995). *Practical English usage.* Oxford: Oxford University Press.

For new teachers, an introduction to grammar from the student's perspective.
- Parrott, M. (2000). *Grammar for English language teachers.* Cambridge: Cambridge University Press.

An informative chapter that gives a good overview of current thinking about grammar and its presentation.
- DeCarrico, J., & Larsen-Freeman, D. (2002). Grammar. In N. Schmitt (Ed.), *An introduction to applied linguistics* (pp. 19–34). London: Arnold.

A popular teacher's coursebook in grammar.
- Celce-Murcia, M., & Larsen-Freeman, D. (1998). *The grammar book: An ESL/EFL teacher's course* (2nd ed.). Cambridge, MA: Newbury House.

Two leading corpus-based descriptive grammars.
- Biber, D., Johansson, S., Leech, G., Conrad, S., & Finegan, E. (1999). *Longman grammar of spoken and written English.* Harlow: Longman.
- Carter, R., & McCarthy, M. (2005). *Cambridge grammar of spoken and written English.* Cambridge: Cambridge University Press.

Classroom Activity: 3.1

Irregular Verbs in English

Most English verbs form the past tense and past participle by adding *–ed*:

word	past tense	past participle
walk	*walked*	*walked*
listen	*listened*	*listened*

But some English verbs are irregular and have different past forms:

see	*saw*	*seen*
throw	*threw*	*thrown*

This exercise explores irregular verbs.

1. How many irregular verbs are there in English today? About _____

2. Write the past forms of the following irregular verbs. The first one has been done for you.

verb	past tense	past participle
bite	bit	bitten
draw	_____	_____
forgive	_____	_____
hurt	_____	_____
lie (position)	_____	_____
ring	_____	_____
shake	_____	_____
speak	_____	_____
spread	_____	_____
tear	_____	_____

3. The following irregular verbs have two past forms, but one form is usually more common. For example, the past forms of *hang* are (*hang → hung* or *hanged*), but *hung* is used more than 75 percent of the time. Both of the past forms are possible.

Circle the one that is more common. The first one has been done for you.

verb	regular past tense	irregular past tense
hang	hanged	(hung)
dive	dived	dove
sneak	sneaked	snuck
slay	slayed	slew

Classroom Activity: 3.2

Irregular Plural Nouns in English

Most English nouns form the plural by adding *-s* (or *-es* in some cases):

word	plural form
boy	*boys*
car	*cars*
bike	*bikes*
dish	*dishes*

But some English nouns have irregular plural forms:

man	*men*
mouse	*mice*

Write the plural forms of the following irregular nouns. The first one has been done for you.

word	irregular plural form
woman	women
foot	_____
goose	_____
child	_____
ox	_____
criterion	_____
phenomenon	_____
sheep	_____
deer	_____
fish	_____
buffalo	_____

4

ENGLISH VOCABULARY

Why Are There So Many Words, and Where Did They Come From?

- *How big is the English lexicon?*
- *How many words does it take to communicate in English?*
- *Where have English words come from?*
- *How are words from different origins used differently?*

Students intuitively know that vocabulary is one of the key elements in learning a second language; they carry dictionaries around, not grammar books. When the language is English, this is especially true, because it possesses a particularly large number of words. Learning enough vocabulary to operate in English is one of the greatest challenges facing students. Unlike grammar, vocabulary is an open-ended dimension of the language, which must be intimidating for the average student. Before we discuss where English words come from historically, let us first explore the challenge that the acquiring of a good vocabulary presents by examining the size of the lexicon and determining just how many words are required to use English in various ways.

The Size of the English Lexicon

English has one of the largest vocabularies of any known language. It has many more words than German, Italian, French, or Spanish. Although it would be impossible to accurately count every word in English, a number of scholars have tried to estimate the overall size of the lexicon. Their calculations have varied widely, anywhere from 200,000 words in common use to a total stretching into the millions. One of the reasons for these very different estimates is variation in the definition of what counts as a word. For example, should *access, accessed, accessing,* and *accesses* be counted as one word or four? Likewise, should the noun form *accessibility,* the adjective form *accessible,* and the adverb form *accessibly* be counted as part of a single "word family" or as individual words? The larger estimates of English vocabulary size have tended to categorize each word form as a different word. Using this system, the forms of *access* would be counted as seven separate words.

This seems a bit excessive, and so one study used the "word family" definition (which would count all of the forms listed previously as one related group) to estimate the size of the English vocabulary.[1] Using *Webster's Third New International Dictionary* (1961) as its source, about 54,000 word families were distinguished. There were of course large groups of words not included in these families, such as proper nouns (*Michigan, Microsoft, Nelson Mandela*), vocabulary specific to certain technical fields (chemistry: *cetylpyridinium chloride;* applied linguistics: *illocutionary force*), and dialect words (*gadgie,* "man," and *owt,* "anything," used in the Middlesborough area of England). Nevertheless, the figure of 54,000 gives a good baseline estimate for discussion of the size of the English lexicon.

Of course, it is highly unlikely that anyone would know all of these 54,000 word families, especially considering that each contains a varying number of individual words. Even very educated native speakers will normally know only a fraction of this total. The study noted found that New Zealand university students knew about 20,000 word families. Matching the achievement of the native speaker would be an extreme challenge for non-native learners. The good news is that a much smaller number of words can still allow learners to use English in various ways.

One of the most basic things a learner might want to do in English is to communicate orally on an everyday basis. It seems that between 2,000 and 3,000 word families can provide enough vocabulary to do this.[2] Of course, learners will not be able to discuss everything, but they will have the vocabulary to get their ideas across for everyday purposes (e.g., describing a trip, asking where a store is). As for written communication, knowledge of around 3,000 word families is the threshold that should allow learners to begin to read non-simplified texts. If learners wish to read English newspapers, magazines, and other authentic material without vocabulary being an intrusive problem, then around 5,000 word families are required. By the time learners have a vocabulary size of around 10,000 word families, they should have a wide enough vocabulary to cope in English at an advanced level, including study in an English-medium university.[3]

APPLICATIONS TO TEACHING

If you are a practicing teacher, you probably have a good idea what the learning goals of your students are. (If you are a teacher-in-training, you hopefully will have in the future!) In addition, your school system will have additional targets set out for them, often explicitly stated in a syllabus. Using the guidelines listed in the previous paragraph, one of your objectives should be to ensure that your students have enough vocabulary to be able to meet these goals and targets. To do this, you first need to determine what vocabulary your learners already have. The vocabulary test at the end of this chapter (see pp. 106–110) was designed to tell you how much vocabulary they know at each of the four levels mentioned: the 2,000, 3,000, 5,000, and 10,000 most frequent word families in English. The results can indicate whether your learners have enough lexical resources available to do what is required of them in the classroom, such as reading authentic materials. If not, additional attention to vocabulary will probably be required. If this is the case, there are recommendations in the Further Reading section that can help you organize a structured and effective vocabulary program.

The Origins of the Modern English Lexicon

Old English Words: The Basic Vocabulary of English

From the historical overview in Chapter 2, we can see that the language that eventually developed into Modern English first arrived in Britain in the 5th century with Germanic raiders and settlers. The Old English dialects spoken at this time were thus (West) Germanic but were influenced to varying degrees by the three other languages with which they had prolonged contact: Celtic, Latin, and Scandinavian. The Celtic languages of the conquered Britons in fact had a negligible influence, probably because there was simply very little interaction between the two language groups and because conquerors often scorn the language of those they conquered. However, Celtic lives on in England mainly in place names, such as *Kent, Cornwall,* and *York,* and in the river names *Thames* and *Avon.* In the regular vocabulary of English, only about 20 words remain. *Bin, crag,* and *dun* are ones you may be familiar with. The others exist mainly in regional dialects, for example, *carr* ("rock") and *bratt* ("cloak"). (Additional Celtic words do exist in Modern English, but these were borrowed much later from Irish and Scots Gaelic; examples are *leprechaun, blarney, clan, whisk[e]y,* and *loch.*)

Latin loanwords came into Old English in three phases. The Germanic tribes had some contact with the Romans on the Continent (mainly through the activities of merchants) and so brought a few dozen Latinisms over to England with them.[4] These were words like *camp, street, mile, cheap, pound,* and *wine.* (It should be noted that in this chapter we give words in the modern forms; their forms in Old English were usually rather different.) The English picked up a handful of Latin words from the Celts in England, for example, *port, tower, mountain,* and *cross.* But the Christian church introduced the most Latin words during this period. Not surprisingly, many had to do with religion, but several words deal with everyday life too:

altar	angel	candle	disciple	hymn
organ	nun	priest	shrine	temple
cap	sock	silk	purple	chest
sack	school	master	grammar	verse
radish	beet	pear	lily	plant

Thus the church gave the English people words to express new ideas. In all, Old English absorbed something on the order of 350–500 Latin words before 1066.

Scandinavian had by far the greatest foreign impact on English during the Old English period, following further invasion and settlement, mostly by Danes, from the 9th century onward. The more than 14,000 Scandinavian place-names in England bear witness to this settlement, especially in the area of the Danelaw in the north and east of England. With such a large Scandinavian population, and with mixing and intermarriage between the newcomers and the native Anglo-Saxons, there must inevitably have been interaction between the languages spoken by the two groups. The various Scandinavian dialects (often simply referred to as Old Norse) and Old English were similar to each other, probably close enough to make communication possible; certainly they had many frequently used words in common, such as *thing, winter, summer, will, can, come, hear, see,* and *think.* Old English remained the dominant language, but it took many new words from Old Norse. This affected the spoken language first, and in fact the Scandinavian influence hardly shows up in writing until after the Norman Conquest. Today, English has at least 900 words taken from Old Norse, most of them borrowed during the later Old English period. The following list gives a sample; as will be seen, most of the words related to everyday things and fundamental ideas.

band	bull	fellow	crook	trust	window
law	rag	sly	take	want	sister
scathe	scorch	score	scrape	scrub	scowl
sky	skirt	skin	skill	scrap	scab
gear	geld	gill	egg	get	give
kick	kilt	kindle	keel	kid	bank

The words on the third and fourth lines all begin with the /sk/ sound. The English had already lost this Germanic sound, changing it to the "soft" /ʃ/, spelled *sc*. Similarly, Old Norse retained the "hard" /g/ (fifth line) and /k/ (sixth line) before or after the vowels *e* and *i*, whereas the English tended to modify the consonants in these circumstances to /j/ and /tʃ/, respectively. Consequently, words having these hard consonant features are very likely to be Scandinavian in origin.

From the sources that still exist, it is deduced that Old English contained around 24,000 lexical items. Over the centuries about 85 percent of those words have disappeared. Nevertheless, the remaining 15 percent are hugely important, for they make up the basic stratum of our present vocabulary, including function words (pronouns, prepositions, auxiliary verbs, and so on) and everyday words such as:

man	wife	child	house	meat
bench	leaf	grass	good	fight
high	strong	eat	drink	live

Because many of the Old English words are so basic, they tend to be used more often and widely than others. As a result, they form the essential foundation for all English usage. A look at Table 5 shows that the Germanic (i.e., Old English) words make up a high percentage of the most frequently used words in English, which provide the backbone for any speech or writing.

TABLE 5
SOURCES OF THE MOST FREQUENT 7,476 WORDS OF ENGLISH[5]

	First 100	First 1,000	Second 1,000	From then on
Germanic	97%	57%	39%	36%
Latin	3%	36%	51%	51%
Greek	0	4%	4%	7%
Others	0	3%	6%	6%

In fact, the majority of words on an average page of writing will be of Old English origin. It is even possible to speak and write well using *only* words of Old English origin, as illustrated here.

> But with all its manifold new words from other tongues, English could never have become anything but English. And as such it has sent out to the world, among many other things, some of the best books the world has ever known. It is not unlikely, in the light of writings by Englishmen in earlier times, that this would have been so even if we had never taken any words from outside the word hoard that has come down to us from those times. It is true that what we have borrowed has brought greater wealth to our word stock, but the true Englishness of our mother tongue has in no way been lessened by such loans, as those who speak and write it lovingly will always keep in mind.[6]

We have noted that some 85 percent of the vocabulary of Old English went out of use. You may wonder why the language needed all those words. The literature of the Old English period, especially the poetry, gives us a part-explanation. Poems were composed using the techniques and style of the oral tradition, which included alliteration (using several words in a line with the same initial sound) and variation (saying the same thing more than once in slightly different ways). Thus, in the most well-known Old English poem, "Beowulf," the monstrous creature Grendel completely eats a warrior, "feet and hands"—or, in the Old English, *fet ond folma*. Now the poet could have said *handa* for "hands," but he wanted a word to alliterate with *fet*, and so he took an alternative beginning with *f* out of his store of words. Elsewhere, within a few lines, he varies his description of Grendel with such phrases as "grim spirit," "lonely wanderer," "dark death-shadow," and "fell spoiler"—drawing again heavily on a rich vocabulary. To compose successfully, the Old English poets thus needed a huge "word-hoard" (their own term for it) to provide them with plenty of synonyms, but many of the words would go out of use, once this poetic style went out of fashion.

Loanwords: Enriching the English Lexicon

Loanwords Entering in the Middle English Period

If most of the original Old English words have been lost, how does the modern language nevertheless have such a large vocabulary? To a great degree, it is a result of the readiness of English to borrow useful vocabulary from other languages. This has been a prominent feature of the language ever since the

11th century. Old English, although influenced by Latin and Scandinavian, remained essentially Germanic, with only about 3 percent of its vocabulary being loanwords. From that point onward, English seemed to prefer to accept loanwords into its vocabulary rather than creating new words by other means, such as coining them from scratch or creating new compound words from existing words (although these processes did take place—see pp. 92–97). Perhaps the explanation is simply that the history of England ensured that new words were always available. Whatever the case, more than 70 percent of Modern English consists of loanwords, and nearly half of them come from Latin or French. Let us look at the loanwords English absorbed during the Middle English period.

Although the transformation of English from a language relying on inflections to a language relying on word order was probably the most important single change in the Middle English period, the main effect of the Norman Conquest itself was in the area of vocabulary. A large number of French words were absorbed into English.[7] Our records for the 11th and early 12th centuries are sparse, but it appears that the words entered quite slowly at first, came at a greater rate later in the 12th century, and then flooded in during the 13th and 14th centuries. One reason for this is that it was not until the 13th century that English was finally becoming established again as the language of administration and creative literature (replacing French), and many specialist terms and words to express new social structures and new ideas, unavailable in the native language, were now needed. Between 1066 and 1250, about 1,000 French words entered English. Since French was the language of the ruling class, it is not surprising that many of these earlier loanwords had to do with government, law, and rank. Examples (given here in their modern forms) are *council, court, justice, accuse, sovereign, parliament, castle, prison, service, duke,* and *prince.* But simpler words included *garden, hour, market,* and *people.* After 1250, more French words were borrowed than at any time before or since. The earliest loanwords were predominantly borrowed from the Northern French dialect of the Normans, and they tended to be the more practical words. Later borrowings were mostly from the Central French dialect (spoken in the area that included Paris), reflecting broader contacts with France, and on the whole these borrowings tend to be more "learned" in nature.

In total, Modern English has more than 10,000 French borrowings, the majority taken during the Middle English period. Table 6 can only give a small impression of the debt English owes to French in its vocabulary.

The Scandinavian languages also continued to contribute loanwords, most notably the third-person plural pronouns *they, them,* and *their.* These are rather unusual, because languages seldom accept "grammatical" words as loanwords;

TABLE 6
FRENCH LOANWORDS IN ENGLISH

Governmental and Administrative Words				
government	administer	crown	state	empire
usurp	council	record	treason	liberty
vassal	duke	countess	madam	slave

Religious Words				
religion	cardinal	penance	sermon	hermit
prayer	friar	solemn	piety	faith
saint	damnation	mercy	preach	divine

Legal Words				
bar	defendant	judge	sue	verdict
arrest	punishment	plead	just	fraud
innocent	sentence	bail	award	prison

Military Words				
army	lieutenant	captain	sergeant	battle
peace	defense	retreat	ambush	combat
navy	vanquish	spy	siege	enemy

Words for Fashion, Meals, and Social Life				
fashion	dress	apparel	robe	gown
petticoat	embellish	luxury	adorn	attire
boots	button	fur	satin	lace

Words for Art, Learning, and Medicine				
art	painting	sculpture	music	beauty
geometry	grammar	noun	clause	chapter
pain	ointment	plague	stomach	poison

such words are part of the basic core of a language. The fact that Old Norse words were able to oust the native pronouns confirms its strong influence, but it is also worth noting that forms of the third-person pronouns in Old English were very confusing, being identical in some cases with singular pronouns (so that *hi*, for example, might mean "she" or "they"). Latin words also continued to filter into English, particularly in intellectual areas, like religion, law, and science. Several dozen loanwords came from Holland and Flanders, principally because of the wool trade.

Sometimes the new loanwords replaced Old English words (*people* displaced *leod, beautiful* displaced *wlitig*), and sometimes both the new loanword and the old word would remain but with slightly different meanings, as in Old English *house* and French *mansion*, Old English *hide* and French *conceal*. This can be clearly seen also in culinary vocabulary, where the Old English words were retained to refer to the animals (*pig, sheep, deer*), whereas the French loanwords referred to the meat on the table (*pork, mutton, venison*). This retaining of old words alongside the new is one factor that has lead to the large degree of synonymy in English today.

Loanwords Entering in the Early Modern English Period

English has borrowed an extraordinary number of words in every period since the Norman Conquest. By the end of the 16th century, it had already accepted words from more than 50 languages.[8] Whereas in the Middle English period most words were borrowed from French, in the Early Modern English period, loans from Latin outnumbered all others. Not only were thousands of individual words borrowed but also affixes (prefixes and suffixes), which allowed the formation of thousands more. An A–Z sample gives a sense of the range of the borrowings:

ambiguous	gladiator	navigate	tangent
biceps	harmonica	opponent	ultimate
census	identical	perfidious	vacuum
decorate	joke	quotation	zone
emotion	lichen	ratio	
fanatic	mandible	scintillate	

French continued to be a major influence with words like *admire, bigot, chocolate, formidable, identity, mustache,* and *parade*. Many words from the New World came from Spanish or Portuguese: *alligator, cigar, coyote, hammock, hurricane, jaguar, mango, mosquito,* and *pagoda*. The Italians were especially influential in the arts; we get most of our musical terms from them: *alto, aria, operetta, solo,* and *sonata*. The Dutch lent us words from their areas of strength, seamanship and painting, such as *cruise, deck, sloop, smuggle, easel, landscape,* and *sketch*. Other languages contributed fewer words in quantity but made up for it in their interesting and sometimes exotic quality.

Examples are *zinc* and *noodle* (German), *trousers* and *whisk[e]y* (Irish and Scottish Gaelic), *jackal* and *yogurt* (Turkish), *tea* and *typhoon* (Chinese), *bungalow* and *jungle* (Hindi), and *moose* and *tomahawk* (American Indian languages). As is evident from this list, English was collecting words from every part of the world, developing a truly international character in its vocabulary.

Interestingly, some Latin and French words borrowed in the Early Modern English period had previously been borrowed during the Middle English period and were already in the lexicon in a different form. This resulted in *doublets* (two words from the same source that enter a language from different routes). Some examples follow.

DOUBLETS IN MODERN ENGLISH

Middle English	Early Modern English	Middle English	Early Modern English
armor	armature	chamber	camera
choir	chorus	frail	fragile
gender	genus	jealous	zealous
prove	probe	strait	strict
strange	extraneous	treasure	thesaurus

With the Old English words as a base and with new loanwords entering the language, English found itself with a huge number of synonyms, as we have seen. Many of these disappeared from use, but a large number survived. A language does not usually retain exact synonyms; they will differ in some way. Geoffrey Hughes shows that this difference has to do with their register. He suggests that the English lexicon developed a three-register structure reflecting the historical origins of the words.[9] Old English words have what might be called a general or popular feeling, the French loanwords have a more formal tone, whereas the Latin loanwords feel right in intellectual and technical contexts. Figure 7 illustrates this relationship between historical origin and register, using three "triplets" of words.

Hughes suggests that virtually any word field reflects this three-register structure, and it is not difficult to find examples covering a range of concepts, as seen in Table 7.

A range of synonyms like this gives English an amazing ability to express nuanced ideas. We can also see again that the willingness of English to keep near-synonyms is another important reason for its distinctively large and varied vocabulary.

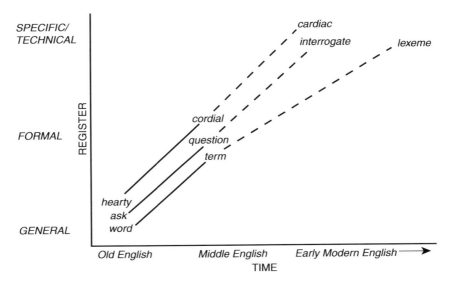

FIGURE 7   The Relationship between Historical Origin and Register

Source: From *A History of English Words* (p. 15), by G. Hughes, 2000, Malden, MA: Blackwell. Copyright 2000 by Blackwell. Reprinted with permission.

TABLE 7
THE THREE REGISTERS OF THE ENGLISH LEXICON

General/ Old English	Formal/ French	Intellectual/ Latin
kingly	royal	regal
rise	mount	ascend
ask	question	interrogate
fast	firm	secure
holy	sacred	consecrated
fire	flame	conflagration
goodness	virtue	probity
fear	terror	trepidation
time	age	epoch
gift	present	donation
lively	vivacious	animated

Source: The information in this table is compiled from *A History of the English Language* (pp. 182–183), by A.C. Baugh and T. Cable, 1993, London: Routledge; *The Cambridge Encyclopedia of the English Language* (p. 48), by D. Crystal, 1995, Cambridge: Cambridge University Press; and *A History of English Words* (p. 15), by G. Hughes, Malden, MA: Blackwell.

Loanwords Entering Modern English

Loanwords have continued to enter English right up until the present time. Between about 1800 and 1920 they included:[10]

French – chauffeur, garage	*Russian* – vodka
Italian – confetti, vendetta	*Czech* – robot
Spanish – bonanza, canyon, patio	*Hindi* – loot, thug

This trend continues, with political, technological, culinary, cultural, and other developments around the world keeping the stream of new words flowing into English. In particular, French continues to be an important donor language: A study of more than 1,000 recent loanwords showed that around 25 percent were of French origin.[11] French borrowings in the 20th century include:

apres-ski	cellulite	insulin
bouffant	discotheque	pacifism
brassiere	film noir	questionnaire

The following is a small sample of more recent loanwords (though some, such as the two Russian words, may already be fading from use):

Russian – perestroika, glasnost	*Japanese* – karaoke
Italian – ciabatta, tiramisu, latte	*Mexican* – fajitas
Arabic – fatwa, intifada	*Chinese* – feng shui
Latin – annus horribilis	*Brazilian Portuguese* – lambada

Although thousands of loanwords have entered English over the years, large numbers of words have also disappeared. It is interesting to have a look at some of these. Although they may seem strange to us now, we might still be using these Old English and Early Modern English words in the 21st century if circumstances had been different.

Lost Old English Words		Lost Early Modern English Words	
anda	(envy)	assate	(to roast)
bleo	(color)	anacephalize	(to sum up)
galdor	(song)	cohibit	(to restrain)
here	(army)	eximious	(excellent)
leax	(salmon)	expede	(to accomplish)
lyft	(air)	illecebrous	(delicate)
racu	(explanation)	mansuetude	(mildness)
tela	(good)	temulent	(drunk)

There are also a number of words that have fallen out of general use but that remain in the language as part of another word. For example, you might not recognize the words *ruth* (compassion), *guma* (man), or *wer* (man) on their own, even though they are components of the words *ruthless*, *bridegroom*, and *werewolf*, respectively.

APPLICATIONS TO TEACHING

Using a Wider Vocabulary

English has a large vocabulary, and one ramification of this is that good usage dictates that speakers use a wide variety of words to suit specific circumstances. One of the main problems learners have is overusing their limited vocabulary. A learner may have to reuse basic vocabulary several times, where a proficient speaker would employ variation:

Learner: My father *bought* a new *car* last year. It was *expensive*. I'd like to *buy* a *car* myself, but they're too *expensive*, so I'll have to *buy* a bicycle instead.

More proficient speaker: My father *bought* a new *car* last year. It was *expensive*. I'd like to *splash out on* a *convertible*, but they're too *pricey*, so I'll have to *be satisfied with* a bicycle instead.

This contrived example illustrates that English users are expected to mix up their vocabulary in a kind of "elegant variation." If learners reuse the same vocabulary too much, the resulting language sounds stilted and mechanical. This means that English learners need to continue to expand their vocabulary far beyond what is required for basic communication. Of course they can get their meaning across even if they repeat too many words, but if they aspire to appropriate usage, there is no substitute for a large vocabulary. Ideally, in addition to learning a single word for a concept, they will learn a number of synonyms as well. Moreover, they need to know the appropriate context for each synonym or phrase, as there are very few, if any, exact synonyms in English. Each one normally has a nuance of meaning or collocation, or a grammatical characteristic, that differentiates it from other synonyms. Mastering this synonymy inevitably entails long-term vocabulary study for students. To avoid boredom, a variety of language activities needs to be employed. Exercises that raise students' consciousness about the origin and role of different kinds of vocabulary can offer an interesting change of pace. Several are included in the Classroom Activities section at the end of this chapter.

The Origins of a Word and Its Appropriacy

The way that words are used in Modern English can sometimes be explained partly by their historical origins. For example, Old English words are often monosyllabic and tend to refer to the basic elements of life and often have a direct, familiar, colloquial feel. On the other hand, loanwords tend to be polysyllabic and often convey a formal or learned tone. To illustrate this, examine two speeches, the first given by Ronald Reagan and the second by Martin Luther King, Jr.[12] The loanwords have been italicized.

Reagan

We're to the end of a bloody *century, plagued* by a *terrible invention—totalitarianism. Optimism* comes less *easily* today, not because *democracy* is less *vigorous,* but because *democracy's enemies* have *refined* their *instruments* of *repression.* Yet *optimism* is in *order because* day by day, *democracy* is *proving* itself to be not at all a *fragile flower.*

King

I have a dream that one day on the red hills of Georgia the sons of former *slaves* and the sons of former *slave* owners will be *able* to sit down together at the *table* of brotherhood ... I have a dream that my four little children will one day live in a *nation* where they will not be *judged* by the *color* of their skin....

King's speech conveys the sense that he was speaking directly to the people without a script. It has a warm and accessible tone because of King's heavy use of everyday, largely monosyllabic, Old English vocabulary. Reagan's speech, on the other hand, sounds much more formal and "official," partly because of the high percentage of loanwords (even though they still make up less than half of the total), which tend to be polysyllabic and Latinate. Thus we see that a different tone is often conveyed by the two types of words—loanwords and those derived from Old English—and there is a tendency for speakers to use each in specific contexts. Students wishing to speak in everyday contexts should begin to have the lexical resources to do this if they know the most frequent 2,000 words of English, almost half of which are Old English in origin. However, if students wish to engage in more formal and abstract communication, they will need a great deal of vocabulary beyond this frequency level, most of which will be loanwords.

Academic Vocabulary

More advanced students, who wish to perform in a range of different discourse situations, need to be able to choose vocabulary with the appropriate stylistic marking. A good example of this is students who wish to use English in an academic setting. They will need to know the type of words common in academic discourse and the ones that can give their texts the right tone. For example, the sentence *The environment is being used mainly to achieve easy profits* is perfectly adequate to express the intended meaning. However, when the boldfaced academic vocabulary is inserted, the tone of the sentence better matches the expectations of academic writing: *The environment is being* **exploited predominantly** *for* **economic** *reasons.* A list has been compiled of 570 word families of this type of academic vocabulary (called the Academic Word List).[13] More than 82 percent of the word families on this list are Latin based, such as *data, export, motivate, remove, origin, survey,* and *temporary.* There are 45 families of Greek origin, including *decade, energy, ideology, sphere,* and *symbol.* Only 38 families come from Old English (e.g., *aware, behalf, goal, shift, team*) and 7 from Middle English (e.g., *available, somewhat, straightforward, enable*). These figures show the importance of loanword vocabulary in texts of an academic nature. Learners wishing to operate in an academic setting will need to use this loanword-rich vocabulary, which suggests it is worth their time and effort to explicitly study the words on the Academic Word List.

English Words That Have Been Created

In addition to borrowing words from other languages, English has created a large number of its own, mostly by using previously existing words and word parts (stems and affixes) in various ways.

Compounding

Many words have been created by **compounding.** This is the process of combining existing words to build a single larger unit, often with a meaning that is in some way different from the component words. For example, *blackboard* is not the same as *black board*—some blackboards are green and so many are now white that *whiteboard* has come into the lexicon to mean a board on which you use a color marker instead of chalk. Two-word compounds are the most common in English, but multi-word compounds are not unusual: *mother-in-law, off-the-*

wall. Compounding is a very flexible process, with words from different parts of speech easily combining with one another, as illustrated below:

	-Noun	-Verb	-Adjective
Noun-	*fingerprint*	*skydive*	*bloodthirsty*
Verb-	*frying pan*	*sleepwalk*	*lookalike*
Adjective-	*software*	*highborn*	*bittersweet*

Compound words can be presented in various ways: as one word (e.g., *songwriter*), with spaces between the words (e.g., *smoke screen*), or with a hyphen (e.g., *laid-back*). There does not seem to be any fixed rule to guide this presentation, but the more established compounds tend to be spelled as single words (*overgrown, broadcast, firearm*). When compound words are relatively new, there is often no consensus about how to render them; for example, would you write *freezedry, freeze-dry,* or *freeze dry?* Only time will tell which version comes to be most acceptable or even if this compound will survive in the language. When it comes to spoken discourse, however, the pronunciation of a compound is much more systematic. If a number of words are merely juxtaposed in normal use, the stresses are approximately even, but in compound words, one of the elements will usually be stressed more strongly than the other(s). For example, in the phrase *a man eating rabbit,* there would be more or less even stressing on *man* and *eating,* with the resultant signification of a man enjoying a meal of rabbit. However, in the same phrase with *man* and *eating* compounded as an adjective, *a man-eating rabbit,* the stress would be much stronger on *man,* signifying that here is a dangerous rabbit that you had better avoid! It is thus the stress that shows us how to interpret the phrase.

Blending

In compounding, the complete component words are retained (*play* + *pen* = *playpen*), but sometimes two or more words are combined together with only parts of each included in the new word. The resulting words are known as **blends.** This process has added a number of words to English, of which the following are a small sample:

    breakfast + lunch = brunch
    smoke + fog = smog
    guess + estimate = guesstimate
    motor + hotel = motel
    breath + analyzer = breathalyzer
    pulse + quasar = pulsar
    aqua+exercise=aquacize

Word Parts: Stems and Affixes

Using word parts is one of the most productive ways of creating new words. English has always done this. However, the process was much more prevalent in Old English than it is in the modern language. For example, more than 100 words were formed from the stem *mōd* (*mood* in Modern English).[14] Modern English still forms many new words from stems and affixes, but some are obviously more productive than others. For example, the prefix *with-* (meaning "against" or "from") is not used in creating new words today but lives on in the words *withdraw*, *withhold*, and *withstand*. Likewise, the suffix-*red* occurs only in *hatred* and *kindred*.[15] Of the affixes that are still used to create new words today, some prefixes (e.g., *after-*, *be-*, *mis-*, *un-*) and some suffixes (e.g., *-dom*, *-ful*, *-ness*, *-ward*) date from the Old English period, whereas others were borrowed later from other languages (e.g., *anti-*, *ex-*, *super-*, *ultra-*, *-al*, *-ese*, *-ize*, *-or*).[16] It is difficult to say exactly how many affixes English has in total, but it is probably too many to teach explicitly. Fortunately for learners, many of them are not used extensively. In fact, English only has about 50 or 60 common prefixes[17] and probably a similar number of common suffixes.

Table 8 shows the most common English suffixes, though not all the variant forms (e.g., *-ible* for *-able*). The list of inflectional suffixes is complete; the list of derivational suffixes has been limited to 50.

Although Modern English has a limited number of common affixes, they are linked to a very large number of words. This can be illustrated by a few statistics: 7,476 relatively high-frequency words were analyzed, and it was found that 97 percent of them were derived from only around 2,000 word stems.[18] Another study found that about one-fifth of the words examined had inflectional suffixes and about one-eighth had a derivational affix.[19] An early study found that almost one-quarter of the words in the *Teacher's Word Book of 20,000 Words* (1932) had prefixes and that 15 prefixes accounted for 82 percent of those words.[20] Thus, these word parts play a large role in English. Perhaps more important, they are often transparent enough to be of use to learners. Four prefixes (*un-*, *re- in-*, *dis-*) were examined, and it was found that about 60 percent of the words containing them could be understood if the most common meaning of the word stem was known.[21] If less common prefix meanings were also known and the surrounding context used to aid comprehension, then around 80 percent of the words could be understood. Knowledge of word stems, prefixes, and suffixes and how they are combined can be a valuable asset for learners of English.

TABLE 8
COMMON SUFFIXES IN ENGLISH

Inflectional suffixes

-*s* plural of noun
-*'s* possessive case of noun
-*s* 3rd-person singular of verb
-*n't* contracted negative of verb
-*ed* past tense of verb
-*ing* present participle
-*ed* past participle
-*er* adjectival comparative
-*est* adjectival superlative

Derivational suffixes

Abstract noun-makers

-*age* frontage, mileage
-*dom* officialdom, stardom
-*ery* drudgery, slavery
-*ful* cupful, spoonful
-*hood* brotherhood, girlhood
-*ing* farming, panelling
-*ism* idealism, racism
-*ocracy* aristocracy, bureaucracy
-*ship* friendship, membership

Concrete-noun-makers

-*eer* engineer, racketeer
-*er* teenager, cooker

-*ess* waitress, lioness
-*ette* kitchenette, usherette
-*let* booklet, piglet
-*ling* duckling, underling
-*ster* gangster, gamester

Adverb-makers

-*ly* quickly, happily
-*ward(s)* northward, onward
-*wise* clockwise, lengthwise

Verb-makers

-*ate* orchestrate, chlorinate
-*en* deafen, ripen
-*ify* beautify, certify
-*ize/-ise* modernize, advertise

Adjective-/noun-makers

-*ese* Chinese, Portuguese
-*(i)an* republican, Parisian
-*ist* socialist, loyalist
-*ite* socialite, Luddite

Nouns from verbs

-*age* breakage, wastage
-*al* refusal, revival
-*ant* informant, lubricant

-*ation* exploration, education
-*ee* payee, absentee
-*er* writer, driver
-*ing* building, clothing
-*ment* amazement, equipment
-*or* actor, supervisor

Nouns from adjectives

-*ity* rapidity, falsity
-*ness* happiness, kindness

Adjectives from nouns

-*ed* pointed, blue-eyed
-*esque* statuesque, Kafkaesque
-*ful* useful, successful
-*ic* atomic, Celtic
-*(i)al* editorial, accidental
-*ish* foolish, Swedish
-*less* careless, childless
-*ly* friendly, cowardly
-*ous* ambitious, desirous
-*y* sandy, hairy

Adjectives from verbs

-*able* drinkable, washable
-*ive* attractive, explosive

Source: From *The Cambridge Encyclopedia of English Language* (p. 128), by D. Crystal, 1995, Cambridge: Cambridge University Press. Copyright 1995. Reprinted with the permission of Cambridge University Press.

Other Processes

Word Coinage

As previously mentioned, creating a new word unrelated to any other is quite rare. Some coinages have initially been trade names that later came into generalized use. Words like *Kodak, Kleenex, Vaseline, Nylon, Dacron,* and *Xerox* fall into this category. *Zipper* was originally the name of a boot with a slide fastener but then came to be the label for the fastener itself.

Other coinages are the result of people just making up new words: *blurb* was coined by the American humorist Gelett Burgess and *googol* (the number 10^{100}) was thought up by the nine-year-old nephew of an American mathematician. A few other words must be considered to be coinages because they have no cognates in the Germanic languages (i.e., there are no words of the same origin) and cannot be traced to other languages as loanwords: *quiz, fun, pun, slang, pooch,* and *snob*. But overall, the number of coinages in the English language is quite small.

Acronyms/Initialisms

Another way new words have been added to the language is through **acronyms** and **initialisms.** These are abbreviations made up of the first letter or letters of other words, names, or phrases and are shorter and easier to use than the full names or phrases involved. When the abbreviations can be pronounced as a single word (e.g., *radar, NATO*), they are known as **acronyms.** Where no word can be made and the separate letters have to be pronounced (e.g., *HTML, YMCA*), they are initialisms; these are still far easier to say than the original full phrases. At first, acronyms tend to be retained as completely capitalized (e.g., *NATO*), but as they become more used they are naturalized as ordinary words, though an initial capital will be retained in the case of the names of organizations *(Nato)*. Examples of both types include:

Science
radar – radio detection and ranging
scuba – self-contained underwater breathing apparatus
HTML – hypertext mark-up language

Organizations
OPEC/Opec – Organization of Petroleum Exporting Countries
NATO/Nato – North Atlantic Treaty Organization
YMCA – Young Men's Christian Association

General
AWOL/awol – absent without official leave
WASP/wasp – white Anglo-Saxon Protestant
SUV – sport utility vehicle
FAQ – frequently asked questions

Sometimes initialisms are used as euphemisms, such as *BO* for "body odor" and *VD* for "venereal disease." Perhaps the most widely used initialism of all time is the ubiquitous *OK*. There have been many theories about the origins of OK, but a recent one confidently asserts that it can be traced to an item in the *Boston Morning Post* of March 23, 1839. There, following a popular fad for facetious abbreviations that was sweeping Boston, OK was used to mean *all correct* (i.e., as though spelled oll korrect).[22]

Shortening Existing Words

New words may also be created by shortening those already in use. For example, *exam, gym,* and *lab* are shortened forms of *examination, gymnasium,* and *laboratory*. It seems as though language speakers prefer shorter words, and this can be demonstrated by Zipf's Law, which says that there is an inverse relationship between the length of a word and its frequency of occurrence. That is, we like the words we use frequently to be short ones. Some of the common words we use today were shortened a long time ago, and most people are not even aware of their original source:

mob – mobile vulgus (Latin for movable, or fickle, common people)
bus – omnibus
taxicab – taximeter cabriolet (now *taxi* and *cab* are both used as
   individual words)
pants – pantaloons

This process of shortening is continuing today, and although both forms of the following examples are still used, the shorter form may well push out the longer form in the end:

gas – gasoline
auto – automobile
phone – telephone
zoo – zoological gardens
flu – influenza
bra – brassiere
decaf – decaffeinated (coffee)

APPLICATIONS TO TEACHING

English does not have a great number of affixes when compared to many other languages. This makes them a good subject for explicit teaching because a limited number of word parts can help students learn and use a great number of words. For example, if a student knows *re-* = "again" and *view* = "see," then *review* should be easier to learn. There is the question of which affixes should be taught and in what order. Paul Nation provides the following list as a guide.[23] (Note that several affixes occur more than once depending on different usages. See the original publication for more details.)

A SEQUENCED LIST OF DERIVATIONAL AFFIXES FOR LEARNERS OF ENGLISH

Stage 1

-able, -er, -ish, -less, -ly, -ness, -th, -y, non-, un- (all with restricted uses)

Stage 2

-al, -ation, -ess, -ful, -ism, -ist, -ity, -ize, -ment, -ous, in- (all with restricted uses)

Stage 3

-age (leakage), *-al* (arrival), *-ally* (idiotically), *-an* (American), *-ance* (clearance), *-ant* (consultant), *-ary* (revolutionary), *-atory* (confirmatory), *-dom* (kingdom, officialdom), *-eer* (black marketeer), *-en* (wooden), *-ence* (emergence), *-ent* (absorbent), *-ery* (bakery, trickery), *-ese* (Japanese, officialese), *-esque* (picturesque), *-ette* (usherette, roomette), *-hood* (childhood), *-i* (Israeli), *-ian* (phonetician, Johnsonian), *-ite* (Paisleyite; also chemical meaning), *-let* (coverlet), *-ling* (duckling), *-ly* (leisurely), *-most* (topmost), *-ory* (contradictory), *-ship* (studentship), *-ward* (homeward), *-ways* (crossways), *-wise* (endwise, discussion-wise), *anti-* (anti-inflation), *ante-* (anteroom), *arch-* (archbishop), *bi-* (biplane), *circum-* (circumnavigate), *counter-* (counter-attack), *en-* (encage, enslave), *ex-* (ex-president), *fore-* (forename), *hyper-* (hyperactive), *inter-* (inter-African, interweave), *mid-* (midweek), *mis-* (misfit), *neo-* (neo-colonialism), *post-* (post-date), *pro-* (pro-British), *semi-* (semi-automatic), *sub-* (subclassify, subterranean), *un-* (untie, unburden)

Stage 4

-able, -ee, -ic, -ify, -ion, -ist, -ition, -ive, -th, -y, pre-, re-

Stage 5

-ar (circular), *-ate* (compassionate, captivate, electorate), *-et* (packet, casket), *-some* (troublesome), *-ure* (departure, exposure), *ab-, ad-, com-, de-, dis-, ex-* ("out"), *in-* ("in"), *ob-, per-, pro-* ("in front of"), *trans-*

Nation also lists a number of principles that can make the learning of word parts more effective:[24]

- It is most effective to address word parts after your learners already know a substantial number of complex words. Then, when they analyze the word parts, they will already know some words containing those parts, which should help them memorize the words.
- The teaching of word parts will necessarily be a long-term process. Using a "mini-syllabus," such as that illustrated, is a way to order the teaching of important affixes systematically.
- It is best to teach word parts individually as required, rather than giving learners a long list to study. The reason is that learners often get confused between the various items on such a list. When they learn the word parts (or words) individually, the words become more fixed in the mind and are less likely to be "mixed up" with other similar affixes and stems.
- You should encourage learners to look for the regular form and meaning patterns that underlie the use of many word parts.
- Learners need to realize that many complex words do not follow regular morphological patterning and will need to be learned as unanalyzed wholes. Learners need to be able to recognize such words.

There is a variety of ways to teach word parts. These range from doing exercises where words are broken down into their parts (*production* → pro / duct / ion) to playing word games in class that focus on the use of word parts. Good sources of word part exercises include *Teaching and Learning Vocabulary*[25] and *New Ways in Teaching Vocabulary*.[26]

The meaning of compounds and new words made up from word parts is usually relatively transparent; indeed this is one of the reasons why a language creates new words in these ways in the first place. However, in some instances the apparent meaning can be very misleading. Two studies found that English learners can sometimes misanalyze such words and come up with erroneous (if amusing) guesses of their meaning:[27]

outline = out of line
discourse = without direction
falsities = falling cities

Overall, it makes sense to encourage learners to use what they know about words and affixes to guess the meaning of unknown words. At the same time, we should also make them aware that these guesses may sometimes be wrong. The best way for learners to confirm their guesses is by using the surrounding context. Unfortunately, they do not always do this. One study found that once students made a guess about an unknown word's meaning, often based on its form or similarity in spelling to another word they already knew, they stuck to that guess even if the context made it quite clear that particular meaning was wrong.[28] We must help our students understand that guessing a word's meaning is only the first step of the process; confirming its meaning against context is an important second step to avoid possible error.

Conclusion

As with other aspects of English, the vocabulary has changed significantly over the centuries. It still is changing, with new words coming into the language every day and other words quietly falling out of use. This vitality has always been a hallmark of English and is unlikely to change. Flexibility, especially the willingness to borrow extensively from other languages, has lead to a very large and varied vocabulary, which must be considered as one of English's greatest strengths.

Unfortunately, the size and variety of the English lexicon create a problem for students. Whereas English mainly increased its vocabulary through loanwords, many other languages relied more on compounding (e.g., German) and affixation (e.g., Spanish) to build their lexicons. In these languages, learners can understand and create a large number of new words simply by knowing the systems underlying lexical construction. As we have seen, English utilizes similar systems of word building but not nearly as much as other languages do. This means that learners have to acquire considerable numbers of words that are not systematically transparent. For example, Germans might say *herzlich* (*Herz* = "heart" and *lich* = "like") to express the concept warm-hearted, whereas in English, learners would have to know and choose between a number of near-synonyms such as *cordial*, *convivial*, and *enthusiastic*, which have no formal similarity. The combination of many differently formed synonyms and English's large number of words means that the learning of vocabulary will be one of the greatest challenges facing students, especially if they wish to use English at higher levels of proficiency.

FURTHER READING

These two recent books give more detailed descriptions of the origin of English vocabulary.

- Hughes, G. (2000). *A history of English words.* Oxford: Blackwell.
- Stockwell, R., & Minkova, D. (2001). *English words: History and structure.* Cambridge: Cambridge University Press.

A short introduction to some of the main issues in vocabulary teaching and learning.

- Nation, P., & Meara, P. (2002). Vocabulary. In N. Schmitt (Ed.), *An introduction to applied linguistics* (pp. 35–54). London: Arnold.

These books provide accessible guidance to good vocabulary teaching practice and the research that underlies it. Nation's book includes numerous exercise examples.

- Nation, P. (1990). *Teaching and learning vocabulary.* New York: Heinle & Heinle.
- Schmitt, N. (2000). *Vocabulary in language teaching.* Cambridge: Cambridge University Press.
- Folse, K. S. (2004). *Vocabulary myths: Applying second language research to classroom teaching.* Ann Arbor: University of Michigan Press.

Classroom Activity: 4.1

Old English Vocabulary in Today's English

English developed as a language between the 5th and 11th centuries, at which period it is called *Old English*. It came from the family of Germanic languages and was much influenced by Old Norse (also Germanic) and by Latin. These exercises will help you become familiar with Old English and its relationship to today's English.

1. How much of Old English's vocabulary do you think still remains in today's English? _____%

2. The Old English words that remain tend to be the most basic and essential words in today's English. Look at the following texts and underline the words you think might be of Old English origin.

   The man with the white carnation in his buttonhole, who enjoyed the grand title Executive Director for Human Resources, went up to the young woman and announced arrogantly that the current economic situation was unsustainable and her employment would be terminated with immediate effect.

   "Are you saying that my work is to end now, at once? Is that right, and must I leave today?" she asked him fearfully.

   "Absolutely correct! Please vacate the office."

   When the woman heard this, she wept and said, "How can I live, with two children to feed and a husband who has long been sick?"

3. Now that your teacher has told you which of the words are Old English, compare the underlined words (Old English) with the others (non–Old English).

What kind of words are the Old English words? _____

_____

What kind of words are the non–Old English words? _____

_____

How are they different? _____

_____

Classroom Activity: 4.2

Where Did Old English Vocabulary Come From?

Most Old English vocabulary came directly from its Germanic roots, but some words were borrowed from Latin and others came from another Germanic source, Old Norse. A list of words derived from Old English that are still a part of today's language follows. Guess the origins of each word.

Here are some hints to help you:

- Since Old English came from the Germanic family of languages, most of the basic words are also originally from this family.
- Old English did not have the *sk* sound *(sky),* so words with this sound probably came from Old Norse.
- Latin was the language of the Christian church, so words connected with religion probably come from Latin.
- Some English merchants who traded in Europe communicated in Latin, so some "trade" words also come from Latin.
- Education in the early Old English period was concerned with Latin learning.

angel	fight	man	score	skill
candle	good	master	scowl	skin
cap	grammar	meat	scrap	skirt
chest	high	paper	scrape	sky
child	house	priest	scrub	temple
at	leaf	scab	silk	wife

The original Old English language (10 words)	Old Norse (10 words)	Latin (10 words)
_____	_____	_____
_____	_____	_____
_____	_____	_____
_____	_____	_____
_____	_____	_____
_____	_____	_____
_____	_____	_____
_____	_____	_____
_____	_____	_____
_____	_____	_____

Classroom Activity: 4.3

Where Did English Vocabulary Come From?

Between 1500 and 1800, English borrowed thousands of loanwords from other languages. Look at the following groups of loanwords and see if you can guess which language they came from. Look up any word you do not know in your dictionary.

A	B	C	D
cruise	admire	bog	alto
deck	bigot	cairn	aria
easel	chocolate	galore	balcony
landscape	entrance	leprechaun	ballet
sloop	formidable	plaid	opera
smuggle	invite	shamrock	solo
sketch	muscle	trousers	sonnet
yacht	vogue	whiskey	violin

E	F	G	H
ambiguous	alligator	bangle	kowtow
census	banana	bungalow	tea
emotion	coyote	dinghy	typhoon
gladiator	cocoa	jungle	
navigate	embargo	loot	
quotation	hurricane	pajamas	
ultimate	jaguar	shampoo	
vacuum	mosquito	thug	

I
moose
pecan
tomahawk

__I__	American Indian languages
_____	Chinese
_____	Dutch
_____	French
_____	Irish and Scots Gaelic
_____	Hindi
_____	Italian
_____	Latin and Greek
_____	Spanish/Portuguese

Can you guess which of these languages contributed the most words to English between 1500 and 1800? _____

Classroom *H*andout

A List of Useful Latin Prefixes

Many words in English have prefixes. In fact, almost a quarter of the most common words in English have them. Although there are many possible prefixes, some are much more useful than others. We know that the most frequent 15 prefixes account for more than 80 percent of all prefix occurrences in common English words. Therefore, it is worthwhile to learn how to use the following frequent prefixes because they will help you understand and use a great many words in English.

Prefix	Meaning	Word	Other forms
ab-	from, away	absent	a-, abs-
ad-	to(ward)	adjacent, arrive	a-, abs-, ac-, aft-, ag-, al-, an-, ap-, aq-, ar-, as-, at-
com-	with, together	comrade, coincidence, contain	co-, col-, con-, cor-
de-	down	decrease	
de-	away	deflect	
dis-	not	disagree	
dis-	apart, away	discard	di-, dif-
ex-	out, beyond	extreme	e-, ef-
in-	not	inadequate, improper	ig-, il-, im-, ir-
in-	in (to)	include	il-, im-, ir-
inter-	between, among	international	
mis-	wrong(ly)	misuse	
non-	not	non-standard	
ob-	against	object, oppose	o-, oc-, of-, op-
ob-	to(ward)	obtain	o-, oc-, of-, op-
over-	above	overhang	
per-	through	perforate	
pre-	before	prepare	
pro-	forward	progress	pur-
pro-	in favor of	promote	
re-	back	recline	
re-	again	recur	
sub-	under	submarine, suspend	suc-, suf-, sug-, sum-, sur-, sus-
trans-	across, beyond	transmit	tra-, tran-
un-	not	unusual	

Source: From *Teaching and Learning Vocabulary* (p. 268), by P. Nation, 1990, New York: Heinle & Heinle. Copyright 1990 by Heinle & Heinle. Adapted with permission.

The Vocabulary Levels Test

The Vocabulary Levels Test can be used to estimate the vocabulary size of second language learners of general or academic English. It provides an estimate at each of four frequency levels. You can use this test to discover whether your students are likely to have the lexical resources necessary to cope with certain language tasks, such as reading authentic materials, as outlined at the beginning of the chapter. The information can also be used to identify possible lexical deficiencies that might need addressing. Before using this test, you should read the detailed background information available in Schmitt, Schmitt, and Clapham,[29] Nation,[30] and Read.[31] Another version of this test is available in Schmitt.[32]

This is a vocabulary test. You must choose the right word to go with each meaning. Write the number of that word next to its meaning. Here is an example:

1 business
2 clock   _____ part of a house
3 horse   _____ animal with four legs
4 pencil   _____ something used for writing
5 shoe
6 wall

You answer it in the following way:

1 business
2 clock   __6__ part of a house
3 horse   __3__ animal with four legs
4 pencil   __4__ something used for writing
5 shoe
6 wall

Some words are in the test to make it more difficult. You do not have to find a meaning for these words. In the previous example, these words are *business, clock,* and *shoe.*

If you have no idea about the meaning of a word, do not guess. But if you think you might know the meaning, then you should try to find the answer.

The 2,000 Word Level

1 copy
2 event   _____ end or highest point
3 motor   _____ this moves a car
4 pity   _____ thing made to be like
5 profit   another
6 tip

1 admire
2 complain   _____ make wider or longer
3 fix   _____ bring in for the first time
4 hire   _____ have a high opinion of
5 introduce   someone
6 stretch

1 accident
2 debt   _____ loud deep sound
3 fortune   _____ something you must pay
4 pride   _____ having a high opinion of
5 roar   yourself
6 thread

1 arrange
2 develop   _____ grow
3 lean   _____ put in order
4 owe   _____ like more than something
5 prefer   else
6 seize

1 coffee
2 disease   _____ money for work
3 justice   _____ a piece of clothing
4 skirt   _____ using the law in the right
5 stage   way
6 wage

1 blame
2 elect   _____ make
3 jump   _____ choose by voting
4 manufacture   _____ become like water
5 melt
6 threaten

1 clerk
2 frame   _____ a drink
3 noise   _____ office worker
4 respect   _____ unwanted sound
5 theater
6 wine

1 ancient
2 curious   _____ not easy
3 difficult   _____ very old
4 entire   _____ related to God
5 holy
6 social

1 dozen
2 empire   _____ chance
3 gift   _____ twelve
4 opportunity   _____ money paid to the
5 relief   government
6 tax

1 bitter
2 independent   _____ beautiful
3 lovely   _____ small
4 merry   _____ liked by many people
5 popular
6 slight

The 3,000 Word Level

1 bull

2 champion   _____ formal and serious manner

3 dignity   _____ winner of a sporting event

4 hell   _____ building where valuable

5 museum   objects are shown

6 solution

1 blanket

2 contest   _____ holiday

3 generation   _____ good quality

4 merit   _____ wool covering used on

5 plot   beds

6 vacation

1 comment

2 gown   _____ long formal dress

3 import   _____ goods from a foreign

4 nerve   country

5 pasture   _____ part of the body which

6 tradition   carries feeling

1 administration

2 angel   _____ group of animals

3 frost   _____ spirit who serves God

4 herd   _____ managing business and

5 fort   affairs

6 pond

1 atmosphere

2 counsel   _____ advice

3 factor   _____ a place covered with grass

4 hen   _____ female chicken

5 lawn

6 muscle

1 abandon

2 dwell   _____ live in a place

3 oblige   _____ follow in order to catch

4 pursue   _____ leave something

5 quote   permanently

6 resolve

1 assemble

2 attach   _____ look closely

3 peer   _____ stop doing something

4 quit   _____ cry out loudly in fear

5 scream

6 toss

1 drift

2 endure   _____ suffer patiently

3 grasp   _____ join wool threads together

4 knit   _____ hold firmly with your

5 register   hands

6 tumble

1 brilliant

2 distinct   _____ thin

3 magic   _____ steady

4 naked   _____ without clothes

5 slender

6 stable

1 aware

2 blank   _____ usual

3 desperate   _____ best or most important

4 normal   _____ knowing what is

5 striking   happening

6 supreme

The 5,000 Word Level

1 analysis
2 curb   _____ eagerness
3 gravel   _____ loan to buy a house
4 mortgage   _____ small stones mixed with
5 scar   sand
6 zeal

1 contemplate
2 extract   _____ think about deeply
3 gamble   _____ bring back to health
4 launch   _____ make someone angry
5 provoke
6 revive

1 cavalry
2 eve   _____ small hill
3 ham   _____ day or night before a
4 mound   holiday
5 steak   _____ soldiers who fight from
6 switch   horses

1 demonstrate
2 embarrass   _____ have a rest
3 heave   _____ break suddenly into small
4 obscure   pieces
5 relax   _____ make someone feel shy or
6 shatter   nervous

1 circus
2 jungle   _____ musical instrument
3 nomination   _____ seat without a back or
4 sermon   arms
5 stool   _____ speech given by a
6 trumpet   priest in a church

1 correspond
2 embroider   _____ exchange letters
3 lurk   _____ hide and wait for someone
4 penetrate   _____ feel angry about
5 prescribe   something
6 resent

1 artillery
2 creed   _____ a kind of tree
3 hydrogen   _____ system of belief
4 maple   _____ large gun on wheels
5 pork
6 streak

1 decent
2 frail   _____ weak
3 harsh   _____ concerning a city
4 incredible   _____ difficult to believe
5 municipal
6 specific

1 chart
2 forge   _____ map
3 mansion   _____ large beautiful house
4 outfit   _____ place where metals are
5 sample   made and shaped
6 volunteer

1 adequate
2 internal   _____ enough
3 mature   _____ fully grown
4 profound   _____ alone away from other
5 solitary   things
6 tragic

The 10,000 Word Level

1 alabaster
2 chandelier _____ small barrel
3 dogma _____ soft white stone
4 keg _____ tool for shaping wood
5 rasp
6 tentacle

1 dissipate
2 flaunt _____ steal
3 impede _____ scatter or vanish
4 loot _____ twist the body about
5 squirm uncomfortably
6 vie

1 benevolence
2 convoy _____ kindness
3 lien _____ set of musical notes
4 octave _____ speed control for an
5 stint engine
6 throttle

1 contaminate
2 cringe _____ write carelessly
3 immerse _____ move back because of fear
4 peek _____ put something under
5 relay water
6 scrawl

1 bourgeois
2 brocade _____ middle class people
3 consonant _____ row or level of something
4 prelude _____ cloth with a pattern of gold
5 stupor or silver threads
6 tier

1 blurt
2 dabble _____ walk in a proud way
3 dent _____ kill by squeezing someone's
4 pacify throat
5 strangle _____ say suddenly without
6 swagger thinking

1 alcove
2 impetus _____ priest
3 maggot _____ release from prison early
4 parole _____ medicine to put on
5 salve wounds
6 vicar

1 illicit
2 lewd _____ immense
3 mammoth _____ against the law
4 slick _____ wanting revenge
5 temporal
6 vindictive

1 alkali
2 banter _____ light joking talk
3 coop _____ a rank of British nobility
4 mosaic _____ picture made of small
5 stealth pieces of glass or stone
6 viscount

1 indolent
2 nocturnal _____ lazy
3 obsolete _____ no longer used
4 torrid _____ clever and tricky
5 translucent
6 wily

5

THE SOUNDS OF ENGLISH

Why Does the Pronunciation of English Vary, and Why Doesn't It Always Match the Spelling?

- *Why doesn't* police *rhyme with* lice *or* swan *with* man?
- *Why does English have silent letters (e.g., the* k *in* knight*)?*
- *How has the pronunciation of English changed in the past, and how is it changing now?*
- *What is accent?*
- *What is Received Pronunciation (RP) in British English?*

Variation in the Pronunciation of English

It is a curiosity of language use that speakers who understand each other perfectly well may nevertheless speak in dissimilar ways: Their **accents** may be different, and they may pronounce specific words in quite distinct ways. In fact, the authors of this book come from two separate continents and say some words in very different ways, but we have no difficulty in communicating. Most languages are indeed very tolerant of variation; it is not the sounds themselves but their relation to other sounds that determines the level of success in communication. The degree of toleration varies. To communicate the word *often*, for instance, it is only necessary that we articulate the pair of consonants *ft* clearly and supply a vowel before them: We could supply almost any vowel and there would be no comprehension problem because there are no even remotely similar words to cause possible confusion. On the other hand, if we say *bit*, we have to be more careful. There are the words *beat* and *bat* to consider as well as *bid* and *pit*. So we cannot stray too far from a recognizable "average" sound of the word *bit*. Yet even if we did pronounce *bit* as though it were *beat* or *bid*, the context might still enable listeners to guess easily what was meant, especially if we were a non-native speaker and they were already making allowances for that fact: "Can I have a *bit/beat/bid* of help?"

But pronunciation is not simply something that varies according to the region we come from or our competence in the language. It changes over time, too. When we read the poetry of Shakespeare and find that he makes *pierce* rhyme with *rehearse* (in *Richard II*), we realize that the pronunciation of one of the words, at least, must have changed in the last 400 years. In fact, both *-ier-* and *-ear-* would probably have rhymed with *ear* in today's *bear*. Moreover, the pronunciation of English has changed much more recently than this; you have only to listen to the commentary on an old newsreel or the dialogue of a film from the 1940s to realize that many of the sounds of the language are as dated as the cars and the clothes. For example, if it is a British film, the word *platform* will probably sound as though it were spelled *pletform*.

Mismatches between Pronunciation and Spelling in English

One thing that is sure to cause students problems at some point is the mismatch between how some words are pronounced and how they are spelled. Indeed, there are so many inconsistencies and irregularities that students may wonder whether there is any system at all. Take a group of words such as *through, though, bough, cough,* and *hiccough,* which all contain the element *-ough.* In each of these the pronunciation of *ou* is different, and *gh* is either left silent or pronounced as though it were an *f* or a *p.* The Irish dramatist and critic George Bernard Shaw, who spent much of his life railing against what he considered to be the absurdities of English spelling, summed up the problem nicely. The word *fish,* he asserted, might as well be spelled *ghoti*—*gh* as in *cough, o* as in *women,* and *ti* as in *nation!* It was a clever point, but in fact English spelling is much more systematic than this.

The problem is that it does not **consistently** and **regularly** follow pronunciation. Yet it is worth noting from the outset that the majority of the letters used in the spelling of English give us no serious problems in pronunciation: Consider *d, f, j, k, m, n, p, q, r, v, w, x, z,* and we could add *b* and *l,* as long as we remember that sometimes they may be "silent," as in *walk, would, debt,* and *dumb.* The consonants *c, g, h, s, t,* and *y,* however, can be rather more problematic, and the vowels *a, e, i, o,* and *u,* along with the diphthongs derived from them (*ai, au, ei, eo,* etc.), are a lot more so.

This was not always the case. In the days of the Anglo-Saxons one thousand years ago, Old English spelling consistently followed the way a word was spoken. The conflicts between sound and symbol that plague us today have accumulated over the centuries since then. One of the most profound influences in respect of vowel pronunciation was a radical and systematic change, taking place mainly in the 15th and 16th centuries, known as the Great Vowel Shift, when all the main long vowels underwent a shift in their values. Other changes resulted from the efforts of foreigners (among them Norman scribes and early printers) to spell English sounds in what, in their view, were more accurate ways. Some modern spellings reflect scholarly attempts to make a word more etymologically correct by reintroducing original spelling features long lost in pronunciation. Last, English's prolific borrowing over many centuries of words from other languages with their own peculiar spelling patterns has added to the problem. So the modern correspondences, or lack of them, between sound and spelling are in a profound way historical. Many of today's spellings give us an accurate picture of how a word used to be pronounced in, say, the 14th or 15th centuries, before the sorts of changes outlined here took place.

To be able to answer interesting questions about sound changes and the relationship of sound to spelling, we first need a way to precisely classify and describe the sounds of English.

Describing the Sounds of English

English uses a little more than 40 sounds, the exact number depending on how they are counted, which is more than the average language, as discussed in Chapter 1. This large inventory of sounds facilitates the substantial vocabulary that English possesses, but it does have a downside: There are only 26 letters in the Modern English alphabet. This means that many letters must represent more than one sound, which is an underlying cause of many of the spelling inconsistencies in English today. There is also the difficulty of precisely describing the sounds of English using only the alphabet. We need a system that describes all the different sounds available, using a comprehensive series of symbols to differentiate between them, wherein each symbol represents one, and only one, sound. Such systems are used by dictionaries to illustrate the pronunciation of words. However, each learner's dictionary we consulted employed a slightly different phonemic alphabet system, and so we selected the symbols most commonly used. From these we compiled a phonemic system illustrated on the following pages. It uses the letters of the regular alphabet supplemented by others (e.g., ʃ, æ, ɔ, and ʌ) to represent unambiguously each meaningful sound or **phoneme** (conventionally indicated between slashes, e.g., /d/) of Standard English. These sound representations are used throughout this chapter and the rest of the book.

Consonants

There are 24 consonant sounds in most English accents, conveyed by 21 letters of the regular English alphabet (sometimes in combination, e.g., *ch* and *th*).

THE CONSONANTS OF ENGLISH	
Sound	Examples
/p/	pair, cup
/b/	bad, crab
/t/	tall, hit
/d/	dark, head
/k/	cab, lack
/g/	good, tag
/f/	fine, wife
/v/	very, above
/θ/	thing, both
/ð/	this, father
/s/	saw, house
/z/	zap, goes
/ʃ/	shape, push
/ʒ/	pleasure, beige
/h/	her, ahead
/x/	loch
/tʃ/	cherry, match
/dʒ/	judge, raj
/m/	man, team
/n/	nail, tan
/ŋ/	ring, singer
/l/	let, tall
/r/	right, scary
/w/	wet, away
/j/	you, soya

There are several ways in which linguists classify consonants, according to how they are pronounced. For example, p, b, m, and w are called **labials** because they are formed by pressing the lips together. The group comprising the pairs f/v, θ/ð, s/z, and ∫/ʒ are called **fricatives** because, when they are articulated, two of the speech organs in the mouth come so close together that audible friction is produced as the air passes through; and k/g, t/d, t∫/ʤ, and p/b are called **stops** because the mouth passage is completely closed off at some point in their articulation. You can test such definitions very easily by articulating each consonant slowly and deliberately and noting the behavior of your tongue, lips, and vocal chords.

We have grouped the fricatives and stops in pairs to illustrate another aspect of their pronunciation, the presence or absence of **voicing**—that is, vibration of the vocal chords. In each case, the first member of the pairs is unvoiced (no vibration), the second one voiced (vibration). Try pronouncing the members of each pair in turn, feeling your throat as you do so, and you will understand the difference between them. As we shall see, voicing is also an important characteristic of vowel production.

We shall sometimes use these linguistic terms in talking about consonants in later chapters.

Vowels

Vowels are the major constituents of syllables, the smallest uninterruptible units of spoken language: All syllables consist of a vowel alone or a vowel preceded and/or followed by a consonant. Although the spelling system of English allows representation of only 5 vowels (*a, e, i, o, u*), there are at least 12 in the spoken language, though some linguists would distinguish as many as 20. In fact, vowel quality—the specific sound that enables us to distinguish, for example, between *bad, bed,* and *bud*—can be varied almost infinitely by alterations in the position of the tongue and lips and the opening or closing of the mouth. Differences in vowel quality are one of the criteria, too, by which we identify different accents (see pp. 136–141).

THE VOWELS OF ENGLISH

Sounds	Examples
/ɪ/	b<u>i</u>t, p<u>i</u>n
/ɛ/	b<u>e</u>t, p<u>e</u>n
/æ/	b<u>a</u>t, r<u>a</u>n
/ɒ/	p<u>o</u>t, <u>o</u>ften
/ʌ/	sh<u>u</u>t, en<u>ou</u>gh
/ʊ/	b<u>oo</u>k, p<u>u</u>t
/ə/	<u>a</u>bout, butt<u>er</u>
/i/	prett<u>y</u>
/i:/	b<u>ea</u>n, s<u>ee</u>
/u/	infl<u>u</u>ence
/u:/	s<u>oo</u>n, cl<u>ue</u>
/ɑ:/	f<u>a</u>ther, b<u>ar</u>n
/ɔ:/	c<u>au</u>ght, l<u>aw</u>
/ɜ:/	b<u>ir</u>d, f<u>ur</u>

Vowels are *voiced* sounds, produced when the vocal cords vibrate (thus giving voice) and the mouth cavity is open. If the nasal passage is also left open, so that some air can escape this way too, we get *nasal* vowels, which are a particular feature of American English. The short unstressed sound /ə/ is known as "schwa." Vowels are classified according to two main criteria:

- The position of the highest part of the tongue relative to the roof of the mouth: high or low. When the tongue is at its highest, pressed against the roof of the mouth and restricting the passage of air, the vowels produced are described as *close* (or *high*); when at its lowest, leaving the mouth cavity at its most unrestricted, the vowels are said to be *open* (or *low*). When its position is somewhere between, the vowels may be said to be *half-open* (or *mid*).
- The extent of retraction of the tongue: unretracted at the front of the mouth or retracted right to the back of the mouth. When the tongue is unretracted, the vowels produced are described as *front* vowels and when retracted they are *back* vowels; when the tongue is pulled back only part of the way, the vowels may be described as *central*.

Each vowel, then, may be defined according to its degree of closeness/openness (highness/lowness) and frontness/backness. This may be displayed diagrammatically in a slightly assymetrical box that represents the vowel-producing space of the mouth (looking from the side, with the front of the mouth to the left, as shown in Figure 8). For each vowel, the approximate position for its articulation, and therefore its quality (how it sounds), can thus be illustrated. But it is essential to note that the precise point of articulation of a particular vowel is impossible to pin down: It will vary between speakers and even within the discourse of a single speaker.

Thus, the *a* in *father*, represented in the phonemic alphabet as /ɑ/, can be described as "an open back vowel"; *a* in *back* /æ/ is "an open front vowel," and *e* in *met* /ɛ/ is "a half-open front vowel."

In earlier periods of English, vowels varied in length more than they do today, so that the short and long versions might be perceived as different sounds, and this could be a distinguishing factor between different words. Today, vowels still vary in length to some extent, but it depends on the variety of English as to whether such differences are recognized as establishing distinct sounds. For most speakers of American English, the distinction is lost, and indeed it is very difficult for American ears to even hear it. On the other hand, many speakers of British English do pronounce the relatively short *u* in *influence* differently from the relatively longer *u* in *soon*. To the extent that British English and its offshoots recognize differences in vowel length, it is possible to distinguish two main groups: the short (æ, ɛ, ɪ, i, ɒ, ʌ, ə, ʊ, u) and the long (ɑ:, ɔ:, ɜ:, u:, i:). In

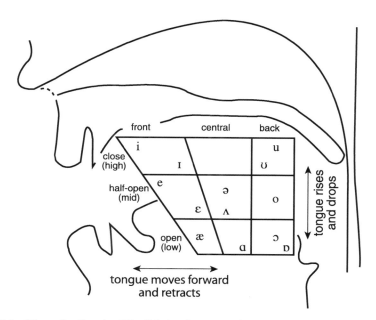

FIGURE 8   Where the Vowels of English Are Pronounced

most of the back vowels, lip-rounding plays an important part, and the closer (i.e., higher) the vowel, the more rounded the lips will be, a fact that can be verified easily enough in the mirror: For the back-closed vowel of *boo*, the lips are pushed forward and rounded, as though for blowing out a candle. The front vowels are not made with lip rounding in Standard English, but in some non-standard forms, as in many foreign languages, rounding produces a dramatically different sound—like the *u* in French *tu*, or the *ü* in German *müde*.

When two vowels are combined, we call the result a **diphthong** or **glide.** In diphthongs, the speech organs move (or glide) during utterance into the position of a second vowel. Thus, in *boy*, the speech organs begin in the position to produce the sound /ɔ:/ as in *saw* but immediately move into the position to produce /i:/ as in *see*. The first part of the diphthong is usually much longer and louder than the second. These are the eight diphthongs usually identified in British and American English:

THE DIPHTHONGS (GLIDES) OF ENGLISH	
Sounds	Examples
/aɪ/	r<u>igh</u>t, b<u>uy</u>
/ɛɪ/	w<u>ai</u>t, r<u>ai</u>n
/ɔɪ/	t<u>oy</u>, v<u>oi</u>ce
/əʊ/	g<u>o</u>, alth<u>ough</u>
/aʊ/	m<u>ou</u>se, all<u>ow</u>
/ʊə/	poor
/ɛə/	hair
/ɪə/	hear

British English speakers do not normally pronounce the final /r/ in the last three examples given (*poor, hair,* and *hear*). American speakers use short vowels in these words and add the /r/ sound (/ur/, /ɛr/, and /ir/); thus typically they only use the first five diphthongs in the list.

The following two vowels are not normally used in standard American or British pronunciation, but they would have been heard in the Old and Middle English periods and will be used later in this chapter in our discussion of these periods:

/e/ This sounds something like the *ai* in *bait*, but it is a pure and
     clipped vowel, with none of the gliding that makes *ai* into a
     diphthong. Speakers of French (*été*) or Italian (*tre*) will be familiar
     with this sound, which can be short or long.

/o:/ Again, this is a pure vowel (also in French, *eau*, and Italian, *uno*),
    very like the name of the letter *o*, but with no glide or falling away.

Stress

When we speak English we use vowels and consonants in varying combinations
to produce the units we recognize as words. But that is only the start. **Stress** is a
basic identifying feature of all words of more than one syllable; characteristically,
English words are stressed on the first syllable: *lóvely, módern, básic, cónsonant.*
Sometimes meaning may depend on stress: Compare the noun *récord* with the
verb *recórd*. It is the stress system of English, in combination with variations in
speed and in intonation, that give it its characteristic rhythm.

Like other aspects of pronunciation, stress is subject to change through
time. We soon realize this when we try to read Shakespeare's verse. In *She bears
a duke's revenues on her back* (from *Henry VI*), the metrical structure of the
line shows that the stress in *revenues* must be on the second syllable (*revénues*),
not (as today) the first. Other trisyllabic words that followed this pattern in
early modern times include *advértise, charácter, demónstrate,* and *siníster*. On
the other hand, some words in which we now stress the second syllable used
to be stressed on the first: *ántique, cónvenient, dístinct, éntire, éxtreme, Júly*. In
others, where we stress the first syllable now, the stress used to be on the last:
aspéct, expért, paramóunt, parént, yesterdáy. In some cases, stress seems to have
been variable in Shakespeare's day, as in *cómplete* or *compléte*. How did this
situation of variation and change come about? It is not always clear, but in many
cases it may have been because of the confusion that arose when a language
(English) in which natural stress was on the first main syllable of a word was
invaded by hundreds of words from a language (French) in which stress was
characteristically at the end of a word.

Variable stress is still a feature of English. Sometimes it depends on how
a word is used. Very often it seems that, in noun/verb pairs, we prefer to stress
the first syllable in the noun (e.g., *ínsult, éxport, díscount*) but the second in the
verb (e.g., *insúlt, expórt* [though this is variable], *discóunt*). On the other hand,
excess as a noun is stressed on the second syllable and as an adjective on the first
(*éxcess baggage*). Again, however, regional differences emerge. American speakers
stress the first syllable of *address* when it is a noun and the second when it is a
verb, as in the previous examples. British speakers, however, stress the second
syllable in both cases. Sometimes regional British stress patterns will concur
with American against standard British English; thus Americans and northern
English people will tend to stress *advertisement* on the first and third syllables
(as in the verb *ádvertíse*), whereas standard British English favors stress on the

second syllable, with corresponding loss of distinct quality for the first and last vowels. In a similar way, *harass* and *harassment* have traditionally been given stress on the first syllable in standard British English but the second in American; in this instance, the American way is more and more commonly followed by British speakers. Other variations in stress patterns are frequent among regional varieties of English, especially in the case of loanwords. For example, American speakers tend to retain the original stress pattern in French loanwords, as in *brochúre* and *ballét*, whereas speakers of British English anglicize the stress: *bróchure* and *bállet*. We discuss these differences in more detail in Chapter 7.

APPLICATIONS TO TEACHING

Teachers who wish to teach pronunciation obviously need to have an understanding of the mechanics of sound production. This book assumes some knowledge of the sound system of English and so only gives a brief overview. Teachers who would like more detail on the system and how the various sounds are produced can consult the books listed in the Further Reading section.

If pronunciation is to be an important component of the language curriculum, then the teacher should consider whether it is worthwhile teaching students a phonemic alphabet. Because there is not a straightforward correspondence between the English sound system and the English alphabet (about 40 phonemes but only 26 alphabet characters), trying to explain pronunciation using only this alphabet are awkward and can cause confusion. Many teachers have found that the time and effort expended initially on teaching a phonemic alphabet are rewarded over the students' whole course of study, as explanations about pronunciation can be much more direct and precise. There is also an added benefit: The phonemic practice should enable students to better use the phonemic pronunciation guides in their dictionaries.

Any discussion of pronunciation in the classroom needs to include the more global pronunciation features such as stress in addition to the vowel and consonant phonemes. These global *(suprasegmental)* features play a large part in conveying the speaker's emotions and stance as well as indicating the key information in a piece of discourse. This is illustrated by the following sentence, which can have several meanings depending on where the stress is placed:

I took the train to New York on Friday.

(not someone else)

I took the <u>TRAIN</u> to New York on Friday.

(not some other means of transportation)

I took the train to <u>NEW YORK</u> on Friday.

(not some other city)

I took the train to New York on <u>FRIDAY</u>.

(not some other day)

Why Does Pronunciation Change?

Languages never stand still, and the history of English is primarily the history of changes made in the spoken language. The ancestor languages of English were perpetually changing too. To give just one example, in words beginning with a *bh* sound (a sort of aspirated *b*) in Indo-European (spoken perhaps 6,000 yeas ago), as in *bhrater* (brother), that sound became /f/ when the words evolved into Latin (*frater*) but /b/ in Germanic languages such as English and German (*brother, Bruder*). So sound changes helped to shape English as a separate language. Such changes in retrospect appear radical and systematic, but in practice they happen slowly and piecemeal. It seems that divergences from the "standard" in the pronunciation of certain words begin within a speech community quite arbitrarily, and eventually the modified sound may (or may not) be adopted generally and become the new standard. We can in fact imagine a long period during which linguistic conservatives consciously strive to retain the older pronunciations, before the new finally take over. This is seen frequently today. Until late in the 20th century, for instance, the British pronunciation of *amok* (as in "to run amok") was traditionally /əmʌk/, rhyming with *muck*, and indeed the word was sometimes spelled *amuck*; but increasingly speakers unfamiliar with the word have simply pronounced it as spelled /əmɒk/, rhyming with *mock*, to the annoyance of those who assert the old pronunciation to be the "correct" one.

A number of theories as to why the sounds of a language—how we pronounce it—change through time have been put forward. Some of them, such as those that blame the effect of alterations in climate affecting the organs of speech or the influence of racial characteristics, have no demonstrable basis in fact. Other theories have identified influences that definitely do have an effect on language change, though no single influence can satisfactorily explain all change. We should probably accept that sound change is caused by a complex combination of influences, rather than a single one. A number of the most significant factors that cause pronunciation to vary over time follow.[1]

The "Lazy Principle"

This widely accepted influence explains a large range of sound changes, and its effects are quite easy to demonstrate. It could be expressed also as "the principle of the minimalization of effort," which is to say that we are always happy to take shortcuts in our articulation of words, especially those of several syllables, or even to expand slightly if that helps to smooth away awkward combinations of sound. These changes make words easier to pronounce and are readily adopted, as long as they do not make a word sound too much like another and therefore cause confusion. The principle operates in five ways:

1. **Assimilation.** In this process, neighboring sounds become more like each other. The basic aim always is to reduce the activities of the tongue or mouth as they change to produce successive sounds. This can be seen in current English in *pancake*, where /n/ becomes /ŋ/ under the influence of /k/ in the next syllable; for /n/, the tongue presses against the front tooth ridge, but in both /ŋ/ and /k/, it is pressed against the roof of the mouth. By using /ŋ/ before /k/, the tongue does not have to move as much.[2] Listen carefully, and you may sometimes hear something similar happening with *football*, where the /t/ may become /p/ under the influence of following /b/: /fʊpbɔ:l/. In *cupboard*, the *p* is completely assimilated into the *b* and lost, so the word is pronounced /kʌbəd/.[3] An "analytical" pronunciation—with *cup* and *board* articulated separately—would sound very strange today. Just such a pronunciation is, however, now usually given to *clapboard* (*clap* plus *board*). Yet the assimilated pronunciation /klæbəd/ was once the more commonly heard form, perhaps when the building of clapboard houses (with overlapping weatherboards) was more widely familiar.

   Assimilation explains also why *swan* is pronounced with a back vowel /ɒ/, rhyming with *con*, not a front vowel /æ/, rhyming with *man*. Until about 1700 it did rhyme with *man*, but when the lips are rounded and the tongue retracted to produce /w/, it is far easier to keep things that way and produce /ɒ/ than to pull the lips back again and push the tongue forward to produce /æ/. The same lazy principle explains why *wash* today rhymes with *posh*, not (as it used to) with *hash*.

2. **Dissimilation.** This is a process by which neighboring sounds become less like one another. The two sounds /f/ and /θ/ in the middle of **diphthong**, for instance, require some effort to distinguish, because they are pronounced very close together and require an awkward change within the mouth to pronounce: /dɪfθɒŋ/; the easier option is to replace /f/ with the stop /p/, which is what many speakers do. In this example, it is likely also that the spelling of the word, where /f/ is represented graphically by *ph*, has influenced the pronunciation, and the word is often mispelled *dipthong*.[4] Another example is *chimney*, in which the second of the two nasal sounds /n/ is often replaced with /l/, as though the word were spelled *chimley*.

3. **Simplification.** There is a regular tendency for consonant clusters to be simplified. At the start of the Early Modern English period, the initial /k/ in words like *knight* and *know*, /g/ in *gnat*, and /w/ in *write* were still usually pronounced, as they had been in the Old English period. By 1700 the first sound of each pair had been dropped (see p. 134). So too had the /t/ in *castle*, though we retain it today in the related verb *castellate*. The /t/ in *Christmas* is still often heard, but more and more it is being dropped also. In the case of *often*, the *t* was originally pronounced until about the 17th century, after which it became fashionable to drop it; but in recent times, it is common to hear it again. Unfortunately, the spelling of words did not change to match the lost sounds, and this is one cause of the silent letters in English. It is also interesting to note that the loss of /k/ from *knight* produced potential confusion with *night*, but in practice the context of use of the two words is so different that English was able to retain both **homophones** (words with the same sound) with little danger of confusion between them.

4. **Elision.** Another process of simplification occurs when whole syllables are dropped in frequently used words, especially where successive unstressed syllables begin with a vowel or the same consonant. Thus *temporary* is often shortened to *tempory* or *temprary* or even *tempry*, *family* to *famly*, and *deliberately* to *delibrately*. Unstressed prefixes tend to be dropped also: *perhaps* → *praps*. Theoretically, these pronunciations could affect spelling in time, though in the latter case, at least, our fondness sometimes for ironical

emphasis, when we pronounce the two syllables very distinctly, with stress on the second: *per-háps*, may make it unlikely.

5. **Addition of sounds.** Sometimes, rather than simplify, we add sounds, in a process known as ***intrusion.*** The Old English word for *thunder*, for instance, was *þunor*, which might have produced modern *thunner*, but from at least the 13th century an additional phoneme /d/ began to intrude, probably because the transition from /n/ to the final syllable (in which the vowel was probably lost, so that /r/ became a syllable in its own right) was a difficult one, which the insertion of /d/ made easier. A similar process produced *bramble* from Old English *bremel*: When the lips are already together for /m/, it is a natural progression to produce the consonant /b/ before the following vowel. The same process explains the commonly heard intrusive /p/ in *hamster* /hæmpstər/, which is going the same way as the area of London called Hampstead, which started life as *ham-stede* but has been spelled (and thus certainly pronounced) with a *p* since the 17th century.

Social Influence

Radical changes in social hierarchies can have a dramatic effect on language. It has been noted that, after the Russian Revolution of 1917, the upper-class pronunciation that had previously carried great prestige soon became undesirable, and speakers tried to disguise it. A more gradual but similar change may have taken place in 17th-century England, when an ambitious middle class, made wealthy through trade, began to pervade the landed gentry and carried some of their speech habits into upper-class pronunciation.[5] In England during the closing decades of the 20th century, a conscious process of social leveling gave a certain fashionable cachet to accents that had previously been considered undesirable, while the accent associated with the old aristocracy became marginalized and often ridiculed. An example of an accent that has become fashionable is that of "Estuary English," the name given (rather inaccurately) to a regional London form of speech that spread eastward through the counties adjoining the estuary of the River Thames, especially Essex and Kent, during the 1980s. It contains many elements of London Cockney speech and has been cultivated by some television personalities. But its influence has spread far beyond the Thames estuary to areas of the north and west of England, many of them in easy reach of London by train. Its success has been explained as perhaps a combination of two factors—the down-market trend of middle-class people anxious to avoid being seen as "posh," and the upward mobility of people from London settling in new areas.[6] Estuary English has thus been responsible for several features of pronunciation now becoming much more common in everyday spoken British English:[7]

- The final /t/ in words is dropped and replaced with a glottal stop (*There's a lo' of i' abou'*).
- The short final vowel /i/ in words like *happy* and *very* is lengthened to /iː/ (/hæpiː/).
- The syllables without vowels occurring in Received Pronunciation (see later in this chapter) are "filled out" with an unstressed schwa vowel (/mɪdl/→/mɪdəl/).

Hypercorrection

Sometimes pronunciation is deliberately altered in an effort by speakers to speak in what they take to be a more correct or socially acceptable way. A Yorkshire woman of our acquaintance recalls how, fresh down from the north and keen to be accepted as a southerner, she asked in a pharmacy for some /ɑːsprɪn/ (with the first syllable sounding embarrassingly like *arse*), on the mistaken assumption that in the south the "short" northern *a* /æ/ was always pronounced "long": Compare northern British *ask* /æsk/ with the usual southern version /ɑːsk/. Similarly, you will sometimes hear *m* intruding at the end of *who* in unexpected places, where someone is trying to show off their credentials as a speaker of "correct" English: "Whom is there?" They have failed to understand that the old inflected form of the pronoun *who* is only appropriate as an object form, as in "To whom it may concern," at least as prescribed by traditional grammar. Misunderstandings like this only serve to highlight the problematic nature of many of the prescriptive rules that exist in traditional grammar. In any case, it is rare for such hypercorrected pronunciations to catch on and become the norm.

The Influence of Spelling

A more pervasive sort of change occurs when pronunciation is modified to bring it in line with new spellings that themselves have resulted from a process of misguided "correction."[8] The word that we now spell *schedule* was borrowed from Old French *cedule* in the 14th century and was spelled and pronounced *sedule*. However, a mistaken attempt in the 16th century to give the word an "etymological" spelling, imitating its then current Latin form, resulted in the form *scedule* and then *schedule*, and from the mid-17th century the pronunciation of the first syllable as /ʃɛd/ became standard. In the 18th century, Noah Webster recommended /skɛd/, on the basis that the word was of Greek origin, like *scheme* (though in fact it was not), and hence the usual American pronunciation today. *Receipt* and *indict* are both words taken from Anglo-French, as *receite* and *endite*, respectively, but they too were respelled to give them a Latin look, with inserted *p* and *c*, respectively (and, in the case of *endite*, a more Latinate prefix, *in*, also). No one has seriously tried to pronounce the *p* in *receipt* (it would be very difficult), but it is not unusual today to hear *indict* pronounced /ɪndɪkt/, instead of traditional /ɪndaɪt/. These mistaken "etymological" respellings are another source of the silent letters of English. There will be more on this in Chapter 6 on spelling.

The standard British pronunciation of *metaphor* is /mɛtəfə/, with the last syllable very weak, as though spelled *-er* (with the *r* unpronounced in British English), but a pronunciation that gives some clarity to the last syllable is also often heard /mɛtəfɔːr/; perhaps this is caused by analogy with words in *-ore*, such as *carnivore*, in which the last syllable is always pronounced clearly. On the other hand, American English has a tendency to pronounce all of the syllables in a word in a way similar to how it is spelled, and so *metaphor* would be pronounced as /mɛtəfɔːr/ in most American English varieties. An interesting example of the influence of spelling on pronunciation is the name *Magdalen*. It was borrowed as French *Madelaine* in the 14th century and took the form *Maudeleyn*, with a pronunciation like that of the derived adjective *maudlin* (originally meaning "weeping, tearful," with reference to Mary Magdalen), which we still use. But the name later became respelled in a way that brought it nearer to its ecclesiastical Latin form, *Magdalena*, and so today we say /mægdælɛn/—unless we are talking of the Oxford and Cambridge colleges of that name, when we are required to use the old pronunciation /mɔːdlɪn/ and may indeed feel ourselves at a social disadvantage if we get it wrong.[9]

APPLICATIONS TO TEACHING

The pronunciation of words has changed over time and that change continues for many words today. This can be seen in words like *Christmas* and *often*. Does the correct pronunciation include the /t/ or not? In fact, there is no "correct" answer, as these words are in the middle of change, with some proficient speakers pronouncing the /t/ and others not. There are many other words like this in English. Dictionaries are a useful source for pronunciation guidance but often do not alert students to this kind of variable pronunciation. The more we understand that English is a living language and constantly changing, the less confident we can be that any reference source, including dictionaries, can always provide absolute answers.

It is probably safe to say that all students are sometimes frustrated by the numerous spelling inconsistencies in English. Although it may not make it any easier to learn the idiosyncratic spellings of the exception words in English, our experience shows that students appreciate logical explanations of these exceptions. A short explanation of the historical basis of the silent letters in English, for instance, seems much more satisfying than the "That's just the way it is" explanation that many ESL teachers offer. Such uninformative vague responses give students the impression that English is fundamentally unsystematic and illogical and therefore difficult to learn. Anything teachers can do to give the impression that English is systematic and learnable can only help students' motivation and improve their eventual achievement.

Languages vary in how transparently their pronunciations match their spellings. Some languages, like Spanish, have a relatively close sound-symbol correspondence, and one can be quite confident about a word's pronunciation based on its spelling and vice versa. At the other end of the spectrum, some languages have sound-symbol correspondences that are less transparent, which can lead to learning difficulties. An example of this is Scottish Gaelic, which contains complex phonological changes in its spoken form. Although its spelling follows these changes in a regular way, the complexity of the sound system often creates confusion in spelling for students trying to learn the language. English is somewhere between these extremes as a language, being largely systematic but with numerous exceptions. Students coming from loose correspondence languages may not be particularly bothered by the spelling exceptions in English and indeed may expect them given their experience with their own L1s. However, students coming from close correspondence languages may simply apply their L1 spelling strategy of confidently spelling out words from their sounds, not even realizing that in English this sometimes leads to mistakes. Teachers may have to make these students aware of such potential problems. In mixed classes, teachers also need to be aware that close correspondence students may become more frustrated with English spelling than loose correspondence students.

Historical Sound Change and Its Effect on Modern English Pronunciation

Sounds in the Past: How We Know

To understand how the sounds of Modern English were established and why change continues, we need to know how earlier forms of the language sounded. But how is this possible—how can we know how Old or Middle English sounded or even the Early Modern English language of Shakespeare? By the early 16th century men of learning had in fact already become preoccupied with the question of the "right" pronunciation of English and, although their phonemic descriptions fall far short of the sort of precision we are used to today, they and their successors provide us with invaluable information about how English was spoken at various times during the early modern and modern periods. Another valuable source of information is poetry, for poets using regular metrical and rhyme schemes preserve traditional pronunciations. Thus from Shakespeare we learn that *loyalty* rhymes with *lie (Richard II)*, showing that the last syllable of *loyalty* (then spelled *-ie*) carried more stress than it does today and sounded something like the /aɪ/ sound in modern *lie*.

For the Middle English period, matters are more difficult, though poetry again may be an enormous help, for at this time poets start regularly to use end rhyme and, in some cases, metrically regular lines. Modern regional dialects, too, can act as signposts to the past, for they tend to be conservative, often staying unaffected by major changes in the standard language. After that we can apply linguistic science. Sound change in languages is continuous and in general seems to follow regular and thus predictable patterns, so we can use our knowledge of these in trying to work backward and recover old pronunciations. As for the earliest forms of English, when Christian monks first started writing Old English in the early 7th century, they naturally used the Latin alphabet already familiar to them. As we know more or less how each Latin letter was sounded, we can assume that the Old English sounds represented by those letters were very similar. This is confirmed by the fact that additional symbols were eventually supplied for sounds that evidently were not in Latin (see p. 154).

Sound Change

As we have indicated, the sounds of English have been subject to variation and change since the earliest stages of the language. But change is not inevitable.

Take the following Old English words, used more than 1,000 years ago, and followed here by their equivalents in the modern language:

asc	ash
bedd	bed
ford	ford
full	full
mann	man
sacc	sack
scip	ship
twentig	twenty
þæt	that
þis	this

These words were pronounced 1,000 years ago more or less as they are today—though there have been some minor changes in spelling (the sound /ʃ/ was represented by *sc* in Old English but by *sh* now; the letter þ gave way to *th*). As the Old English language evolved in the centuries following the Norman Conquest into what we now call Middle English, and then on into Modern English, little of significance happened to the way the relevant vowels and consonants of these words, and others employing the same sounds, were pronounced.

But now look at this list of Old English words (given with their approximate pronunciations) and their Modern English equivalents:

tīma	/tiːm/	time
grēne	/greːnɛ/	green
brecan	/brɛkɑn/	break
nama	/nɑmɑ/	name
bāt	/bɑːt/	boat
mōna	/moːnɑ/	moon
hūs	/huːs/	house

The differences are quite marked: The Old English (OE) word for *time* sounded more like modern *team*; that for *green* something like *grain*; for *moon* like *moan*, for *boat* a bit like *bart(er)*, and so on. Moreover, the changes occurred in a large number of words with these vowels. Thus Old English *līm* /liːm/ became Modern English *lime*, *fēt* /feːt/ became *feet*, *sōna* /soːnɑ/ became *soon*, and *mūs* /muːs/ became *mouse*. In most cases, the changes center on a long vowel and the consonants remain unaffected. (The exceptions are the *a* in *nama* and the *e* in *brecan*.) What these changes bear witness to is a process known to historical linguists as the Great Vowel Shift, and it is important because it explains much about the shape of the modern language, including the exasperating gap between spelling and pronunciation in so many words and the great variety of ways of representing the same sounds.

The Great Vowel Shift

By Chaucer's time, the pronunciation of English long vowels had already changed a little since Anglo-Saxon times—in words like *nama* ("name" OE /nɑmɑ/) and *brecan* ("break" OE /brɛːkɑn/), where a short vowel was followed by a single consonant plus another vowel, the first vowel had lengthened, and in the first case had been "fronted" also (/næːm/, /brɛːk/). But roughly between the death of Chaucer in 1400 and that of Shakespeare in 1616, there were further changes by which all of the seven long vowels of Middle English—iː, eː, ɛː, æː, uː, oː, and ɔː—moved in a systematic way to take on new values. Table 9 shows these changes, with the new values reached. In three cases, the new vowels or diphthongs shifted further during succeeding centuries in Standard English, as indicated, though some of the 17th-century qualities may still be heard in some varieties of Modern English (the /ɔʊ/ of *house*, for instance, in some parts of the United States and Canada).

TABLE 9
THE GREAT VOWEL SHIFT

The Great Main Vowel Shift				Later Developments		
14th Century			17th Century	21st Century		
tim	iː	>	əɪ	→	aɪ	time
grene	eː	>	iː	=	iː	green
brek	ɛː	>	eː	→	ɛɪ	break
nam	æː	>	ɛː	→	ɛɪ	name
boote	ɔː	>	oː	→	əʊ	boat
mone	oː	>	uː	=	uː	moon
hus	uː	>	əʊ	→	aʊ	house

Just how systematic these changes were can be seen in Figure 9. Five of the vowels, eː, ɛː, ɑː, oː, and ɔː, had been raised. As for iː and uː, these were already articulated as high as they could be in the mouth and no more raising was possible, and so they shifted "sideways" into the diphthongs /əɪ/ and /əu/, respectively.

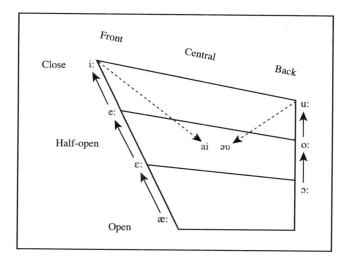

FIGURE 9   How the Long Vowels of Middle English Shifted

The causes of the Great Vowel Shift are little understood, though dialectal variation may have played a part. In historical terms, the shifting took place fairly rapidly, between the early 15th and the beginning of the 17th century. Even so, people at the time would not have been aware of it as such, but they probably would have been conscious of much fluctuation and variation in the long vowel sounds of their language, especially around 1500. It is only in retrospect that we see a clear systematic pattern emerging and becoming fixed—giving us the form of the "standard" pronunciation of English that we now recognize. There are other languages that have undergone similar drastic vowel shifts at times, including Chinese in the 9th century. The key aspect of such shifts is not the individual changes in themselves. What matters is that the language's system of difference remains intact: The specific quality of a particular vowel in pronunciation is always less important than the difference between it and other vowels in the system. What is important in English is that the individual words in groups such as *main, mean, mine, moan,* and *moon* or *bane, been, bone,* and *boon* should be distinguishable from each other.

The fact that the Great Vowel Shift had such a dramatic effect on the spelling of English was largely the result of unfortunate timing: It began just at the time when spelling conventions were beginning to be established, during the 15th and 16th centuries. After the advent of printing in England, in 1476, there was at first no great effort on the part of the printers to establish consistency and uniformity in their spellings, though in general they took spellings that had become usual in manuscripts in the later 14th or earlier 15th centuries. But the shift had hardly begun then. Thus, even as the representation of a particular sound was being fixed, that sound might be changing radically. To some extent, then, at least in respect of the long vowels, English ended up with a Middle English orthography matched to an Early Modern English sound system—and even after that, there would be some more shifting to add to the inconsistencies. Indeed, the process continues, and no doubt today's vowels will sound distinctly odd from the perspective of the 22nd century.

Results of the Great Vowel Shift: Odd Couples

The timing of the Great Vowel Shift has caused many anomalies in Modern English, especially notable in the contrast between pairs of words that seem to contain the same elements but are pronounced differently. Why, for example, does *police* not rhyme with *lice*? Or *vine* with *ravine*? Or *polite* with *elite*? In the first pair, *lice* has been in the language since Old English times (as *lys*, with a long vowel), so naturally it was subject to shifting in the later 15th century. *Police*, on the other hand, was not borrowed into English (from French) until late in the 16th century, after the major shift in English vowels had taken place, and so we still pronounce it (more or less) as the French did (and still do). Similarly, *vine* was borrowed in the 13th century and was thus subject to the Great Vowel Shift, but *ravine* was not borrowed until the 17th century and so the vowel remained unchanged. As for the third pair of words, *polite*, like *police*, was a loanword, but it entered English (from Latin) in the earlier 15th century and did not escape the Great Vowel Shift. It began with a pronunciation something like /pɒliːt/, but the long vowel /iː/ soon shifted, first into the diphthong /əɪ/ and then to /aɪ/. *Elite*, however, was not borrowed (from French) until the 18th century and was never subject to any shifting; we pronounce it more or less as the French do, /ɛɪliːt/, even putting the stress on the second syllable.

It seems, then, that we can make reasonably good deductions about when foreign borrowings entered English simply by observing the way we pronounce them. This is especially apparent when we consider words that have been borrowed once and then reborrowed. Take the words *chief* and *chef*, which both derive from French *chef*. The first, describing something or someone in paramount position, was borrowed into English (first as an adjective, meaning "leading") as early as the 12th century, as *chef*, with a pronunciation reflecting that of French at the time: /tʃɛːf/. Later, it underwent the inevitable shift in its vowel, from /ɛː/ to /iː/, and this happened early enough for the shift to be recorded in a spelling change also, hence *chief*. The second borrowing of *chef*, in the restricted sense "head cook," did not take place until the 19th century. By this time the French pronunciation of initial *ch* had changed from /tʃ/ to /ʃ/, and this is the way we still pronounce the word. In respect of French borrowings with *ch*, you can usually tell which are early and which are late loanwords from the pronunciation. *Chamber, check,* and *choice* are early, reflecting the Old French pronunciation /tʃ/; *chauffeur, chic,* and *chevron* are late, showing the French shift to /ʃ/.

In many of the earliest borrowings from French, we can see preserved differences between the Norman dialect (often called Anglo-Norman French) of William the Conqueror and his followers and the Central French dialect (Old French) that came to prevail in France (see p. 27). Borrowings such as *wage* and *warranty* retained the initial consonant /w/ characteristic of the Norman dialect, but English later reborrowed these two words, this time from the Central French dialect, in which Norman initial /w/ was pronounced /g/, and so the new words became *gage* and *guarantee.* Similar pairs of borrowings are given in the Applications for Teaching of this chapter.

Where we put the stress in French borrowings is another interesting indication of history. In English, "natural" stress is usually on the first main syllable of a word, but in French it is on the last syllable. In general, in older borrowings, the stress pattern in borrowed words has become thoroughly anglicized with first-syllable stress, as in *cárriage, cólour, cóurage, lánguage, sávage, víllage,* and *fígure,* whereas, in later borrowings, it is more likely that the French stress pattern still prevails: *brunétte, connoisséur, elíte, ensémble, prestíge, rappórt, vignétte.*[10] In the case of *chauffeur,* British English speakers tend to naturalize the word to the extent of putting the stress on the first syllable, but Americans nearly always retain the French stress on the second syllable. The same pattern of difference is seen in the pronunciation of such words as *brochure, garage, ballet, cafe, bureau, debris,* and *cliche.* For more on these differences, see pp. 186–188.

Other Changes in Early Modern English

In addition to the changes of the Great Vowel Shift, there have been a few others since Chaucer's time, and they are worth noting because they help to explain some of today's apparently inconsistent spellings.

Shortening of Long Vowels

The spelling of a number of words with short vowels in Modern English betrays the fact that, until changes that took place in the Early Modern English period, their vowels were long. Examples are *bread* /brɛːd/ and *sweat* /swɛːt/ and *blood, book,* and *good,* where Modern English /oː/ first became /uː/ before relaxing to /ʊ/ or, in the case of *blood,* to /ʌ/.

Loss of Consonants

Several consonant pairs were simplified during the Middle or Early Modern English periods, with loss of one of the letters in pronunciation but not usually in spelling, because such losses were not established early enough for that. This is the explanation for some of the silent letters in today's English. The consonants included *k* and *g*, lost before *n*, and *w*, lost before *r* and after *s*: thus *knight* (OE *cniht*), *knee* (*cnie*), and *gnat* (*gnæt*); *write* (*writan*); and *sword* (*swurd*) and *answer* (*answarian*). In words like *knight* and *gnat*, the initial *k/g* had been syllabic in Old English—that is, pronounced as a separate syllable in its own right: /kə-níxt/, /gə-nǽt/ (as it still is in modern German). In some cases, the fact that the unpronounced consonants had been kept in the spellings eventually influenced restoration of the old pronunciation. This happened with *swoon* and *awkward*. The former word sounded like *soon* in the 16th century, but now we pronounce the old *w*. In the case of *awkward*, a colloquial pronunciation that ignores the second *w* /ókəd/ is still heard in British English, as well as in some dialects, but in general the *w* is pronounced.

New Consonant Sounds

The phoneme /ʒ/ arose from the coalescence of the two elements /z/ and /j/. For instance, *vision* would originally have been pronounced *viz-jun*. The sound was also borrowed in French words, such as *rouge* and *garage*.

The Pronunciation of *r*

Until about 1700, /r/ was always pronounced before another consonant (as in *carve, person*) and finally (as in *far, mother*). In modern standard British English, however, and in most regional British dialects and in Australian, New Zealand, and South African English, it is ignored: "Is it far?" /izitfɑ:/. An exception is when *r* comes at the end of a word and is followed by a word beginning with a vowel: "Far and wide" /fɑ:rəndwaɪd/. Even here, however, the *r* is often avoided and the initial vowel of *and* is dropped also: /fɑ:ndwaɪd/. The tendency to drop the final *r* probably began in the 17th century but was completed only in the 18th. In some varieties of English, however, the change did not take place and *r* continued, and continues, to be pronounced in all positions. Such varieties are termed **rhotic,** while standard British English and other varieties in which *r* is dropped are **non-rhotic.** Within the United Kingdom, the traditional speech of the West Country, Scots, and Irish English is rhotic. So is American English, with the exception of the varieties spoken in New England and some coastal areas in the Southeast. This is one of the most distinctive features of American pronunciation for non-Americans.

APPLICATIONS TO TEACHING

Historical sound changes explain a number of English phenomena of interest to ESL teachers, though of course the explanations do not make the English pronunciation any easier to learn.

In borrowed words, especially those from French, the date of borrowing can explain some curious differences between English versions of the same French words. In the first column are words borrowed from Anglo-Norman French (which tend to be earlier borrowings, though not always); this was the dialect spoken by the Norman conquerors. In the second are the same words borrowed again, this time from the Parisian dialect of Old French (or from the language that developed from this into Modern French); this was very different from the Norman dialect:

Anglo-Norman French	Old French/French
wage (13th century)	gage (14th century)
warranty (14th century)	guarantee (17th century)
warden (13th century)	guardian (15th century)
cattle (13th century)	chattel (13th century)
catch (13th century)	chase (13th century)
leal (13th century)	loyal (16th century)

Differences between other cognate (related) pairs stem from differences between Old French and Modern French:

Old French	French
feast (13th century)	fete (18th century)
hostel (13th century)	hotel (17th century)

The explanation of why some polysyllabic words have their stress on the first syllable (typical in English and a feature of earlier loanword borrowings) and some on the second syllable (more typical of later borrowings) again has to do with chronology. In the first column, the words were borrowed from French comparatively early (most in the 13th or 14th centuries), and their stress patterns have become anglicized. In the second column, the words have been borrowed far more recently, and the original stress patterns have been preserved:

Earlier borrowings	Later borrowings
mústard	duét
léttuce	panáche
cárriage	brunétte
cólor	elíte
cóurage	ensémble
lánguage	prestíge
sávage	rappórt
víllage	velóur
fígure	vignétte

Most important, historical sound changes explain the origin of many of the silent letters in English spelling. A summary is given in Table 10.

The phoneme /r/ is one of the most telling indicators of variety or dialect, and students' pronunciation of it (or lack thereof) will have a strong influence on the type of English they are perceived to speak.

Accent

The aspect of speaking that distinguishes one person, or group of people, from another is known as **accent**. The most common criterion of difference between accents is region, a fact that has been commented on since the time of Chaucer. Although most speakers of English can readily identify different regional accents (American or British, for instance), analyzing the differences can be more difficult. A Briton identifying an American accent would probably recognize the rhotic *r* (see p. 134), a tendency to nasality in many words, the clear articulation of the ends of words such as *comfortable* or names such as *Birmingham*, the placing of stress in unexpected places (see p. 186), and so on. These same criteria, in reverse, are among those that would be used by an American detecting a British accent. But can we really talk about a single American or a single British accent? Clearly not, if we listen carefully. Not all American speech is rhotic, for instance, and there are huge differences between the accent of, say, a native of Brooklyn, New York, and one of Texas. Within Britain, when people talk of a British accent, they usually mean southern English; the speech of a Scot would be easily distinguishable from this (though in fact there several quite distinct Scots accents).

TABLE 10
ORIGIN OF SILENT LETTERS IN ENGLISH SPELLING

Silent letter	Examples	Reason
k before n	*knight, knee*	**k** ceased to be pronounced during 17th century
g before n	*gnat, gnaw*	**g** ceased to be pronounced during 16th century
m before n	*mnemonic*	Greek spelling; **m** never pronounced in English
p before n	*pneumonia*	Greek spelling; **p** never pronounced in English
p before s	*psyche, psychology*	Greek spelling; **p** pronounced by learned people probably until 18th century
w before r	*wrist, wrong*	**w** probably no longer pronounced after mid-16th century
w after s	*sword*	**w** no longer pronounced after mid-17th century
l after a and before f or v	*calf, half*	**l** probably not pronounced after Middle English period
l after a and before k	*talk, chalk*	**l** probably not pronounced after Middle English period
l after a and before m	*calm, palm*	**l** probably not pronounced after Middle English period
l in modal verbs	*should, could*	**l** ceased to be pronounced soon after the Middle English period in *should;* never pronounced in *could* (added to spelling by analogy with *should*)
g after a vowel and before m or n	*sign, paradigm*	**g** reflects French/Latin original spellings but was probably never pronounced in English
word-final **b** after m	*bomb, thumb*	**b** in some words never pronounced *(crumb)*, in others it ceased to be pronounced quite early *(thumb)*, in still others in Early Modern period *(dumb)*
word-final **n** after m	*autumn, column*	**n** reflects original French spelling but never pronounced in English
t after s or f and before -en	*listen, soften*	**t** ceased to be pronounced in Early Modern period
word-initial **h**	*honest, hour*	The loanwords are French, where **h** not pronounced; English usually follows this, but sometimes not (e.g., *host*)

It is important not to confuse accent and dialect. In general, we might say that dialectal identity involves a range of characteristics, including vocabulary and syntax, and that accent (the way that the dialect is pronounced) is just one of these. One of the pronouncing characteristics of northern English dialects, for instance, is the short front *a* in words such as *last* /læst/, in contrast with the longer back *a* of the south /lɑːst/. But using this pronunciation to speak English that is standard in other respects does not produce a dialect.

Accent has wider social implications, too, for it is a way that individuals identify themselves as belonging to certain social groupings that may cross regional boundaries.

Accent in History: The Fixing of "Standard" Pronunciation

We know nothing about the social implications of accent (if there were any) in the Anglo-Saxon period, nor in the Middle English period. Chaucer, in his *Reeve's Tale*, does make it clear that his two students from the north of England speak differently from the miller who lives in the south, but there is no implication that one regional accent is better than another. Little is known about what was fashionable in speech during the 16th and 17th centuries, either, but there are references as early as the 1580s to an evaluative comparison between the accents of northern and southern England, the latter being considered more "courtly."[12] The English of London was already being seen as socially desirable at this time, though Sir Walter Raleigh apparently always spoke with a Devonshire accent. The 18th century saw a concerted attempt by men of learning and authority to "fix" the language in terms of grammatical usage, style, and spelling, and inevitably pronunciation became an important issue also: There must be a "proper" way to say words. Proper pronunciation was that of the gentlemen of London—"the present practice of polished speakers in the metropolis," as one writer put it[13] —and the "imperfect" accents of other parts of Britain were condemned. The concept of a standard pronunciation was much trumpeted. In his *Course of Lectures on Elocution* (1762), Thomas Sheridan declared: "[I]t cannot be denied that an uniformity of pronunciation throughout Scotland, Wales and Ireland, as well as through the several counties of England, would be a point much to be wished."[14] One of the aims of Samuel Johnson's *Dictionary* of 1755 was to fix pronunciation, but this could only be done very crudely. It is interesting to note that Johnson himself apparently always retained the accent of his native Staffordshire, and specifically of the town of Litchfield.[15]

By the end of the 19th century, the concept of a standard pronunciation, based not on the population as a whole but on the speech of an elite (to which those commenting and prescribing belonged), was well established.

The corollary was an attitude of condemnation toward variations from the standard. Thus we find that in pronunciation, just as in grammar, judgments were made about "correctness" based on arbitrary criteria (usually favoring people in power), rather than on a consideration of how the majority of people actually spoke English at the time.

History of One Elite British Accent: "Received Pronunciation"

"Received Pronunciation," or RP, is the term that has been in use since the 1920s to describe a model of pronunciation based on the dialect of standard British English spoken by those considered to be the best speakers.[16] Unlike other accents, it was not regional but was based from the later 19th century onward on the speech of the British ruling classes and closely associated with the public schools, though there is no evidence that it was ever deliberately fostered there. Because of its prestige, and the ease with which it could be understood, it was naturally adopted by BBC announcers when that organization was founded in the 1920s and was often subsequently described as BBC English. It was the variety of English promoted as the model for non-British learners of English and keenly emulated by many of them because of its associations with social status. Though disliked by many British people for its connotations of upper-class social privilege and the domination of an elite centered mainly in southern England, it was nevertheless the accent toward which middle-class people tended to aspire. It was seen as a passport for entry into the British establishment and was encouraged in the best schools. It is no coincidence that the heyday of RP, as originally understood, was the period 1890–1940, which coincided with the heyday of the British Empire.

During the second half of the 20th century, following the Second World War, the grip of RP gradually loosened or, rather, the accent itself became diluted, being generally thought of now as the educated accent associated with the middle classes of southeastern England; in fact educated accents varied widely and the term became less and less precise. As its social preeminence declined, it lost (for most users) some of the more exaggerated aspects of the original and these then became associated exclusively with the accent of the beleaguered aristocracy and tended to attract ridicule. RP and BBC English remained more or less synonymous, but the accent continued to undergo dilution and become less socially exclusive. Its base remained southern England. In a process that accelerated rapidly during the closing years of the 20th century, the concept of the "educated" regional accent led to a wider acceptance of variation from RP. Such accents are now the norm alongside RP, but a diluted kind of RP—a form of standard British English without noticeable regional accent—still influences the phonetics chapters of textbooks produced by British publishers, even though some would argue that several of its sounds are not easy for the foreign learner.

A Feature That Varies among Accents: The Pronunciation of h

Along with the pronunciation of /r/ (see p. 134), the pronunciation of /h/ is one of the markers that varies considerably among different accents. In the realm of British English, it also has strong social implications. Indeed, the pronunciation of /h/ at the beginning of words (with a breathing sound known as **aspiration**) has been one of the most potent markers of the prestigious RP accent in modern British English usage. As Linda Mugglestone puts it, the dropping of /h/ has been "a convenient form of social shorthand" for linguistic impropriety and class inferiority.[17] In British literature or popular entertainment, characters who drop /h/ are assumed to be uneducated and lower class or to be speaking a comic regional variety of English. Thus, a British television series of the 1980s had the title "Some Mothers Do 'Ave 'Em." Such has been the prominence of this aspect of pronunciation as a social marker, and such the consequent anxiety caused in those aiming for social status, that hypercorrection has been common, with aspiration given where it is not needed, a fact that itself can be exploited for comic effect: "*Hi'm hextremely 'appy to be 'ere.*"

Yet it seems that no one had taken much notice of /h/ in relation to the idea of "proper" English until late in the 18th century, the period when prescriptivism in the language in general became prominent (see Chapter 2). Before then, the habit of dropping /h/ was probably frequent in most varieties of English and attracted no criticism. In Anglo-Saxon times, initial /h/ had been regularly aspirated (as in *hand* "hand," *hus* "house," and *hund* "dog"), but the issue had been made complex after the Norman Conquest with the influx of French loanwords beginning with *h*. The phoneme /h/ had been lost in the Anglo-Norman dialect, and sometimes the *h* was lost in spelling too, when words were borrowed into English, as in *erbe* (originally *herbe*) and *ost* (originally *host*). Eventually, however, the known Latin origin of these words (*herba* and *hostem*) influenced a respelling with *h*, and they joined many other loanwords, such as *heir, horrible, honour, humble,* and *humour,* in which the *h* was spelled but continued for the time being to be omitted in pronunciation. By analogy, the same possibility of omission was eventually extended also to *h*-words that were not French at all but of Old English origin, and there is good evidence that dropping became very common. Before the end of the 18th century, some writers questioned whether *h* should really be considered a letter at all. Quite why attitudes changed, and the dropping of *h* suddenly became such an infallible marker, not only of low class but of lack of education also, is not clear. The playwright Thomas Sheridan seems to have been the first to label it a "defect," in his *Course of Lectures on Elocution* (1762).[18] By the end of the 19th century, in British English, it was permissible to drop the *h* only in four French loanwords: *heir, honest, honour,* and *hour* (and their derivatives).

So we have the situation in British English where the aspiration of initial *h* is part of the prestigious accent, even though historically it was often dropped and continues to be dropped in many British regional dialects. However, this is not the case everywhere. In American English, the "problem" of *h*-dropping as a social marker never arose. Americans generally pronounce initial /h/, although some French loanwords are unaspirated, most notably *heir, honest, honor, hour,* and (in a clear difference between American and British habits) *herb.* Of course there is variation in America as well, with many people beginning to pronounce *herb* with /h/ because of the spelling. Also, non-aspirated *humor* and *humble* may also be heard, the latter especially in the south. But the dropping of *h* was never widespread enough in America to become associated with low prestige or poor education.[19]

APPLICATIONS TO TEACHING

English is spoken with a wide range of accents around the world, and these accents are made up of a variety of phonological features. No accent is inherently any better than any other (see the discussion about varieties and dialects of English in Chapter 7), but it makes sense to teach pronunciation features that are as standard as possible, simply because this should promote maximum comprehensibility and entail the least chance of stigmatization. In former times in the context of British English, this would have entailed the teaching of RP. However, RP is no longer the gold standard, and native Britons may actually find it distracting to hear L2 speakers use an RP accent. Most modern British pronunciation guides use a form of standard British English that avoids the most idiosyncratic elements of RP pronunciation.

With the case of word-initial *h* and whether it is pronounced or not, we have a feature that will strongly affect listeners' impressions of our students' speech, depending on the listeners' origins. It is probably best to teach students to pronounce the *h* in most words, because this is the normal pronunciation in American English and is the prestigious pronunciation in British English as well as most Commonwealth varieties of English (e.g., Australian English, New Zealand English). If students drop their "aitches," either by choice or through lack of ability, they need to realize that there may be a stigmatizing effect in British English circles, although in America it will probably just be assumed that they originally learned English in a non-American school where aspiration was not an issue.

Perhaps a more important task for students is identifying the words where *h* should <u>not</u> be pronounced. When should *h* be pronounced as it appears in spelling, and when is it a mysterious silent letter? We have seen that the reason behind the non-pronunciation of *h* is that it is normally not pronounced in French, and when French loanwords were borrowed into English, sometimes the French pronunciation was kept and sometimes not. Unfortunately, this historical explanation does not produce a usable rule for students to follow, and so the silent *h* words must be learned—but there are very few of them. The consensus seems to be that the following words belong to this category: *heir, honest, honor, hour* (and *herb* in American English).

FURTHER READING

A well-respected guide to the teaching of pronunciation, including an extensive description of the sound system of English. It focuses mainly on North American pronunciation.

- Celce-Murcia, M., Brinton, D. M., & Goodwin, J. M. (1996). *Teaching pronunciation*. Cambridge: Cambridge University Press.

A detailed discussion of pronunciation and how sounds are produced by the human vocal tract.

- Clark, J., & Yallop, C. (1990). *An introduction to phonetics and phonology*. Oxford: Blackwell.

This book focuses on pronunciation teaching where the goal is mutual intelligibility between non-native speakers (rather than the imitation of native speakers).

- Jenkins, J. (2000). *The phonology of English as an international language*. Oxford: Oxford University Press.

Two teachers' handbooks filled with activities designed to help students learn pronunciation in a holistic manner rather than through drills.

- Laroy, C. (1995). *Pronunciation.* Oxford: Oxford University Press.
- Henrichsen, L. E., Green, B. A., Nishitani, A., & Bagley, C. L. (1999). *Pronunciation matters: Communicative, story-based activities for mastering the sounds of North American English.* Ann Arbor: University of Michigan Press.

A detailed history of how accent became so important as an aspect of Received Pronunciation.

- Mugglestone, L. (1995). *Talking proper: The rise of accent as social symbol.* Oxford: Clarendon Press.

Classroom Activity: 5.1

When Did Words Come into English?

English has thousands of words that were originally French. It has been borrowing these French loanwords for more than 1,000 years. The modern pronunciation may give clues about when the loanwords were borrowed.

- If *ch* in the loanword is pronounced like <u>ch</u>air, it came into English before about 1600.
- If *ch* in the loanword is pronounced like <u>sh</u>ape, it came into English in more recent times.

Pronounce each word and decide whether it was borrowed into English before 1600 or more recently. Mark the correct blank. The first two have been done for you.

	Before 1600	More recently
brochure	_____	___×___
chalet	_____	___×___
chamber	_____	_____
chamois	_____	_____
champion	_____	_____
chance	_____	_____
change	_____	_____
charge	_____	_____
chase	_____	_____
château	_____	_____
chauffeur	_____	_____
check	_____	_____
chef	_____	_____

chevron   _____   _____

chic   _____   _____

chiffon   _____   _____

choice   _____   _____

machine   _____   _____

match   _____   _____

merchant   _____   _____

Here are some less common French loanwords that you may not have heard before. Their meaning and the first date of their use in English are given. Should the *ch* in these words be pronounced as <u>ch</u>air or as <u>sh</u>ape? Circle the best pronunciation.

chargé d'affaires	(1767 – deputy ambassador)	<u>ch</u>air	<u>sh</u>ape
chateaubriand	(1877 – a large steak served with a sauce)	<u>ch</u>air	<u>sh</u>ape
chemin de fer	(1767 – a card game)	<u>ch</u>air	<u>sh</u>ape

Classroom Activity: 5.2

Find the Silent Letter

The words in each set include a silent letter. For each set, decide which letter is not pronounced and write it in the blank. Then identify the position of the silent letter. The first one has been done for you.

Word	Silent letter	Silent letter position
1. knee knock knight	k	before "n" at the beginning of a word
2. write wrong wrist	____	_____
3. half calf halves	____	_____
4. talk chalk walk	____	_____
5. calm palm balm	____	_____

6. could   _____   _____

   should

   would

7. sign   _____   _____

   impugn

   paradigm

8. bomb   _____   _____

   thumb

   lamb

9. listen   _____   _____

   soften

   hasten

10. honest   _____   _____

    hour

    heir

Classroom Activity: 5.3

Many Spellings for One Sound

A. The sounds and spelling of English do not match exactly. For example, the sound "sh" in *shirt,* can be spelled 14 different ways. Can you work out these 14 ways? Write words to illustrate each one below. Two are done for you.

1. _____ shirt _____   8. _____

2. _____ ocean _____   9. _____

3. _____   10. _____

4. _____   11. _____

5. _____   12. _____

6. _____   13. _____

7. _____   14. _____

B. We can avoid the problem of too many sounds by making a new alphabet where every sound matches with only one letter. Dictionaries use this kind of system to show the pronunciation of words. Use your dictionary to answer the following questions.

1. What symbol is used in your dictionary for the *sh* sound in Exercise A? _____

2. Write the words for these pronunciations:

/drɪŋkɪŋ/   _____ drinking _____

/gəʊldən/   _____

/aɪdɛntɪfaɪ/   _____

/nɒk/   _____

/mədʒɒrəti/   _____

/njuːmərəs/   _____

/ɔːt/   _____

/pærəgræf/   _____

/ʃædəʊ/   _____

/juːniːk/   _____

6

THE SPELLING OF ENGLISH

How Did the Writing System of English Develop?

- Where did the writing system of English come from?
- How did capital and small letters develop?
- How variable has English spelling been over the ages?
- How did today's standard spellings evolve?
- Why are many American spellings different from those of British English?

The Origins of the English Alphabet

The Beginnings of Writing

Compared to spoken language, written language is a relative newcomer. What we would accept as spoken language originated as long as 100,000 years ago. Before that, our ancestors probably engaged in crude forms of verbal communication, like shouts of warning or grunts of intimidation, perhaps for millions of years. The oldest forms of human writing, on the other hand, are Egyptian hieroglyphics and Sumerian pictographs, which can only be dated back to 3000–3200 BC.[1] Of course, there are rock paintings in caves that are much older, but it is speculative to suggest that they were a formal means of communication. Writing, then, has been used for a mere fraction of the time that speech has. Yet for all its relative recency, it is a key to history and progress, promoting the accumulation of knowledge across the centuries. Through writing, we can read historical peoples' own accounts of what their lives and the contemporary world were like; without it, for the prehistoric period, we must rely on indirect evidence, such as that of archaeology.

The main means of writing English is the Latin (or Roman) alphabet. A second sort of alphabet, Germanic runes, was used in the early Old English period but only for brief messages carved on wood or inscriptions on stone or bone. To trace the history of the Latin alphabet, we must look back to a time before Rome, even before Greece. The earliest writing systems were **pictographic,** employing pictures to represent objects and ideas (e.g., hieroglyphics). But such systems needed a vast array of symbols for that purpose. For example, Sumerian writing included about 600 symbols, most of which had multiple values. Although only about 300 were in use at any one time, it still must have taken considerable study to read and write with ease using this system.[2] Thus writing remained the preserve of a highly trained elite.

A major breakthrough came with the idea of representing sounds, not meanings, with symbols. Such a system requires only one symbol for each sound in a language, and these can then be combined to represent any spoken word. Writing was thus transformed into something that could be learned relatively quickly. As a result, literacy spread rapidly, and soon more civilizations were supplementing the oral transmission of culture and knowledge with a written one. The idea of a phonetic writing system is thought to have originated with the Phoenicians. It was not yet a true alphabet in the modern sense of the word, however, because it usually represented consonants only (see Figure 10).

By the 9th century BC, the Greeks had borrowed the Phoenician symbols. Fortunately, the language of the Phoenicians used some sounds that did not

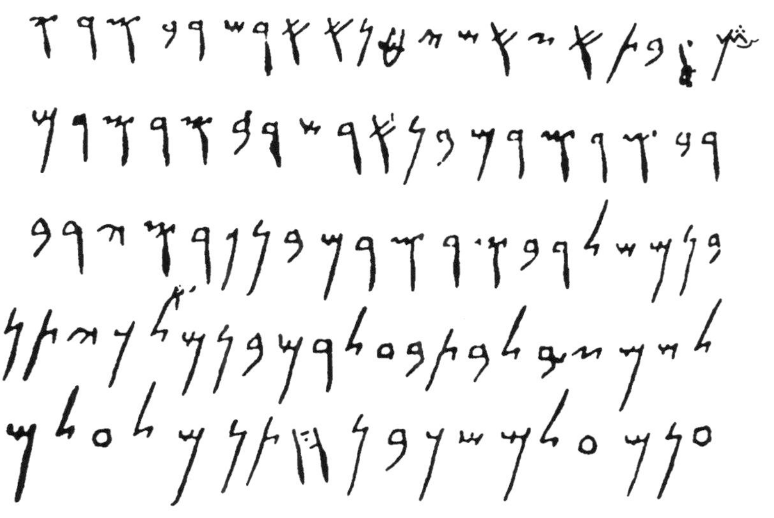

FIGURE 10   The Phoenician Alphabet in Use

exist in Greek. The symbols for these unpronounced sounds were thus unnecessary to the Greeks, but ingeniously they employed them to represent their vowels, creating the first true alphabet (see Figure 11). In fact, 14 of these Phoenician symbols, modified by the Greeks, should look very familiar, as they are retained in the Modern English alphabet with no change. Also, the Phoenician names for the symbols were retained; the first two were *aleph* "ox" and *beth* "house," from which we get the word *alphabet*.

Later, the Romans in turn adopted the Greek alphabet via the Etruscans (a people living earlier in Italy). Many of the symbols were given a more rounded shape, some were adopted unchanged, and some were not taken at all (e.g., $\theta\xi\phi\psi\omega$). The Romans began by writing the large letter forms that since the 14th century we have called **capitals** (the word deriving from the Latin word for "head"), but smaller systems of characters that took up less space and were faster to write were developed, which we now usually call **small letters.** The Latin alphabet eventually spread with the Roman Empire and Christianity

Form		Equivalent	Name
A	α	a	*Alpha*
B	β	b	*Beta*
Γ	γ	g	*Gamma*
Δ	δ	d	*Delta*
E	ε	e *(short)*	*Epsīlon*
Z	ζ	z	*Zeta*
H	η	e *(long)*	*Eta*
Θ	θ ϑ	th	*Theta*
I	ι	i	*Iota*
K	κ	k *or hard* c	*Kappa*
Λ	λ	l	*Lambda*
M	μ	m	*Mu*
N	ν	n	*Nu*
Ξ	ξ	x	*Xi*
O	o	o *(short)*	*Omīcron*
Π	π	p	*Pi*
P	ρ	r	*Rho*
Σ	σ ς	s	*Sigma*
T	τ	t	*Tau*
Υ	υ	(u) y	*Upsīlon*
Φ	φ	ph	*Phi*
X	χ	kh	*Chi*
Ψ	ψ	ps	*Psi*
Ω	ω	o *(long)*	*Omĕga*

FIGURE 11   The Greek Alphabet

throughout Europe, including England, where eventually it came to be used to write Old English.

Ideally, perhaps, an alphabet would have only one symbol for each sound, but this is rarely possible, not least because sounds vary so much, even between speakers of the same language (see p. 111). For varying reasons, languages often use different symbols for the same sounds. The Romans, for instance, used C, Q, and K to represent the /k/ sound, and this contributed to our current spelling confusion because of all the Latin words we borrowed into English.

Writing During Anglo-Saxons Times: Runes

In about the 3rd century, Germanic peoples on the Continent developed their own alphabet, the runic alphabet (or *futhorc/futhark*, a name that uses its first six letters), which was either based on or influenced by the Latin alphabet. In its original form, it had 24 characters, but it was modified for the various Germanic varieties in which it was written. As used in England, the runic alphabet had from 28 to 33 symbols (see Figure 12). They were generally long and angular, suitable for carving onto wood, stone, or bone. Runes were not practical for extended writing but were still widely used in commerce and administration, for religious or magical purposes, and for memorial writing. Each rune represented a sound but also had a name, usually beginning with that sound. Thus the character we call [d] had the name *dæg* ("day"), [w] was *wynn* ("joy"), and [i] was *isern* ("iron"). From the remaining evidence, it seems that runic writing was not as commonly used in England as on the Continent, and by the 6th century it was almost completely replaced by the Latin alphabet, introduced on a large scale to the Anglo-Saxons when Christianity was established among them. However, two runic characters did survive, for they were added to the new alphabet to represent sounds not used in Latin (see p. 155).

The Use of the Latin Alphabet

The writing of Old English in the Latin alphabet began after the Anglo-Saxons became Christians. As we saw in Chapter 2, the Celts of Britain had been Christianized from the 2nd century and the religion survived in the Celtic areas, but the Anglo-Saxon settlers themselves were pagan. Christianity eventually came to them from two directions—from Rome (with St. Augustine, whose mission to Kent began in 597) and from Ireland (with the mission of Aidan, a Celtic monk from the Irish monastery on Iona, who began his mission to

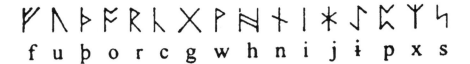

f u þ o r c g w h n i j i̵ p x s

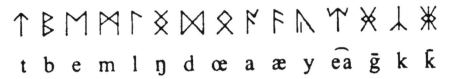

t b e m l ŋ d œ a æ y êa ḡ k k̂

FIGURE 12   The Runic Alphabet (Futhorc)

Northumbria in 635). Christianity is essentially a religion of "the book" (based, that is, on the witness of written scriptures), and it was Christian monks, accustomed to making copies of the Bible and other religious works in Latin, who introduced the idea of using the Latin alphabet to write English too.

The alphabet used by the monks was not, however, completely adequate for Old English, which had a wider range of sounds than Latin. Their alphabet had only 23 letters, lacking *v* (whose function was shared with *u*), *j* (which was not distinguished from *i*), and *w*. The letter shapes of the Latin alphabet then were those we recognize today, though the scripts developed by the Anglo-Saxons showed much variation and evolution during the five centuries of writing in Old English.

As nearly as possible, the Christian monks who first wrote Old English in Latin characters must have tried to represent the language as they heard it. The spelling of Old English thus began by being more or less phonetic, matching sound to symbol. However, the fact that Old English had, according to one estimate, some 35 phonemes (fewer than Modern English, see p. 113), shows that some overlap in the representation of sounds was inevitable. Just as in Modern English, for instance, *s* and *f* were voiced between vowels, as in *arisan* (/ɑriːzan/ "to arise") and *ofer* (/oːvɛr/ over) but unvoiced in other positions, as in *sittan* (/sɪttan/ "to sit") and *fisc* (/fɪʃ/ "fish"). But the Anglo-Saxon scribes felt no necessity to represent these pairs as separate sounds. Only during the Middle English period would *z* and *v* (or its orthographical variant *u*), respectively, come to be used for the voiced varieties of the two sounds.

There were a few sounds of Old English not present in Latin (i.e., distinct phonemes) that the Christian monks felt they needed to represent. New letters were required. They were either borrowed from the old runic alphabet or simply created by modifying existing letters:

- For the unvoiced Old English phoneme /θ/ ("*thing*") and the voiced version /ð/ ("*this*"), both of which we now represent with "th," two symbols were adopted: the rune þ "thorn" and the invented symbol ð "eth", adapted from a *d*. The two Old English symbols were used interchangeably for both of the "th" sounds; scribes seem to have picked whichever they pleased and sometimes used both within a single word.
- For the Old English sound /w/, the rune ρ "wynn" was borrowed.
- For the vowel /æ/, a sound distinct from that represented by *a* (/ɑ/, /ɑː/), Latin *a* and *e* were combined to form *æ*, a character known to the Anglo-Saxons as *æsc* ("ash").

In the Middle English and Early Modern English periods, the English alphabet went through various changes. Some of the more noticeable alterations were the dropping of þ, ð, ρ, and *æ* but the addition of ȝ, a letter we call yogh (a modification of an Anglo-Saxon *g*), which could represent a variety of sounds, including *g* as in *gear* and *y* as in *year*. Yogh was abandoned by about 1500. To give some sense of the historical progression of spelling, the same sentence (contrived for the purpose) is written here in the typical orthography of the four major historical periods. Classroom Activity 2.0 from Chapter 2 gives a more extended illustration of the development of the English orthography.

Old English:	He siehþ twelfe cyningas ond cwena togædere in ðam huse.
Middle English:	He seeth twelf kingis and queanes toȝider in þe hous.
Early Modern English:	He seeth twelue kynges and queenes together in the house.
Modern English:	He sees twelve kings and queens together in the house.

Capital and Small Letters

What we now call small letters (also known as lowercase letters, a term that described their location in the lower part of a printer's case of loose type) developed in the early Middle Ages when Latin, originally written in what we now call capitals, began to be written extensively in faster and smaller scripts. Thereafter, the capital forms (uppercase letters) were reserved for special functions, including titles. Even in Anglo-Saxon times, the larger letters were sometimes used in manuscripts for the first letter of the word that started a new sentence (and sometimes for the whole word or for all the words in the first line), but the regular use of capitals in this way, and for the first letter of proper names, became general only in the later medieval period. Not until about 1800 had the present usage more or less been established.

The conventions for the use of capital letters at the start of a word in English today seem to be as follows: Capitals are always used for (a) the opening word of a sentence, (b) proper names, and (c) names of the days of the week and months. They are usually used also for (d) names of the deity and religious celebrations (God, the Lord, Mass); (e) key temporal events or epochs (the New Year, the Middle Ages); (f) abstract nouns to which we may want to draw attention (Liberty, Education), along with scholarly or medical disciplines (Mathematics, Psychotherapy, Gerontology) and institutional labels (the State, Government); and (g) the main words in titles and other words to which we may want to give emphasis. In categories d, e, f, and g, it is often a matter of personal preference (or, in the case of publications, house style) whether capitals are used, and so there are no hard-and-fast rules. For instance, a chapter heading could be "The sounds of English" or "The Sounds of English."[3]

The Standardization of English Spelling

During the time that the English alphabet was evolving toward its present state, English spelling was also developing. Often, words were simply spelled the way they were pronounced, whereas at other times factors came into play that forced a divergence between a word's pronunciation and its spelling. Moreover, attitudes toward English spelling in the past have on the whole been relatively relaxed. Our modern insistence on correct spelling as a virtue almost on a par with godliness and cleanliness is quite recent. Only toward the end of the 18th century was the final "fixing" of spelling as we now know it more or less achieved, after which deviation from the standard was frowned upon.

Why is spelling important? There are good reasons for desiring a standard orthography:

- Writing is a method by which we communicate over both time and distance to an infinitely wide audience. A high degree of consistency and uniformity is necessary if we are to convey information or ideas efficiently and accurately to this audience.

- Writing does not have the advantage of the non-linguistic clues (e.g., gestures, intonation) that spoken discourse uses to convey meaning, so the clarity that is essential for good communication must be conveyed primarily in the unadorned words and sentences. Therefore, the spelling of these words and sentences must be precise and unambiguous.
- Unlike speaking (which most native speakers, at least, acquire naturally), writing has to be taught, and obviously it makes good sense that the same system be taught to everyone.

On the face of it, then, a good case can be made for standardization in the spelling of English, and the story of spelling is the story of how that was achieved.

An Early Spelling Standard: The Wessex Standard

Old English was never really a single language but a collection of varieties or dialects, each with its own spelling conventions. However, after Wessex became the dominant kingdom from the end of the 9th century, thanks to King Alfred, the distinctive spelling system that we now associate with Old English began to be used widely. By the 11th century, although uniformity was never total, scribes seemed to be keeping to a general orthographical norm, rather than allowing their own local or personal variations to intrude. The Norman Conquest of 1066 brought cataclysmic political and social changes to England, but these did not immediately affect the writing of English, and the "Wessex standard" seems to have continued in use for several generations. But as the volume of new writings in English inevitably declined under the Norman French rulers, so the hold of the Wessex standard loosened. Wessex ceased to be the political and cultural "center" of England, that role now being taken over by the East Midlands, with the focus on London. When, in the 14th century, English did come to be written extensively again, it was in a context of diversity and instability. The old spelling conventions had been forgotten. In effect, there was as much variety in the writing of English in the later 12th, 13th, and 14th centuries as there was in the speaking of it, with great differences according to region. There were new influences at work, too, including the habits of French-trained scribes, whose orthographical conventions soon became visible in English writings.

The Middle English Period: Free Spelling

Writers of English by the 13th century were spelling more or less as they pleased. A good way to illustrate the confusing variety of spellings that we find in the manuscripts is to cite biblical texts, of which we find numerous copies and which remain relatively stable because they are translated from the same original Latin texts. Here are seven versions of the opening line of the Lord's Prayer. The first, for comparison, is a well-known one taken from the King James version of the Bible (first issued in 1611; there have been many other versions since). Thus it is actually in Early Modern English, but it is still well known in this form today and takes us back a little nearer to the Middle English versions:

1. Our father, which art in heaven, hallowed be thy name
2. Fader ure, þu þe eart on heofenum, si þin nama gehalgod (c. 1020)
3. Fader ure, þu þe ert on heofene, sye þin name ʒehalged (c. 1200)
4. Vader oure, þet art ine heuenes, yhalʒed by þi name (c. 1350)
5. Owre fadur þat art in hewon, Blessud be þi name (c. 1350)
6. Our fadyr þat art in heuyn, halwyd be þy name (c. 1360)
7. Oure fadir that art in heuenes, halewid be thi name (c. 1390)

There are some small variations in grammar and syntax, of course, and a form of the French borrowing "blessed" appears in one case, instead of the "native" "hallowed," but the variations in orthography are what concern us here. In none of these examples is the digraph *th* used, to replace þ, until the latest. We note that until about 1200, *f* is used in forms of "heaven," even when the sound represented was more like a *v*; after that, it is represented by *u*, which was commonly used until well into the Early Modern English period. On the other hand, the initial *v* of *Vader* in the fourth sentence, where all other versions have *f* (pronounced /f/ in both Old and Standard Modern English) reveals that it was written in Kent, where the local pronunciation did use the voiced sound even at the beginning of a word. This reminds us of the important fact that regional differences account for much of the spelling variation that characterizes the Middle English period. As we saw, such variation had more or less disappeared during the later period of Old English, with the dominance of Wessex spelling. In the Middle English period there was no such standard, and none would begin to assert itself until later in the 15th century.

Another way to illustrate the remarkable flexibility of spelling during this period is to look at the word *merry*. Its meaning has remained about the same for 1,000 years: "pleasant," "cheerful," "sweet," or "tuneful." However, it has been spelled in an astonishing number of ways. Even during the Old English period, it can be found as *myrig, mirig, mirge, myrge,* and *murge* (in all of which the *g* was pronounced "soft," more like a *y*). But the spelling variations exploded during the Middle English period, with at least 20 being recorded between about 1200 and 1500:

miry, mirye, mury, murye, miri, mirre, mirie, mirrie, mirry, myrrie, myrry, mery, merye, mere, meri, merey, merie, merrye, meary, merrie

But even as the variation continued, certain new spelling conventions introduced by Norman scribes were becoming established. Several of these are already apparent in the previous versions of the first line of the Lord's Prayer and are still integral to English spelling today. Here are some of them:

- The sound /v/, represented by *f* in Old English, was now represented by *v* or *u* (*fif* → *fiue* "five," *heofen* → *heouen* "heaven"). The orthographical distinction between *v* and *u* that we use today was not fully established until the 17th century.
- The Old French convention of using an *h* to signal modification of a consonant in pronunciation produced several changes. *Ch* was now written for *c* in Old English words where the sound was "palatalized" as /tʃ/, that is, generally before or after *e* or *i* (so Old English *cirice* became *chirche* and eventually *church*).
- Similarly, /ʃ/ was now used for the sound represented by *sc* in Old English, as in *scip*, which became Middle English *ship*.
- *th* increasingly replaced Old English *ð* and *þ*, though the latter remained in frequent use throughout the Middle English period, persisting especially in the north of England. It even occurred in some printed books as late as the 17th century. A curiosity of early printing was the use by some typesetters of *y* to represent *þ*, probably because that is what some scribes' writing of *þ* tended to look like. It was used especially for the words "that" (*yat*) and "the" (*ye*), and this explains the origin of quaint labels such as "Ye Olde Tea-Shoppe," prevalent in English tourist towns today; but *ye* in the medieval manuscripts and early printed books was pronounced with /θ/ and never /j/.
- *qu* replaced *cw* in Old English words; thus OE *cwen* "woman" or "queen" became *quen*.
- The Old English consonant pair *hw* was turned into *wh*, so that OE *hwi* became *whi* and later *why*, and *hwit* became *whit(e)*. This produced the silent *h* in such words, though some speakers of Standard English (and of several regional varieties) still use aspiration here.

Among the spelling conventions that were gradually established during the later medieval period was **diacritic** spelling—that is, the use of a letter not in its own right but as a signal about the pronunciation of another letter. The most frequently used letter in this connection was final *e*. Now almost always silent in itself, it came to be used in two ways:

- To show the quality of the preceding consonant. Thus *g* followed by *e* was to be pronounced /ʤ/ (*rage*; compare this to *rag*), and *c* was to be pronounced /s/ (*entice*; compare to *antic*). In American spelling, the *c* in this position was often changed to *s* (*defense*).
- To show lengthening or diphthongization of the vowel in the preceding syllable. Thus *hate* (compare to *hat*), *write* (compare to *writ*), and *rote* (compare to *rot*).

The Modern Standard Develops: Chancery English, Printing, and Dictionaries

As we have seen, the spelling of English was relatively unrestrained during the Middle English period, with each scribe essentially spelling words the way he or she heard them. But eventually a new standard asserted itself. Just as the political dominance of Wessex in the 10th century had led to the establishment of the Wessex variety of written English as an early standard, so in the 14th and 15th centuries the political and economic dominance of London eventually ensured that the spelling conventions established there would be adopted nationwide—a standard that was more or less divorced from the systems of specific dialects or regional varieties of English.

Initially, there were several independent standards, but ultimately the most important influence on the emerging standard orthography was the Royal Chancery.[4] This was a large and important administrative department, part of what today we call the Civil Service. It sent out official documents to every corner of England—legal writs and summonses, customs and tax documents. More of these documents came to be written in English during the second half of the 14th century as the influence of French in government was fading, and the conventions used by the Chancery scribes eventually were generally adopted by the country as whole.

Another important influence on the standardization of spelling was the introduction of printing. England's first printing press was set up at Westminster by William Caxton in 1476. However, although the new technology offered the opportunity for rapid standardization of orthography, in practice there is little evidence during the first hundred years of its use that printers were much concerned with such matters. As his own translations and the prefaces to his works show, Caxton himself was wildly inconsistent in his spellings. Within a few sentences in his prologue to *Caton* (c. 1484), for instance, we find *boke*, *booke*, and *book*, and *lytel*, *lytell*, and *lytyl* (and from another contemporary work of his we may add *lityl* and *lityll*). One factor involved in variation was that early printers often achieved line "justification" (that is, making all the lines the same length) by lengthening or shortening words rather than adjusting the spaces between them. The formative period of English spelling in fact lasted some 200 years; not until 1700 was the standard that we recognize today, with all its familiar conventions, just about in place.

In Chapter 5, we noted the importance of key changes in the pronunciation of English (those of the Great Vowel Shift) that coincided with the period when efforts were being made to standardize spellings. The effect was to establish many of the apparent disjunctions between sound and spelling, and the inconsistencies between the ways that similarly spelled words are pronounced, that are still with us.

The final impetus for the fixing of spelling was given by the publishing of dictionaries.[5] The earliest dictionaries, which began to appear in the later part of the 16th century, were not comprehensive surveys of the language but simply guides to the spelling of hard words. The schoolmaster Richard Mulcaster published a list of about 9,000 words in 1582. Robert Cawdrey is credited with the first substantial dictionary in the modern sense—one that gave definitions as well as spellings. The first edition appeared in 1604 with the impressive title *A Table Alphabeticall, contayning and teaching the true writing and understanding of hard usuall English words, borrowed from the Hebrew, Greeke, Latine, or French, with the Interpretation thereof by plaine English words, gathered for the benefit and help of all unskilfull persons.*

The great period of dictionary making was about 1650 to 1750, with that of Nathaniel Bailey one of the most prominent. First published in 1721 as the *Universal Etymological English Dictionary*, it went through 30 editions before the end of the century. The role of the dictionaries in respect of orthography was a thoroughly conservative one. The dictionary makers knew very well that, because of variations and perpetual changes in pronunciation, phonetic spelling could not ever be achieved. They tended to codify the current practice of the printers, rather than set new trends. Thus, they had the effect of fixing the spelling of English as it was in the later part of the 17th century.

It was Samuel Johnson's *Dictionary* of 1755 that became the arbiter for spelling. Johnson could be pedantic and opinionated, but he was also pragmatic. As he noted in his long preface to the dictionary: "I have often been obliged to sacrifice uniformity to custom; thus I write, in compliance with a numberless majority, *convey* and *inveigh*, *deceit* and *receipt*, *fancy* and *phantom*." In other words, Johnson adopted the spellings actually used at the time by writers, rather than making arbitrary prescriptions. In this respect, he was a precursor of modern corpus linguists, who do the same thing with modern dictionaries, only with the advantage of large corpora. The result of this use-based approach, coupled with Johnson's perceived authority, was that there are very few spellings in the dictionary that we do not follow today.

Other European countries had, at various times during the Modern English period, made official efforts to regulate the spelling of their languages, either through academies (in Italy since 1582, France since 1634, and Spain since 1713) or through action by the government (in German-speaking countries in 1901 and in Dutch-speaking countries in 1883 and 1947). An academy had been proposed for English by Jonathan Swift in 1712, but nothing came of it, and no governmental action has ever been taken to dictate correct English language. In a sense, the role of such an academy was taken over unofficially by the dictionaries—in England itself by Johnson's dictionary first and then the *Oxford English Dictionary* (from 1888) and in the United States by *Webster's Dictionary* (1828). Today there is a great consistency of spelling, with all British dictionary-makers using essentially the same spellings; likewise all American dictionaries are uniform in their spellings. Although dictionaries are not perfect (not least because they have trouble reacting to the constant flux of new words coming into a language), their authority in arbitrating spelling is usually not questioned.

Changing the Spellings of Words

Forcing English into a Latin Form: "Etymological" Respellings

A notable, but far from useful, tendency of the 16th century (already visible in the 15th) was the promotion of etymological respellings.[6] These had a scholarly aim, to ensure that the origin of a word was visible in its spelling. The process was applied especially to French loanwords to show their Latin origins. Here are some examples:

Modern Word	As Borrowed into English from French	Ultimate Latin Source
adventure	aventure	advenire
advice	avis	ad + visum
debt	dette	debitum
doubt	doute	dubium
receipt	receite	recipere
indict	endite	indictum

In each case, a key Latin consonant had been lost after the words had been borrowed into French, but it was replaced after they were borrowed in turn into English. In the case of *adventure* and *advice*, the new spellings eventually influenced pronunciation, and we now sound the *d* in both words. The *b* added to *debt* and *doubt* and the *p* to *receipt*, however, were quite unpronounceable. Although *indict* is traditionally still pronounced without the inserted *c*, it will often be sounded today by people unfamiliar with the word, probably by analogy with words like *predict*. We can see that the effect of etymological respellings (see also pp. 125–126) was often to widen the gap between sound and spelling, thus creating many of the silent letters that cause problems for both native speakers and learners of English.

Going Their Own Way: The Development of American Spellings

One of the profound effects of the American Declaration of Independence of 1776 was a conscious severing of ties with the mother country, and European ideas in general, and a consequent rise in patriotism. One of the most ardent of the patriots was Noah Webster (1758–1843), a lawyer turned teacher of English whose books on the language set him on a course that would end with the publication in 1828 of his two-volume *An American Dictionary of the English Language*.[7] Earlier, between 1783 and 1785, Webster had published a three-part work grandly entitled *A Grammatical Institute of the English Language*, the first part of which was to become an amazing best-seller. Under the title *The American Spelling Book*, it sold 80 million copies in the next 100 years. Oddly, Webster began his career as a conservative in spelling matters, expressly commending in *A Grammatical Institute* the spellings of Samuel Johnson (such as *honour*, not *honor*, and *judgement*, not *judgment*). But within only six years his position had changed dramatically, and he had become a radical advocate for change. His aims were both practical—like other reformers, he aimed to rationalize the spelling of English—and, at this period in his life, nationalistic: He wanted to make American spelling distinct from British. In his *Dissertations of the English Language* (1789), he wrote, "As an independent nation, our honor requires us to have a system of our own, in language as well as government." Among his proposals were these: *bred* for *bread*, *bilt* for *built*, *giv* for *give*, *laf* for *laugh*, and *arkitecture* for *architecture*. He recommended the use of diacritics too, such as a bar over vowels to indicate length and a stroke through *th* to indicate voicing (the sound in *bathe* rather than that of *bath*).

However, during another 50 years of energetic thinking and writing, Webster gradually edged back toward conservatism again. By the time that the great *Dictionary* was published in 1828, his most radical proposals had been dropped, and others had disappeared by the time of the last revision of the *Dictionary* supervised by him in 1841. His successors quietly continued the process, partly because of the pressure of a competitor, Joseph Worcester, whose own *Comprehensive Dictionary of the English Language* (1830) favored conservative spelling, and partly with a more international market in mind; the *Dictionary* would in fact acquire the description *International* in 1890. Nevertheless, it is fair to say that it was Webster's advocacy that helped to establish the forms that today we specifically associate with the English of America. The fourth edition of 1865 (called "the unabridged" edition) and its successors were increasingly recognized by Americans as authoritative, so that Webster's role can be seen in retrospect as comparable with that of Johnson in Britain as a "fixer" of spelling. In the 18th century, some forms now identified as American were in fact still current as alternatives in Britain (including *-or* for *-our*), but one effect of Webster's championing of such forms was to push British printers to adopt consciously what were now seen as British forms. In some cases, America took the lead; it is Webster who advocated the dropping of *k* in words such as *musick*, a step that was soon followed in Britain.

The differences between American and British spelling established through Webster's efforts were not in the end radical, but they were conspicuous, especially to the British, who have tended to regard them unfavorably. Webster had the instincts of most reformers to simplify and rationalize (as is shown in the change of the ending *-our* to *-or* in many nouns, which brings spelling into line with pronunciation), but even these more efficient spellings might still feel odd to Britons used to the British English versions. However, today there is an increasing tendency for the British to accept (often without even noticing) American spellings, though the *-or* endings remain unattractive.

The main differences between American and British spellings are listed on p. 165, with the American version given first. (See Chapter 7 for other differences between American and British English.) However, when reviewing this list, you should keep in mind that the vast majority of words are spelled the same in American and British English and that the spelling differences really are minor, not usually causing comprehension problems. American and British versions of a word (e.g., *flavor* and *flavour*) are still the same word and are typically pronounced the same regardless of the spelling differences. There are even cases where a word is spelled quite differently and still has the same pronunciation in American and British English (American *jail* and *curb*; British *gaol* and *kerb*). In other cases, difference in spelling is reflected in pronunciation (American *aluminum* /ælúːmɪnəm/; British *aluminium* /æləmíniəm/).

1. *-or/-our:* This group includes words such as *color/colour* and *flavor/flavour.* Inconsistently, however, British English spells many similar words without a *u,* such as *error, mirror,* and *terror,* as well as most words referring to people, such as *actor, author,* and *emperor.*

2. *-er/-re:* This group includes words such as *center/centre* and *fiber/fibre.* In the case of *meter,* British English uses *metre* for the measurement but *meter* for the measuring instrument, whereas American English uses *meter* for both.

3. *-e-/-oe-:* This group comprises words such as *estrogen/oestrogen* and *diarrhea/diarrhoea,* mostly of Greek origin.

4. *-e-/-ae-:* Examples include *arch(a)eology, gyn(a)ecology,* and *(a)esthetics.* However, British English increasingly uses the *e* forms, notably in *encyclopedia, medieval,* and *primeval.* In words beginning with *aer-,* however, the simplification does not occur, so that American English and British English share *aerate, aerobics,* and *aerosol.*

5. *-ll/-l:* This group mainly comprises verbs of two syllables, usually stressed on the second, in which American English prefers *ll.* Examples are *distil(l), fulfil(l),* and *skil(l)ful.* In verbs with *a* in the second syllable, American English again doubles the *l,* as in *appall, befall, enthrall,* and *install,* but British English is inconsistent: *appal, befall, enthral, install.*

6. *-ize/-ise:* American English prefers *-ize,* as in *apologize, civilize,* and *organize.* Both *-ise* and *-ize* are used in British English, though many British publishers now prefer *-ize.* In Australia, *-ise* is generally preferred. In a small group of nouns, the alternatives *-lyze* and *-lyse* are available and have been used fairly consistently by American and British English respectively; however, the *-lyze* forms are becoming increasingly popular in Britain also (e.g., *analyze, paralyze*). For a number of words, there is no choice in either variety: *capsize, advise, chastise, exorcise, improvise,* and *revise.*

7. *-nse/-nce:* The conspicuousness of this difference is out of proportion to its occurrences. The most common examples are *defense/defence, license/licence, offense/offence,* and *pretense/pretence.* In the case of *license,* British English (like American English) uses the *-nse* form for the verb.

8. *-dg/-dge:* Only a few words are involved in this distinction, such as *abridgment/abridgement, acknowledgment/acknowledgement,* and *judgment/judgement.*

9. *-og/-ogue:* Again, few words are involved. They include *analog/analogue, catalog/catalogue,* and *dialog/dialogue;* in others, such as *monologue* and *prologue,* American English usually retains the *-gue* used in British English.

10. *-ection/-exion:* Words involved include *connection/connexion* and *inflection/ inflexion*, but in fact the American spellings are most often used in British English now. However, both varieties invariably use *complexion*.

Other differences between American and British English in the spelling of individual words include *ax/axe* (though the British form is also frequently used in America), *check/cheque* (a money order), *donut/doughnut, draft/draught* (an air current), *mold/mould, story/storey* (in a building), *pajamas/pyjamas, plow/plough, program/programme, sceptical/skeptical,* and *tire/tyre.*

It is possible to make two generalizations about British and American spelling conventions.[8] First, where spelling differences do exist between British and American English, the American spellings tend to be shorter than the British ones. Second, a spelling used in Britain is more likely to be acceptable in America than an American spelling is in Britain. However, in an age of international communications, users of each variety are increasingly exposed to the other's spelling conventions and the differences are usually slight in any case; the chances of miscommunication because of spelling are not great.

APPLICATIONS TO TEACHING

In this chapter we have seen that the spelling of English was not always fixed but at times showed a huge amount of variation, with people often spelling words phonetically, according to the sounds of their own dialect, and using widely different conventions to do so. For instance, *wattyr, watyr,* and *watter* were equally valid ways of spelling *water.* However, with the publication of dictionaries, the spelling of English became relatively fixed. Of course, we need to help our students master standard spellings, but when they are struggling with them, it might be somewhat motivating for them to know that many of their phonetically correct spellings (which are errors according to the standard) may well have been acceptable in the past. In some ways they are just unlucky to be learning English in a time when spelling has been fixed, often in a phonetically confusing way.

But even with today's standardization, there are still some words that remain flexible in their spelling, especially compound words and words that may use hyphens. This can easily be illustrated by analyzing the spellings of the following compound words in the 100 million-word British National Corpus (BNC). In general, we find that the more established a compound word is, the more likely it is that it will be spelled as one orthographic unit. From this, it can be argued that *lookalike* and *throwaway* are further along the road to becoming a single conceptual unit than *go-between* and *bleary-eyed*, which still are predominately spelled with a hyphen.

ALTERNATIVE SPELLINGS OF COMPOUND WORDS IN THE BRITISH NATIONAL CORPUS (100 MILLION WORDS TOTAL)

Spelling	Number of Occurrences
(someone who mediates between two or more other people)	
go between	8
go-between	123
gobetween	0
(someone or something that looks like someone or something else)	
look alike	1
look-alike	66
lookalike	111
(something with little value that can be easily discarded)	
throw away	4
throw-away	37
throwaway	102
(tired, red, watery eyes)	
bleary eyed	5
bleary-eyed	64
blearyeyed	0

In the last chapter, we explained the origins of many of the silent letters in English, an issue of interest to any student who wishes to spell well. This chapter added to the explanation, focusing on etymological respellings, in which the arbitrary reintroduction of letters into words to reflect the forms they had in their source language (usually Latin) has all too often resulted in the silent letters that cause so much confusion for learners today.

FURTHER READING

Two thorough studies of the subject, although neither brings us up to the present day.

- Vallins, G. H. (1965). *Spelling* (Rev. ed.). London: Deutsch.
- Scragg, D. G. (1974). *A history of English spelling*. Manchester: English Universities Press.

An advanced discussion of the Early Modern English period.

- Salmon, V. (1996). Orthography and punctuation. In R. Lass (Ed.), *The Cambridge history of the English language, Volume 3: 1476–1776* (pp. 13–55). Cambridge: Cambridge University Press.

Many useful entries, including one on spelling reform.

- McArthur, T. (Ed). (1992). *The Oxford companion to the English language*. Oxford: Oxford University Press.

This book provides numerous examples of English texts ranging from the Old English period to today.

- Burnley, D. (1992). *The history of the English language: A source book*. London: Longman.

A resource book with activities for practicing common spelling patterns.

- Shemesh, R., & Waller, S. (2000). *Teaching English spelling: A practical guide*. Cambridge: Cambridge University Press.

A short book on spelling for non-specialists that is filled with interesting bits of information.

- Cook, V. (2004). *Accomodating brocolli in the cemetary or why can't anybody spell?* London: Profile Books.

Classroom Activity: 6.1

Comparing British and American English (Spelling)

Many of the same words used in British and American English are spelled differently. Below are some of the major differences. Write the American spellings of the words.

	British		American
-our	colour	*-or*	___color___
	flavour		_____
	honour		_____
-re	theatre	*-er*	_____
	centre		_____
	litre		_____
-ce	pretence	*-se*	_____
	offence		_____
	licence		_____
-ise	normalise	*-ize*	_____
	jeopardise		_____
	standardise		_____
-ae-	archaeology	*-e-*	_____
	haemorrhage		_____
	anaesthetic		_____

Sometimes different spellings relate to individual words. Can you write the British spelling of these American English words?

check (money)   _____   pajamas   _____

curb (road)   _____   plow   _____

donut   _____   program   _____

draft (air)   _____   skeptical   _____

mold   _____   tire   _____

7

ENGLISH AROUND
THE WORLD

How Is English Different in Various
Countries around the World?

- Is English really very different as spoken in different parts of
  the world?
- What is "Standard English?"
- What are the differences between American and British English?
- How does the English spoken in native-speaking and
  non-native-speaking countries differ?

The Uniformity of English around the World

We have seen how English has changed throughout its history, and the most
noticeable feature of that change in the last 200 years or so has been the
emergence of national varieties of English. (A *variety* is a national or regional
version of English; a *dialect* is one of several versions within a variety. For
example, British English is a variety, and Lower North English is one dialect
in that variety.) This is partly a lingering consequence of the British Empire,
which brought English to many parts of the world where it had never been
heard before. Now English is spoken as a first language in places as diverse as
Australia, South Africa, and Canada. The different varieties of English used
around the world obviously have their own unique characteristics, and it is
becoming the norm to speak of Englishes rather than just a single monolithic
English language.

This chapter illustrates how these Englishes differ from one another. It
is important to stress that the differences are not great. Given that English
is spoken almost everywhere around the globe (at least by L2 speakers), it
is a remarkably uniform language. Its grammar varies only slightly from one

variety to another, and the vast bulk of its vocabulary is also shared. Of course, each variety has its own words (in Australian English, for example, there are *chook* [chicken] and *billibong* [pond]; in Indian English, *shoe-beat* [beating someone with a shoe is considered grossly insulting in India] and *interdining* [eating together by members of different castes]),[1] but they are a very small minority.

If we compare written texts from the various Englishes, it becomes clear that the extent of the differences is small and does not usually cause comprehension problems. English speakers from all parts of the world routinely write for each other in novels, news reports, and journal articles. Any perception that the varieties of English are dramatically different from one another probably comes from spoken English, as pronunciation is the one linguistic aspect in which English does vary widely around the world. The way various varieties are pronounced can make them sound very different even though the underlying language is basically the same. You might find people speaking another variety of English virtually incomprehensible when listening to them, but if they wrote their messages down, they would probably be perfectly understandable.

Trudgill and Chambers nicely summarize the uniformity of English, with the exception of pronunciation:

> The vast majority of native speakers around the world differ linguistically from one another relatively little, with more differentiation in their phonetics and phonology than at other linguistic levels. Most English people, for example, betray their geographical origins much more through their accents than through their vocabulary or grammar. This vast majority speaks mainstream varieties of English, standard or non-standard, which resemble one another quite closely, and which are all reasonably readily mutually intelligible. Differences between these mainstream varieties…are generally linguistically rather trivial, and where not trivial, quite regular and predictable. Grammatically, in particular, these varieties are very close to standard English.[2]

Our discussion of the differences of English around the world is only possible because the language is comparatively homogenous, allowing us to highlight the relatively minor differences. Those illustrated in this chapter are useful to know, but they amount to only a very small proportion of the language overall. Thus it is probably worthwhile to highlight the global homogeneity of English to your students while introducing them to the differences between varieties with which they are likely to come into contact.

Standard English

What Is Standard English?

The notion of "Standard English" carries a lot of emotional baggage. To some, it is a sacred treasure, the correct way to speak that should be protected from contamination and change. To others, it represents an oppressive imperialist ideal that is very difficult for non-natives to master and that does not acknowledge the validity of non-standard varieties. For still others, it is simply the type of English that appears in textbooks and so should not be questioned. Given this range of ideas and the corresponding emotions attached to them, what is the most reasonable way to think about Standard English?

For some languages there is a government-sponsored academy that regulates the usage of those languages and that prescribes the correct forms to use. French is one of the most notable of these languages with its *Académie Française*, though the power of this institution actually to control changes in French is quite limited. English does not have such an academy, and thus there is no "official" Standard English. Nevertheless, there is still a Standard English that is widely recognized, and it is the variety codifed in numerous dictionaries, grammars, and handbooks of usage. Most people accept the norms and conventions published in these reference books, and so this variety of English is most often used for education and public discourse. The media and most international publishers use it, which is one reason why written English is so uniform around the world. The wide use of this standard variety also serves to further solidify its status as the best norm to follow. Thus Standard English is essentially a product of a consensus between its users, enshrined in the reference books.

We have seen how such books (particularly the prescriptive grammars of the 18th century and later) may actually encourage language usage that goes contrary to the norms followed in current practice, but luckily most reference books today are based on large database corpora that allow them to describe accurately how language is ***actually used,*** rather than dictate how it ***should be used.*** For example, the *Longman Grammar of Spoken and Written English* is based on a corpus of 40 million words of native-speaking discourse, and the *Cambridge International Dictionary of English* was compiled from a corpus of about 100 million words, also of native-speaking discourse. (The vast majority of both these corpora consists only of British and American English.) The corpus evidence allows the writers of reference books to describe the features of English used across a range of native dialects while excluding features restricted to local varieties.[3] With modern reference books describing the elements of English that are broadly used in native-speaking contexts, and with Standard English being based on these reference books, we find that Standard English is simply the variety of English that is most widely accepted in native-speaking communities, particularly by educated speakers.

A standard language has been described as having maximal variation in function but minimal variation in form, and we have seen that English is indeed fairly uniform around the world. Yet to suggest that there is a single, all-purpose Standard English would be misleading. The native speakers in each country or region add their own personalities to the English they use, and so there are actually a number of standard forms, one for each of those areas (e.g., Standard American English, Standard New Zealand English, and Standard South Asian English). These national or regional Standard Englishes will not differ from each other greatly, and it has even been suggested that the features they share could be thought of as having truly global usage and would thus make up a "World Standard English." Figure 13 usefully illustrates how English, although relatively uniform overall, varies around the world today. The further from the center, the more linguistic variation there is: World Standard English consists of the most accepted and universal features of English; the national and regional Standard Englishes would vary from this World Standard English to some degree, and the dialects within these national and regional Englishes would have even more diversity. Thus the forms of English closer to the center will be the most comprehensible to the greatest range of speakers.

It is important to note that our discussion of Standard English has mainly concerned written English. Written texts are relatively permanent, and the widespread interchange of texts between different parts of the world allows some consensus on the form of written English to be achieved (and thus standardization). Speech lasts only for a moment and so is mainly a local phenomenon, occurring as people talk to one another. The result is that speech has had much more freedom to diversify in the different locations where it is spoken, and so we find that spoken language typically has much more variation than written language. Even individual speakers will sometimes use relatively more standard forms at some times and relatively more dialectal forms at others. It would be difficult to describe a standard for spoken English, and so discussions of Standard English almost always refer to the written language.

For most native users, the notion of Standard English is something that makes little difference in everyday life. Written Standard English is so ubiquitous in newspapers, magazines, and books that it would be surprising to find anything else. Speakers of various national varieties and dialects regularly read this written standard without a second thought. In spoken discourse there

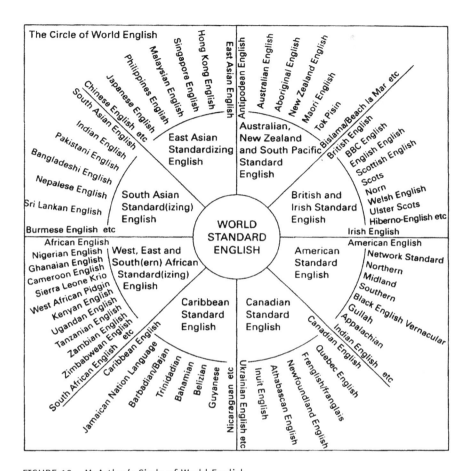

FIGURE 13   McArthur's Circle of World English

Source: From "The English Languages?" by T. McArthur, 1987, *English Today, 11*, p. 11. Copyright 1987 by Cambridge University Press. Reprinted with permission.

is much more variation, but people speaking the different dialects routinely interact with each other without major problems, without having to refer back to some standard form of English to be mutually intelligible.

The idea of standardization mainly comes into play in education, particularly ESL/EFL education, where choices about the type of English to be taught need to be made. In an ideal world, we would teach students all of the features of all of the varieties and dialects of English so that they would be perfectly prepared, regardless of which English speaker they came across. Of course, this is impossible in reality because of time constraints and because no teacher can be expected to know the idiosyncrasies of every English variety and dialect. Thus, it makes sense to focus on a widely understood form of the language, and the most widely accepted form within a native-speaking community—Standard English—seems a reasonable choice.

In making this pragmatic choice, however, it is important not to scorn other forms of English. No national variety (or dialect for that matter) is any better or worse than another one; they simply represent the language characteristics of a group of speakers from a certain area. Each variety and dialect is equally good and useful for its own group of speakers. From this perspective, the value of Standard English lies in its power to facilitate communication across a wide range of people, not because it is any more eloquent or correct than other varieties or dialects. Standard English can be widely understood because it is in general use, but this means that it does not contain any localized language features that may be important for communication in those local contexts. Thus, it makes perfect sense to teach any language features of a local variety or dialect in conjunction with Standard English, if they will enhance communication.

This would go against some people's feelings that Standard English is the best form of English and should be taught exclusively. But these feelings undervalue the usefulness of local varieties and dialects. They are also based on an assumption that Standard English can be exactly described and quantified. Although many of its features are relatively straightforward to describe, based on corpus evidence, it is actually quite difficult to determine unambiguously whether some features are sufficiently common to be considered "standard" or whether they are too "dialectal" and should be excluded from a reference book. In many cases, this will be a subjective judgment and different people will have different ideas about what Standard English consists of. With this in mind, it is best to consider the information in reference books as the authors' and editors' best attempts at describing English, rather than as an unquestionable truth. In the end, Standard English is not an actual form of English that exists and is spoken by a particular group of people somewhere. Rather, it is a useful idealization we can use to help our students, as long as we do not become limited by it.

The Development of Standard British and American English

Although every variety of English has its own standard form, the two main varieties usually looked to as norms are British English and American English. However, these two varieties are not completely homogeneous but are made up of a number of dialects. How did a standard form of English arise from these numerous dialects in either country? As is often the case, the answers to these questions have a historical basis.[4]

Standard British English

In England, the standard form of British English began to be established in the late 14th century. At this time, the Middle English dialects could be clustered into one of four principal groups: Northern, West Midland, East Midland, and Southern (which included Kentish) (see Figure 14 on p. 178). For various economic, political, and educational reasons, the East Midland dialect gained ascendancy over the others to develop into what we call Standard British English today (though the process was far more complex than this simple account suggests). Those reasons included:

- The East Midland dialect occupied the middle position between the linguistic extremes of the northern and southern dialects, acting as a kind of compromise between them.
- The East Midland area was the largest and most populous of the major dialect areas, being the best for agriculture.
- The universities of Oxford and Cambridge were in this area.
- The most popular poet of the day, Chaucer, wrote in the dialect.
- The commercial, political, and legal center of England—London— came to speak the East Midland dialect (and this was perhaps the most important reason).

The dialect first became the standard for written English, especially after printing became widespread. Eventually, it also became accepted as a spoken standard, used in interraction between speakers of varying regional dialects.

Standard American English

In America, the inhabitants were of such diverse origins and moved around and mixed so much as the country grew that no one dialect dominated, and the various dialects of English that they spoke seem to have blended together into a comparatively uniform new one. Although the northern and southern areas of the United States do have their own dialects, the great central part of the country uses the blended dialect (the Midland dialect in Figure 17 on p. 184). Thus, in America's case, the dialect destined to become the standard was simply that spoken by the vast majority of the country. Furthermore, even the differences between the three major American dialects are relatively small compared to the differences between some British dialects. With the exception of the East Coast of America, there is a uniformity in American English that one might not expect from a language spoken in such a large country.

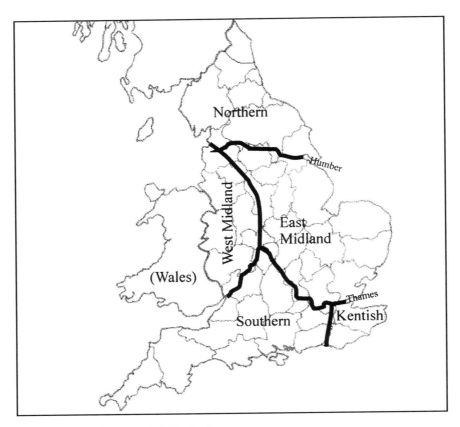

FIGURE 14   The Dialects of Middle English

The Three Circles of Global English Usage

In today's world, English is spoken as much by non-native speakers as by natives. In fact, there are now probably more L2 speakers than L1 speakers, and this imbalance will only become more pronounced in the future. So we must also consider the types of English spoken by these non-natives. Braj Kachru has analyzed the international use of English and described it in terms of three "circles" of usage: an inner circle of users, an outer circle of users, and an expanding circle of users.[5] The inner circle consists of native speakers who live in countries where English is the dominant language, such as Canada, New Zealand, and Ireland. The inner circle also contains the forms of English most often looked on as models, particularly American and British English, and so can be thought of as "norm-producing." The outer circle is made up of L2 speakers who live in countries where English is established and perhaps has some special status, as for example India, Nigeria, and Malaysia. (See the list in Chapter 1, pp. 5–8, for more countries.) English in these areas is vibrant enough for them to begin developing their own unique standard forms, and so they can be seen as "norm-developing." The expanding circle has L2 speakers who live in countries where English has no special status, such as Vietnam, Sweden, and Argentina. Speakers in these countries usually look elsewhere for norms of English usage and so can be seen as "norm-dependent." See Figure 15 for one version of this three-circle model.

This model is useful in conceptualizing the international use of English, but it is not perfect. Sometimes it is difficult to decide in which category a country belongs. For example, Sweden is in the expanding circle; yet English is taught comprehensively in its school system and the level of English proficiency among its population as a whole must be far higher than in many outer-circle countries. Another problem with the model is that it puts the L1 speakers in

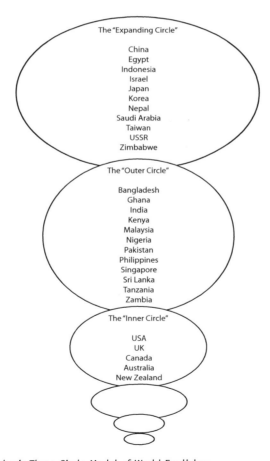

FIGURE 15   Kachru's Three-Circle Model of World Englishes

the middle of the English universe, implying that the most "correct" English, the best teachers, and the finest materials all come from the inner circle.[6] However, the number of English speakers in the outer and expanding circles is growing much faster than the numbers in the inner circle. For instance, the population growth rate of countries of the outer circle was an average of 2.3 percent in 1995–96, while in the inner-circle countries it was only 0.8 percent.[7] Eventually the outer and expanding circles may become more influential than the inner circle by sheer force of numbers.

Despite these limitations, the three-circle model gives us a basis from which to discuss international English. Perhaps it is best to start with a discussion of the inner circle, as it is still most influential in terms of the ELT materials it generates, and because many teachers still consider it to be the source of the best models of correctness for English.

What Are the Differences between American and British English?

A number of countries where English is spoken as the dominant L1 have their own national variety of English (and often several dialects within the national variety)—Scotland, Canada, Australia, and South Africa. But of the various national varieties, it makes sense to pay special attention to British English (because English began and developed in Britain) and American English (because of the influence it has around the world). British English and American English also have the largest numbers of native speakers and the most extensive literatures and are the varieties normally taught to non-native speakers.[8] As most other national varieties have strong ties with either British or American English, an understanding of these two major varieties and their differences should prove useful whatever national variety is being taught.

The Range of Dialects within British and American English

British English

English has been spoken for 1,500 years in Britain, and there have been different dialects from the start. Today, there are 16 major dialects according to one count and numerous local ones (see Figure 16 on p. 183). Although the underlying written grammar is nearly the same, the dialects can differ considerably in terms of vocabulary and pronunciation. Consider the following passage illustrating the Middlesborough dialect from northeast England, which is part of the larger Lower North dialect of British English. It was written to demonstrate a variety of the features that occur in this dialect.

NOW YOU'RE TALKIN'

Ee, well us Teessiders have finally been recognised by the posh Cockneys coz of the class way what we talk, eh?

It was on the telly news and everything. Did yer see it, eh?

What it is, right, there's this new dictionary out this week - which is good news like coz I've finished reading the other one now, like, and - get this - we only get a mention!

Honest. They reckon more new words and phrases are made up on Teesside than anywhere else...well me and the lads in the Streetfighters Arms do anyway, like. Hey, this dictionary, it's huge! Its been genetically modified I reckon. It's not like them rubbishy efforts at school with all the mucky words underlined in red and that.

This one's got 18,000 smart official new words in it. I didn't know there were that many words in the world, me - mind, to be fair I reckon Our Lass gets through at least that many when she's got a right cob on with us, like!

I swear down dead, it's got all these top Teessidisms in it like "ee," "gadgie" and "parmo" - words what we're learning the rest of the country, like.

Not that they're new words or owt like, just ones what all the eggheads down Oxford have finally figured out what we've been saying all along, eh?[9]

You probably have some problems understanding this passage. Partly, this is because it has been written deliberately to represent spoken discourse. As we have seen, spoken grammar is different from written grammar and is usually more flexible because it is produced in real time and is not restricted by being "fixed" to a printed page. The Middlesborough dialect has some distinctive grammatical properties, such as using *What it is, right* as a way to introduce a topic. But it is likely that a more serious problem in comprehending the passage is the unknown vocabulary. Some of it relates to the geographical reference context:

Teessiders – people mainly from the Teesside towns of Middlesborough and Stockton

Cockneys – people from east London but used here to mean anyone from England south of Teesside

Some words are particular to Middlesborough:

gadgie – man, similar to codger

parmo – a late-night breaded-pork and cheese dish claimed to be of Italian origin but actually peculiar to Middlesborough

The use of *Ee* in place of *Oh* (also representing scandalization, exasperation, or surprise) will be unfamiliar, as will *eh*, used as a "tag" (a recurrent expression tagged onto a clause or sentence) inviting agreement. *Owt* is heard in other northern dialects, too, and is a form of *aught* (commonly used in the standard language until recently in sayings such as *For aught I know*), meaning "anything."

These words are more widespread in the United Kingdom:

mucky – dirty, rude
smart – good, cool
telly – television

To hear the passage actually spoken would cause more problems. In general, pronunciation probably causes more comprehension problems between dialects and varieties than any other feature of language.

This passage is intended to show the individual features of one local British dialect, chosen because of its differences from Standard British English. From this you might get the impression that British dialects are so different from one another that people have trouble communicating, but this is not the case. Although there are a large number of local dialects, in daily life it doesn't cause major problems. Speakers routinely communicate with each other, not thinking anything of it. Just as English teachers adjust their language to the level of their students, so do native speakers in ordinary life adjust their language to the persons they are talking to, and they downplay any dialectal features they think might be difficult.

American English

When compared to British English, American English is remarkably uniform. This is partially because it has only existed on American soil for around 300 years compared to Britain's millennium and a half and therefore has had less time to change. But there are other factors connected to the history of American settlement. Most early English immigrants came from southern and eastern England, particularly from around London. After arrival in eastern America, their dialects tended to blend into a common speech. Later, in the 18th century, Americans began moving westward, spearheaded by the Ulster Scots looking for new land. Groups of pioneers from different parts of the Atlantic seaboard crossed paths and mingled their forms of speech as they headed west. By the time they reached Middle America, they spoke essentially the same dialect.

FIGURE 16   Major Dialects of England

In the first half of the 19th century, large numbers of immigrants from many parts of the world began streaming into America, making the eastern cities even more cosmopolitan and further diluting their dialects. The end result of this mobility and cultural mixing is a national variety far more uniform than its English counterpart, which resides on a land mass many times smaller. Scholars divide American English into only three major dialects (Northern, Midland, and Southern—see Figure 17 on p. 184), compared to England's 16 major divisions.[10]

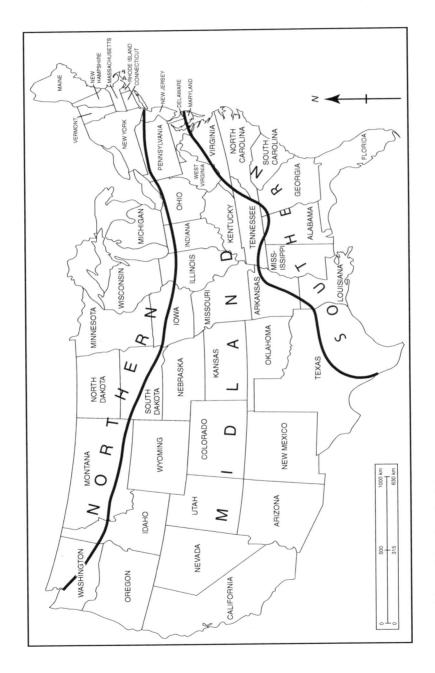

FIGURE 17   Major Dialects of American English

Pronunciation Differences between American and British English

Perhaps the most noticeable difference between American and British English lies in pronunciation, some details of which were referred to in Chapter 5. However, there is considerable variation within each national variety, and often these internal pronunciation differences are greater than the differences between the varieties. Fully describing the phonetic basis for these differences would require a rather technical treatment, which is beyond the scope of this book. The handbook *Teaching Pronunciation* provides an accessible overview of the various differences between British and American English, and this section summarizes the main points.[11]

Common Words with Different Pronunciations in American and British English

WORDS SPELLED WITH THE VOWEL *a*

Many words spelled with *a*, such as *bath, class, last, mask, past,* and *rather,* are pronounced with the vowel /æ/ in American English but with /ɑ:/ in Standard British English. However, it is important to remember that British English contains a number of regional dialects, and many of them, especially the northern ones, use the /æ/ pronunciation.

WORDS SPELLED WITH *-er*

Some words spelled with *er,* such as *clerk* and *derby,* are pronounced as /ɜ:/ in American English but /ɑ:/ in British English.

WORDS ENDING WITH *-ile*

Words ending with *-ile* tend to be pronounced as /əl/ or /l/ in American English and as /aɪl/ in British English: *agile, docile, fertile, missile.*

WORDS USED IN THE TWO VARIETIES WITH THE SAME SPELLING BUT TYPICALLY WITH DIFFERENT PRONUNCIATIONS

Word	American English (AmE)	British English (BrE)
asthma	/ǽzma/	/ǽsmə/
clique	/klɪk/	/kli:k/
vase	/vɛɪs/	/vɑ:z/
schedule	/skɛ́ʤəl/	/ʃɛdju:l/
leisure	/lí:ʒɜ:/	/lɛ́ʒɜ:/
lieutenant	/lu:ténənt/	/lɛfténənt/
z (the letter)	/zi:/	/zɛd/
tomato	/tʌméɪtəʊ/	/tʌmɑ́:təʊ/

Differences in Word Stress

Many words have different stress patterns in American and British English.

WORDS DERIVED FROM FRENCH

Words taken from French usually retain the French syllable–final stress pattern in American English, whereas British English has moved the stress to the initial syllable.

AmE	BrE	AmE	BrE
balLET	BALlet	perFUME	PERfume
blaSÉ	BLAse	debuTANTE	DEButante
bufFET	BUFfet	vaLET	VAlet
garAGE	GARage		

THREE- AND FOUR-SYLLABLE WORDS

In several types of three- or four-syllable words, American English places the stress on the second syllable, whereas it falls on the first syllable in British English (though the latter now often follows the American pattern in the last example).

AmE	BrE
comPOSite	COMposite
subALtern	SUBaltern
arIStocrat	ARistocrat
priMARily	PRImarily

WORDS ENDING IN -ary, -ery, -ory, AND -mony

American English tends to give some stress to penultimate syllables that often are unpronounced in British English, leading to quite different rhythmic patterns in the two varieties.

Word	AmE	BrE
military	/mílətèri/	/mílɪtri/
arbitrary	/árbətrèri/	/áːbɪtri/
cemetery	/sémətèri/	/sémətri/
monastery	/mɒnəstèri/	/mɒ́nəstri/
mandatory	/mǽndətɔ̀ri/	/mǽndətri/
category	/kǽtəgɔ̀ri/	/kǽtəgri/
testimony	/téstəmòʊni/	/téstəməni/
matrimony	/mǽtrəmòʊni/	/mǽtrɪməni/

DAYS OF THE WEEK

The diphthong of -*day* is pronounced fully and carries quite a lot of stress (though less than the first syllable) in American English, whereas in British English the diphthong of -*day* is reduced to a short /i/ (or very short /ɛɪ/) and is unstressed, the first syllable carrying heavy stress.

Word	AmE	BrE
Sunday	/sʌ́ndeɪ/	/sʌ́ndi/
Monday	/mʌ́ndeɪ/	/mʌ́ndi/
Tuesday	/túːzdeɪ/	/tjúːzdi/
Wednesday	/wɛ́nzdeɪ/	/wɛ́nzdi/
Thursday	/θɜ́ːzdeɪ/	/θɜ́ːzdi/
Friday	/fráɪdeɪ/	/fráɪdi/
Saturday	/sǽtɜːdeɪ/	/sǽtɜːdi/

PLACE-NAMES

British English generally gives less stress to the penultimate syllable of words, which leads to a different pronunciation from American English for many place-names that end in -*aster* or -*ester*.

Name	AmE	BrE
Lancaster	/lǽŋkæ̀stər/	/lǽŋkəstə/
Rochester	/rɒ́tʃɛ̀stər/	/rɒ́tʃəstə/
Worcester	/wúəsɛ̀stər/	/wústə/

A similar pattern occurs with place names that end in -*ham*, with the last syllable being reduced in British English.

| Nottingham | /nɒ́tɪŋhæ̀m/ | /nɒ́tɪŋəm/ |
| Birmingham | /bɜ́ːmɪŋhæ̀m/ | /bɜ́ːmɪŋəm/ |

VERBS ENDING IN -*ate*

As we have seen, many words and place-names have different rhythmic patterns in American and British English. Overall, American English tends to retain the distinct syllables in multisyllabic words, often with a light stress, while there is more syllable reduction in British English. American English speakers are also inclined to put stress later in multisyllabic words than British speakers. The class of words ending in -*ate* can be seen as an exception to this tendency, with American English speakers stressing the earlier root syllable and British English speakers stressing the suffix.

AmE	BrE
DICtate	dicTATE
FIXate	fixATE
ROtate	roTATE
VIbrate	vibRATE

MISCELLANEOUS WORD-STRESS DIFFERENCES
In some words, differences in the placement of stress cause the overall pronunciation to be quite different in American and British English.

Word	AmE	BrE
advertisement	/ǽdvɜːtàɪzmənt/	/ædvɜ́ːtəzmənt/
controversy	/kɒ́ntrəvɜ̀ːsi/	/kɒtrɒ́vasi/
corollary	/kɒ̀rələ̀ri/	/kɒrɒ́ləri/
inquiry	/ínkwəri/	/ɪnkwáɪri/
laboratory	/lǽbrətɒ̀ri/	/ləbɒ́rətri/

Vocabulary Differences between American and British English

Beyond pronunciation, the most substantial difference between the two major national varieties probably rests in the area of vocabulary. Although the vast majority of words are used in the same way in both varieties, there is a considerable number that are not. Some words belong only to American English (*druggist* [a dispenser of medicine]), some words only to British English (*noughts and crosses* [the game tick-tack-toe]), and some belong to both varieties but with different meanings (British *chips* = American *French fries*; American *chips* = British *crisps*). Other words are used in both varieties but are more frequent in one than the other; for example, *mail* is preferred in American English, whereas *post* is more frequent in British English, and although *autumn* is the most frequently used word for the season following summer in British English, Americans more often use *fall* as an alternative.[12] Table 11 illustrates some of the more common differences between American and British words, but you should be aware that differences between the word pairs may not always be straightforward. They may vary from each other in any of the previously mentioned ways.

TABLE 11
VOCABULARY DIFFERENCES BETWEEN AMERICAN ENGLISH AND BRITISH ENGLISH

AmE	BrE	AmE	BrE
railroad	railway	elevator	lift
engineer	driver	apartment	flat
conductor	guard	mail	post
baggage	luggage	vacation	holiday
truck	lorry	garbage can	dustbin
hood (car)	bonnet	bar	pub
trunk (car)	boot	druggist	chemist
fender (car)	bumper	French fries	chips
gasoline	petrol	potato chips	crisps
subway	underground	cookie	biscuit
counterclockwise	anticlockwise	trailer	caravan
thumbtack	drawing pin	round-trip ticket	return ticket
flashlight	torch	one-way ticket	single ticket

Although the word pairs in Table 11 may differ in meaning somewhat, they would probably not cause undue problems for most speakers. The exchange of movies, television programs, books, magazines, and newspapers has introduced most of these words to both sides of the Atlantic and has made these lexical differences more a matter of interest and amusement than actual confusion for the most part. Among the words already widely used in the United Kingdom are *French fries, apartment,* and *mail.* However, there are a few lexical differences that might still cause embarrassment, confusion, or even danger, if misused (e.g., *I like the pants you're wearing; Meet me on the first floor; Please walk on the pavement*).

AmE	BrE
underwear	pants
pants	trousers
vest	waistcoat
diaper	nappy
first floor	ground floor
second floor	first floor
sidewalk	pavement
pavement	road

This list illustrates differences in individual words, but there are also differences in idioms. For example:[13]

AmE	BrE
a home away from home	a home from home
leave well enough alone	leave well alone
sweep under the rug	sweep under the carpet

If a person is familiar with either British or American English, these differences in vocabulary, both individual words and phrases, are unlikely to cause much confusion in comprehension. After all, tourists from Britain and America regularly visit each other's countries without language problems; moreover, they often end up finding the vocabulary differences enjoyably interesting.

However, to produce these words and phrases accurately, people must memorize them individually, as there is little that is systematic about the lexical differences that might enable the appropriate forms to be chosen. This may be more than our students wish to take on. Learning the vocabulary for one variety of English is difficult enough; expecting students to learn the differences for another variety may well be asking too much. However, because the vast majority of words are shared between British and American English, students should be able to get on well if they know one of the two varieties. They should be able to comprehend the other variety, even though their production will mark them as non-local speakers.

Grammatical Differences between American English and British English

Compared to pronunciation, vocabulary, and spelling, there is not much grammatical difference between American English and British English. The grammar of standard written English is remarkably similar around the world, although the spoken language does contain more grammatical variation, as do the various dialects. The minor differences in grammar that exist between the two national varieties often involve the use of a single word, whether it be a preposition, verb, or article.

Prepositions

One of the most difficult aspects of grammar for most learners to master is the use of prepositions. Luckily, most are used in similar ways in American and British English.[14] However, in a number of cases, one variety has traditionally preferred one preposition over another, although either may be used (and in several cases the American usage is becoming more prevalent in the United Kingdom also). Table 12 illustrates some of these differences.

TABLE 12
PREPOSITION DIFFERENCES BETWEEN AMERICAN ENGLISH AND BRITISH ENGLISH

AmE	BrE
Americans live *on* a street.	Britons live *in* a street.
Americans fill *out* a form.	Britons fill *in* a form.
Americans check *out* something suspicious.	Britons check *up on* something suspicious.
Americans do things *on* the weekend.	Britons do things *at* the weekend.
Americans are *of* two minds about something.	Britons are *in* two minds about something.
Americans can cater *to* all tastes.	Britons can cater *for* all tastes.

As with other words, these prepositions can be tricky to produce correctly but should cause little problem in comprehension. After all, a person invited to go to the beach would surely understand that invitation regardless of whether it was *on* the weekend or *at* the weekend.

Verb Pairs

GOT/GOTTEN
Gotten is used in American English but very rarely in British English. It is often used as an alternative to *have got* (*He has gotten an offer from another company*). It also has a number of other American uses:[15]

She's gotten a new car. (=obtain)

They've gotten interested in yoga. (=become)

He's so busy that he hasn't gotten off the phone in 2 hours. (=moved)

However, to indicate possession, British English uses *have got* much more often than American English (e.g., British: *Have you got a match?* American: *Do you have a match?*)

WILL/WON'T *VERSUS* SHALL/SHAN'T
American English tends to prefer *will/won't* over *shall/shan't*. The *shall* forms are used more in British English, but only with first-person constructions:

"*Shall we* go home now?" "*Shall I* buy it or not?" but "*Will you* go home now?" The same tendency applies to the negative form: "*I shan't* be here tomorrow," but "*They won't* be here tomorrow." Similarly, two British English uses of *will* are much less likely in American English:[16]

That will be the postman at the door.	(=must)
He WILL keep talking loudly right in my ear.	(stressed *will* indicating a disagreeable habit or practice)

The Definite Article

American English uses articles in some cases where British English omits them.

AmE	BrE
in the hospital	in hospital
in the future	in future
go to the university	go to university

Group Nouns

The use of a singular verb with group nouns to indicate a collective unit is shared by the two varieties: *The government is corrupt.* The use of a plural verb to indicate the collection of individuals in the group, however, is chiefly British English: *The government are corrupt.*

Tag Questions

Tag questions (i.e., regular questioning expressions tagged onto a sentence) exist in both American and British English, with British speakers perhaps using them more than Americans: "That's not very nice, *is it?*" Peremptory and aggressive tags tend to be used more in British English than in American English: "Well, I don't know, *do I?*"

English in Non Native–Speaking Countries

Up to this point, we have discussed mainly the English spoken within McArthur's inner circle of English use. However, because the majority of

English speakers belong to the outer and expanding circles, we now turn to varieties of English originating in countries where it is not the primary language. In outer circle countries, English holds a position as a second or compromise official language (see Figure 5 on p. 36). Some countries, like India or Nigeria, contain so many indigenous languages that some compromise language must be chosen for common communication. Political reasons often exclude a native language, making English a logical alternative choice. In other countries, such as Singapore, economic reasons induce the learning of English as a second language. Countries like the Philippines have kept some English as part of their colonial heritage. In addition to countries where English is present for official or historical reasons, the fact that English is a global lingua franca encourages its study in schools all around the world. All of these reasons have prompted the development of national Englishes that are viable in their own right, without necessarily referring back to the more established inner circle Englishes. These are sometimes termed "New Englishes," and their growth and maturation constitute probably the most important trait in the current stage of the history of English.

Of course, no culture wishes to be marginalized by a larger dominant language, and so the speakers of these New Englishes must negotiate a balance between using English as a world language for communication and retaining local languages for identity and cultural purposes. To some extent, these national varieties all serve both purposes in that they are still English and so still provide the communicative benefits, but they are also different enough to identify the speaker as part of an individual national group. The more a culture embraces a national variety of English as its own, the less threatening it becomes. It is not surprising, then, that each national variety contains some features that set it apart from American or British Standard English and that identify the variety as belonging to the individual country, region, or culture.

Illustrating a New English: South Asian English

South Asian English (spoken on the Indian subcontinent) ranks third in the world in number of speakers, after American English and British English, and the largest component of this regional variety is Indian English, which is estimated to have 320,000 L1 speakers and 37 million L2 speakers (see Table 1 in Chapter 1 on p. 6). A few items from this widely spoken variety of English can give a flavor of the unique features a New English can possess. As with other varieties, there is a lot of variation within South Asian English (SAE), and the distinctive features described may be perfectly normal for some SAE speakers but considered substandard by others.[17]

Pronunciation

In most other varieties, English is a ***stress-timed*** language, where the stresses occur at roughly equal intervals. For example,

Álison didn't / finish her / éssay.

       1   2   3

Each of the three segments (1, 2, 3) would take the same amount of time even though they contain different numbers of words and syllables. In other languages, such as French, all syllables occur at roughly equal intervals; these languages are called ***syllable-timed***.[18]

Il / est / ar / ri / vé / à / six / heures.

1 2 3 4 5 6 7   8

"He arrived (is arrived) at six o'clock.

SAE is closer to such a syllable-timed language. This means that weak vowels tend to be pronounced as full vowels and that suffixes are also stressed. This gives SAE a quite different rhythmic character compared to varieties of English that are stress-timed.

Grammar

The following usages are widely encountered in SAE but with much local variation.

- Pluralization of non-count mass nouns:
  - Many aircrafts have crashed there.
  - We ate just fruits for breakfast.
- Questions without subject-verb inversion:
  - What you would like to eat?
  - What this is made from?
- *One* used rather than *a/an*:
  - He gave me one book.
- The progressive form used for verbs expressing continuity:
  - She was having many dresses. (Cf. "She had many dresses.")
  - I am doing it often. (Cf. "I do it often.")
- Variations in noun number and determiners (i.e., the words that limit the meaning of nouns):
  - He performed many charities.
  - She loves to pull your legs.

- Repetition to add emphasis:
  - Cut into small small pieces.
  - Proceed slowly, slowly.
- The auxiliary *may* used to express obligation politely:
  - These mistakes may please be corrected. (Cf. "should be corrected")
- Different use of prepositions:
  - pay attention on
  - discuss about
  - Convey him my greetings. (Cf. "convey to him")
- Tag questions:
  - You have taken my pencil, isn't it?
  - She borrowed my book, no?
  - He is coming, yes?
- Alternative word order:
  - Who you would like to read?
  - They're late always.
  - My all friends are waiting.
- Yes and no agreeing with the form of a question, not just its content:
  - Q: You have no objection?
  - A: Yes, I have no objection.
- Q: You didn't come on the bus?
  - A: Yes, I didn't.

Vocabulary

As in all varieties of English, SAE has a number of its own distinctive words and phrases.[19]

Word/phrase	Meaning
jawan	a soldier in the Indian army
lakh	a unit of counting indicating 100,000
panchayat	a village council
kaccha road	a dirt road
tiffin box	a lunch box
by-two coffee	a restaurant order by two customers asking for half a cup of coffee each
four-twenty	a cheat or swindler (from the number of a section of the Indian Penal Code)
to sit on someone's neck	to watch that person carefully

Languages Born from English: Pidgins and Creoles

In addition to the New Englishes, there are new languages derived from English, and it is interesting to look at these briefly. Under certain conditions, English becomes the basis for a highly simplified type of language called a *pidgin.* Pidgins are created when speakers of one or more mutually unintelligible languages want to communicate, often for trading purposes. If one language is dominant, it becomes the source language, to which parts of the other languages are added, especially vocabulary. Grammar is greatly simplified, and the number of words is kept to a minimum. Some English pidgins have only five vowels and a thousand words. Pidgins begin as nobody's first language; they are merely languages of communicative expediency.

Occasionally, children grow up hearing a pidgin as their native language. This normally occurs when people who speak different languages intermarry. They use pidgin in their homes, and their children acquire it as their first language. When this happens, the pidgin is termed a *creole.* If there is a sufficient number of speakers, a creole can evolve into a separate language. After that, it can develop in one of two ways. If contact with the source language is maintained, the creole can steadily adopt aspects of it until eventually it becomes a dialect of that language. This is currently happening with many of the Caribbean creoles, such as Jamaican. If contact with the source language is lost, the creole may diverge from it until the two languages are mutually unintelligible. An example of this is Sranan, a English-based creole that is the official language of Surinam.

The following passage is in Tok Pisin (from "talk pidgin"), an expanded pidgin that is rapidly becoming a creole in Papua New Guinea where it is the lingua franca.[20] The passage is a news item that appeared in the Papua New Guinean newspaper, *Wantok* ("one talk," i.e., "one language") in April 1994.[21] See if you can understand it.

Ol meri gat bikpela wari yet

Helt na envairomen em ol bikpela samting ol meri long kantri tude i gat bikpela wari long en.

Bikos dispela tupela samting i save kamap strong long sindaun na laip bilong famili na komyuniti insait long ol ples na kantri.

Long dispela wik, moa long 40 meri bilong Milen Be provins i bung long wanpela woksop long Alotau bilong toktok long hevi bilong helt na envairomen long ol liklik ailan na provins. Bung i bin stat long Mande na bai pinis long Fraide, Epril 22.

Ol opisa bilong Melanesin Envairomen Faundesen wantaim nesenel na provinsal helt opis i stap tu bilong givim toktok insait long dispela worksop.

Although English is the source for most of the approximately 2,500 basic words in Tok Pisin, the evolved spellings, word combinations, and language structure are unique to the extent that you were probably not able to work out what the passage meant. In the next box, the same passage has been translated word-for-word into English. Now see if you can understand it any better.

All women got big-fellow worry yet

Health and environment him all big-fellow something all woman along country today he got big-fellow worry along him.

Because this-fellow two-fellow something he know come-up strong along sit-down and life belong family and community inside along all place and country.

Along this-fellow week, more along 40 woman belong Milne Bay Province he meet along one-fellow workshop along Alotau belong talk-talk along heavy belong health and environment along all little island and province. Meeting he been start along Monday and bye (-and-bye) finish along Friday April 22.

All officer belong Melanesian Environment Foundation one-time national and provincial health office he stop too belong give-him talk-talk inside along this-fellow workshop.

This version probably makes more sense, for at least some of the words are recognizable, such as *health, environment, woman,* and *provincial*. However, there are many words in Tok Pisin that will be unknown (*big-fellow, two-fellow, talk-talk*). Now look at the British English translation.

Women still have big worries

Health and environment are two of the major things which women in the country today have big concerns about.

Because these two things often have a strong effect on the situation and life of families and communities within villages and in the country.

This week, more than 40 women from Milne Bay Province are meeting in a workshop at Alotau in order to talk about the difficulties of health and environment in the small islands and provinces. The meeting began on Monday and will finish on Friday April 22.

The officers of the Melanesian Environment Foundation together with the national and provincial health office are there too in order to give talks in the workshop.

Tok Pisin may seem like a completely different language to you, and indeed it is. However, we should not view it as some second-rate descendent of English. Tok Pisin evolved from Modern English, rather as Modern English evolved from Old English (though of course in very different circumstances and with different results). It enables communication in Papua New Guinea just as American English does in America. It is no longer English but a new language in its own right and serves to illustrate another way that English is changing in today's world.

APPLICATIONS TO TEACHING

In this chapter, we have looked at the many faces of English as it is used around the world. The proliferation of varieties has pedagogical implications but mainly for teachers and administrators rather than learners. Learners will study whatever form of English appears in their textbooks and that their teacher teaches. But it is up to administrators and teachers to decide which variety (or varieties) that will be. In making the decision, it is important to escape the notion of one "correct" English. Each national variety and dialect is correct for the people speaking it. Rather, it is better to think in terms of utility: Which form of English will be most useful for students? If the goal is to give them the language resources to use English in a global context, then either American or British Standard English will be the most comprehensible internationally to a wide range of both native and non-native speakers, although other national varieties like Australian or Canadian English are probably equally understandable. If the goal is to allow them to speak in English in their own country, then teaching the national variety might make more sense. Another approach is to teach one of the inner-circle Englishes as a foundation and then add elements from the local variety that students might find helpful in their own country. Students should be encouraged to take advantage of all the English language resources they have, whether it is some local dialect of English in the home and community or a national standard variety in the classroom.

The notion of correctness also confuses the idea of "Standard English." If one feels that there is only one correct or proper form of English, then any deviation from that form must be considered incorrect or substandard. In this view, all of the speakers of other varieties (Indian English, Nigerian English, and even Australian English if one takes British English to be the norm) are using the language poorly. In fact, there is no one correct English, which is why applied linguists use the term "Standard English." There is some variation in each variety, but the most accepted dialect will be acknowledged as the standard form. This pattern of several dialects within a variety, one of which is accepted as standard, is true of American and British English as well. International publishers, authors, lexicographers, and textbook writers have taken the standard forms of American and British English as their norm, and thus they have become the standard form of written English worldwide. However, if a national variety differs from American or British Standard English, it is not incorrect; it is merely a different version of the language and is exhibiting some of the variation in English worldwide.

This is not to say that the differences between the various national varieties of English are great. The grammar and core vocabulary of English are remarkably uniform across the world. The differences we illustrated in this chapter between American, British, and Indian English make up only a very small percentage of the language overall. The same would be true of any other variety. Teachers often like to point out the differences in the varieties, and indeed this can be useful for students who will be exposed to more than one of them. However, they should also emphasize that varieties are for the most part very similar. Students should assume this similarity, because if they know one variety, they should not have much trouble comprehending a different one. If there is something they do not understand in it, they can always ask for clarification. Likewise, the person they are speaking to should be able to understand them. Writing should cause even fewer problems, as the norms for written Standard English are more or less the same across the world.

With this in mind, it is more important to become proficient in whatever variety of English you are learning than it is to master any particular variety, such as American or British. If you speak one of the national varieties well, you are likely to be understood around the world.

In the end, teachers will have to teach a form of English that is comprehensible to the maximum number of people (which would suggest a standard version), while being an English that students identify with and want to learn (which would suggest a national variety or local dialect thereof). Perhaps the most likely form of English will be a hybrid combining standard and local forms. David Crystal summarizes this challenge for teachers and administrators:

> In my view, the chief task facing ELT is how to devise pedagogical policies and practices in which the need to maintain an international standard of intelligibility, in both speech and writing, can be made to comfortably exist alongside the need to recognize the importance of international diversity, as a reflection of identity, chiefly in speech and eventually perhaps also in writing.[22]

FURTHER READING

Three books discussing the internationalization of English.
- Burns, A., & Coffin, C. (Eds.). (2001). *Analyzing English in a global context*. London: The Open University.
- Graddol, D., Leith, D., & Swann, J. (1996). *English: History, diversity, and change*. London: The Open University.
- Jenkins, J. (2003). *World Englishes*. London: Routledge.

A discussion on Standard English that includes many activities.
- Wilkinson, J. (1995). *Introducing Standard English*. London: Penguin.

For a detailed description of the different varieties of English, including American and British English, with a particular emphasis on pronunciation.
- Trudgill, P., & Hannah, J. (2002). *International English* (4th ed.). London: Edward Arnold.

A look at American English from both prescriptive and descriptive perspectives.
- MacNeil, R., & Cran, W. (2005). *Do you speak American?* New York: Nan Talese/Doubleday.

These two books offer a more detailed discussion of South Asian and Indian English.
- Kachru, B. B. (1983). *The Indianization of English: The English language in India*. Oxford: Oxford University Press.
- Nihalani, P., Tongue, R. K., & Hosali, P. (1979). *Indian and British English*. Oxford: Oxford University Press.

Two good sources for further information on pidgins and creoles.

- O'Donnell, W. R., & Todd, L. (1991). *Variety in contemporary English.* London: Routledge.
- Wardhaugh, R. (1992). *An introduction to sociolinguistics.* Oxford: Blackwell.

Classroom Activity: 7.1

Comparing British and American English (Vocabulary)

The two most influential national varieties of English are British and American English. Overall, they are very similar, but they do have some interesting differences. In this exercise, we will explore vocabulary differences.

BRITISH VERSUS AMERICAN VOCABULARY

The following pairs of words are British and American words referring to the same thing. Write **B** (British English) or **A** (American English) before each word. (Note that many American terms are now beginning to be used in Britain and vice-versa.) A few have been done for you.

B	lift	**A**	elevator
A	hood	**B**	bonnet (of a car)
___	boot	___	trunk (of a car)
___	apartment	___	flat
___	line	___	queue (when waiting for something)
___	pub	___	bar/tavern
___	lawyer/attorney	___	solicitor/barrister
___	tin	___	can (of food)
___	check	___	tick (mark with a ✓ symbol)
___	diversion	___	detour (on a road)

_____ nappy	_____ diaper
_____ autumn	_____ fall
_____ paraffin	_____ kerosene
_____ liquor store	_____ off-license
_____ potato chips	_____ crisps
_____ first floor	_____ ground floor
_____ pavement	_____ sidewalk
_____ drawing pin	_____ thumbtack
_____ checkers	_____ draughts (game)
_____ trash	_____ rubbish
_____ lorry	_____ truck
_____ waistcoat	_____ vest
_____ nought	_____ zero
_____ petrol	_____ gasoline
_____ freeway	_____ motorway
_____ chemist	_____ druggist
_____ subway	_____ underground (train)

Classroom Activity: 7.2

Comparing Different Kinds of English

The four boxes contain four different kinds of English. Compare them and decide:

1. What is similar between the forms of English in the boxes?

2. What is different?

3. Does any box contain English that is more "correct" than the others?

A. In Shakespeare's play *Henry VI*, a sergeant instructs the night guards to stay alert:

Sergeant:
Sirs, take your places and be vigilant.
If any noise or soldier you perceive
Near to the walls, by some apparent sign
Let us have knowledge at the court of guard.

Guard:
Sergeant, you shall.
Thus are poor servitors,
When others sleep upon their quiet beds,
Constrain'd to watch in darkness, rain, and cold.

Source: From *The Riverside Shakespeare* (p. 604), 1974, Boston: Houghton Mifflin.

B. At a British post office, a customer is buying a stamp:

Customer: Can I have a second class stamp please?
Clerk: You can … there we are.
Customer: Thank you.
Clerk: [giving just one penny change] And one penny thank you.
Customer: [making a joke] That's for me to spend is it?
Clerk: That's right.
Customer: I bought a new book of ten first class when I was in town
                today and I've left them at home in me shopping bag.
Clerk: Have you?
Customer: And I've got one left.
Clerk: Oh dear. [laughs]
Customer   Bye.
Clerk: Bye.

Source: From *Exploring Spoken English* (p. 92), by R. Carter and
M. McCarthy, 1997, Cambridge: Cambridge University Press.

C. A 16-year-old female describes how she and her
friends were caught skipping school. She speaks
a non-standard Australian dialect called Inner
Sydney English:

We got picked up for jigging school. We was walking down on the wrong
side of the road and the ranger come up an says, 'Why aren't you kids at
school?' and we says, 'Oh, we've moved,' you know, 'and we're allowed to
come down here for the day'. There was five of us there. There was Penny
an Stephen. They was there. An he took us down the ranger's station an
they just sat there, an then he called the coppers. An they knew who we
were.

Source: From "Variation in Subject-Verb Agreement in Inner Sydney
English" (p. 292), by E. Eisikovits, in J. Cheshire (Ed.), *English around the
World*, 1991, Cambridge: Cambridge University Press.

D. A Dutch airport planner gives an academic report about the noise situation at Amersterdam Schipol Airport:

Since 1998, Schipol has been a fully noise-coordinated airport. It has a total noise volume budget, which is also the maximum noise capacity for the airport. The total number of yearly slots has to fit within this budget, so the only way to grow is to make less noise per aircraft movement. There is also a network of [noise] measuring points within built-up areas, each with its own maximum noise limit… National law enforces the total noise impact of the airport. The airport is responsible for operating within the total noise budget. The air traffic control (ATC) for the operations (routes) and the airlines can be penalized if the airlines (without ATC permission) do not follow prescribed routes.

Source: From "Environmental and Economic Factors in Airport Capacity" (p. 219), by J. Krul, in P. Upham, J. Maughan, D. Raper, and C. Thomas (Eds.), *Towards Sustainable Aviation*, 2003, London: Earthscan Publications.

8

ENGLISH IN THE FUTURE

Where Is English Going?

- Will English become more uniform, or will it fragment into a large number of mutually unintelligible varieties?
- Will English maintain, increase, or lose its global status?
- What will English look like in the future?

Will English Become More Uniform, or Will It Fragment in the Future?

As discussed in Chapter 7, a feature of English in the last 200 or so years has been the birth of a number of national varieties. We have stressed, however, that the various varieties are relatively similar to each other and are for the most part mutually intelligible, with the grammar of English being virtually the same around the world. (This does not apply to pidgins and creoles based on English, which may not be mutually intelligible.) The varieties differ in a relatively small amount of vocabulary, which usually serves to make a variety interesting rather than particularly difficult to understand. The main difference between varieties is usually in the pronunciation, which can make comprehension difficult, but this has little to do with the underlying structure of the language itself. English started its international expansion only a few centuries ago and that has not been enough time for major varietal differences to develop. Also, English-speaking countries tend to be highly literate. This, combined with the advent of mass communications, has exposed most speakers to the standard forms of English, which has tended to inhibit major variation. Therefore, when we speak of the differences in national varieties, it is important to remember just how similar all the forms of English are.

So English is relatively homogeneous around the world at present, but will this situation last? In the short term, the answer is probably yes. Language change takes time, and we are unlikely to see big changes in the near future. But beyond this, language change is very difficult to predict. It depends on the factors that support or inhibit language diversification. A key to these factors is understanding the purposes for which a language is used. According to David Graddol, English has two main functions in the world: international communication and as a means to forge cultural identities.[1] The first function serves to push English toward greater uniformity, with the ideal, being a "standard international variety" of English that all people around the world could speak, thus making international communication unproblematic. However, the second function leads to an increasing number of local or regional varieties, each of which is identified with a local culture. In this way, the people of a locality can possess their own version of English, thus maintaining their cultural identity while reaping the benefits of using a language well-known internationally.

Given the prominent position of English in the world today, it may be tempting to assume that the "international communication" function will win out and that English will eventually coalesce into a single variety that would effectively be World Standard English. This may well happen, given English's very strong position at present, but it is not a foregone conclusion. There are a number of factors that may cause a World Standard English not to develop. First, the priority of printing (which leads to standardization) is weakening, with more electronic forms of information available online all the time. The new electronic technology often spawns forms of English that are condensed and are different from the standard written language in various ways. For example, e-mail is currently one of the most common forms of electronic information transfer, and it is often written in a stream of consciousness fashion and sent without being spell-checked or revised. In this way, it often resembles spoken discourse more than conventional written discourse. This is not surprising, because the original reasons for e-mail were its speed and convenience, and the need to revise carefully would detract from these advantages.

Another recent phenomenon is text messaging on mobile phones. Because the phones do not have a full keyboard, keying in text messages via the number keyboard is somewhat awkward. As a result, users use abbreviations and symbols to minimize the number of keystrokes required. Also, some phone companies limit text messages to a certain number of characters (160 for one company in the Nottingham, U.K. area, including spaces), which encourages the use of abbreviations, contractions, and various other short forms. Examples of these include:[2]

Abbreviations		Emoticons	
2d4	to die for	:-)	I'm happy
b4	before	%-)	staring at a screen too long
f ?	friends?	:'-(	been crying
gdm8	g'day mate	:-@	gonna scream
hf	have fun	:-X	my lips are sealed
musm	miss you so much	<:|	dunce
t+	think positive	$-)	greedy
u r	you are	:-|:-|	deja vu

The following text dialogue between two University of Nottingham undergraduate students contains a number of short forms. The "full English" translations are given underneath the text versions.

Student A: Hey hon, went 2 C band last nite wit Matt. Was gr8. Went 4 drink after @ Crown. Got messy. V. hungover. U? x

Student B: Had a good 1 wit Ben. Cooked me meal, Chick + pasta, notin' changes! U in 4 dnr?

Student A: Yep, lectures til 5. CU then. x

Student A: Hey honey, I went to see a band last night with Matt. It was great. We went for drinks after at the Crown pub. I got very drunk. I am very hungover. How about you? kiss

Student B: I had a good one (evening) with Ben. He cooked me a meal, chicken and pasta. Nothing changes! Are you coming for dinner?

Student A: Yes, I have lectures until 5 PM. See you then. kiss

E-mailing and text messaging and the shortcuts they use have raised many questions relating to the spelling and presentation of English. Because speed is important in both, normal conventions of capitalization and spelling are often ignored, and abbreviation is extensive. Will these developments affect the writing of English generally? So far, the effects on orthography seem to be confined mainly to the matter of capital letters. They are not given high priority, and people who would never normally dream of writing their own name without initial capital letters find themselves doing so in electronic addresses (e.g., *richard.marsden@nottingham.ac.uk*). Use of small letters instead of capitals in the text of e-mails is increasingly common, and teachers have noticed the habit creeping into submitted essays too. It is also becoming more common in other areas as well, such as advertising.

Thus, electronic forms of communication are generating new written forms of English and often blurring the distinction between the written and the spoken language. This diversification may be more acceptable to societies now than before, as there appears to be a general movement away from conformity and toward a greater tolerance of diversity. Whereas in former times there might have been an outcry against incorrect written English, nowadays people seem increasingly comfortable with the idea that different types of English might be suitable for different purposes and media. These trends may exert pressure toward more diversification of English rather than standardization.

A second factor potentially acting against the establishment of a World Standard English is the changing nature of broadcasting.[3] Initially, the development of satellite broadcasting had a unifying influence on English, as large numbers of people in many countries around the world were exposed to standard varieties (e.g., through BBC Broadcasting). But the people who watched these programs were mainly the more educated and affluent viewers and formed only a small percentage of the potential audience. Because of this, there is now a trend toward international broadcasters "localizing" their programming to reach a wider audience in each locale. This involves tailoring the programming to the local context, with more locally originated material, using local talent, broadcast in the local language. Examples of this include the news network CNN launching a Spanish version *CNNenEspañol*. Thus, the formerly unifying nature of satellite broadcasting may instead turn into a force for diversification.

A third factor is the nature of English language teaching (ELT). Previously, the existence of the ELT community has generally led to conformity, as most of the internationally available, commercially produced materials have used a small number of varieties, most notably American, British, and Australian English. These materials have been used around the world, leading to a similar underlying English being taught. The existing commercial ELT producers are unlikely to go away, but other producers will probably join them. As regional

Englishes develop, and perhaps become lingua francas for regional economic trade zones, countries in these zones may begin to publish aggressively and promote their own materials. It is not difficult to foresee this happening in China, where there is a massive internal market, and a number of Chinese publishers are scrambling to fill the need. These publishers may attempt to market their materials in the wider Asian region, especially as China inevitably becomes economically more dominant. We can already see similar things happening in other countries. Malaysia is working to become a provider, rather than recipient, of English language education, exporting English materials to other countries in the region and setting up universities to attract students from around the Southern Hemisphere.[4] The overall effect may be that materials in a number of English varieties will vie for ELT business, thus moving away from the more-or-less homogeneous standardized ELT materials in use at present.

In sum, the prominent position of English in the world today suggests that English may well become more unified in the future. However, there are also several factors working against this. Graddol suggests that the most likely scenario for English in the future is that a number of English varieties will continue to compete for usage in the world.[5]

Will English Continue to Be a Prominent World Language?

English is clearly the most influential language in the world today, but will it continue to hold that position in the future? Unless there is a cataclysmic event, such as a war, as a result of which a non-English-speaking country becomes dominant in the world, the answer is probably yes.[6] As the statistics in Chapter 1 show, English simply has too big a head start to be under threat from another language in the near future.

If there is any threat, it may come from technology.[7] In the popular *Star Trek* series, the characters use a universal translator to speak with other species. The components for such a translator already exist—speech recognition software, translation software, and speech synthesis software—but all are still in the developmental stage. Although the translation software can handle straightforward text, it is still incapable of handling the nuances of language or idiomatic speech. To illustrate this, we ran this paragraph through translation software into German and then back again into English.

The first free Internet translation (English→German→English, using *http://world.altavista.com*) came out like this:

> If there is any threat, she can come from the technology. In the popular Sterntrek
> row the letters use a universal translator, in order to speak with other sort.

The components for such translators already exist?speech an acknowledgment software, translation software and speech synthesis software?but everything still are in the development stage. Although the translation software can touch direct text, it is still unable of the language or the idiomatischen speech from the treatment of the nuances. In order to show this, we let this point run by translation software in German and then back again in English.

The second free Internet translation (using *www.freetranslation.com*) was somewhat better:

If there is any threat, it can come of technology. In the popular Sterntrekserie, the characters use an universal translator to speak with other species. The components for such a translator exist are already language recognition software, translation software, and language syntheses software however everyone quiet in the development phase. Although the translation software can treat simple text, it is yet incapable of handling the shades of language or idiomatic language. In order to show this, we ran this paragraph through translation software in German, and then again back in English.

As can be seen from these two examples, there are still far too many mistranslations for the translation software to be considered reliable. The speech recognition software is even further from being ready for universal use, as all current versions need to be trained to an individual's voice, and even then they struggle to maintain 95 percent accuracy (five errors for every hundred words). That may seem quite good, but it would mean six errors in the present paragraph of 122 words. To be part of a usable translator in the real world, the software would have to cope reliably with a wide range of speakers and accents, and at the moment it is still hopelessly inadequate for use with unknown speakers.

So it seems that the potential technological threat to English from automatic translation is still some way off. However, given the startling speed at which technology has advanced in the last 50 years, it will surely come. But by the time it is widely available, it may well be obsolete, as everyone who needs it might already speak an international lingua franca.

Other threats that might erode English's position of prominence have to do with politics and national identity. In former colonies, English's association with colonialism might lead to those countries rejecting English.[8] This distasteful association can indeed be strong, but the age of colonialism is fading into evermore distant history while the advantages of having English as a resource are becoming ever clearer. Thus, it is difficult to see any former colonized countries rejecting English for this reason at this point. However, another kind of colonization may have an influence. English is closely tied to the export of Western, largely American, ideals of life and consumerism, and these ideals are becoming increasingly challenged around the world. If non-Anglophone countries decide that they do not in fact want "the American Dream," they may also decide to make strong efforts to avoid the vehicle of that dream, English, as well. It is certainly possible to reject ideology without rejecting the related language, but some backlash of this sort is not beyond the realms of possibility.

Graddol identifies a number of other factors that have the potential to affect the future of English. Among these are demographics, urbanization, education, and economic changes. Starting with demographics, it is estimated that by the year 2050, Chinese will have 1,384 million native speakers, Hindi/Urdu 556 million, and English 508 million.[9] Thus, English will slip from being the second most-spoken mother tongue to the third. But this is unlikely to disadvantage English greatly, as its strength has largely come from the number of people who speak it as a second language. The increase in the middle class in Asia and Latin America bodes well for English, as professional groups are the most likely to make the greatest use of English. There is also a trend toward urbanization, the moving from rural areas to cities. Now about half of the world's population live in cities (in 2000 the figures were 40 percent in less-developed regions but 76 percent in more-developed regions).[10] Cities are centers for the flow of information and ideas and so are usually more open to English as a global language than rural areas. But cities are also places where languages mix and change, and this may have an effect on generating hybrid forms of English and perhaps other rival lingua francas.

English is likely to maintain a strong presence in the world if large numbers of people continue to learn it.[11] In the early 1990s, more than 60 percent of all school students in Europe studied English, and subsequent changes in national curricula that have highlighted the importance of modern languages may well have increased this figure. The situation is similar in many other countries as well. For example, in the Russian Federation, 60 percent of secondary school students take English. At the university level, English is also getting stronger globally, with some subjects, such as the sciences, taught in the language itself, because the most up-to-date books and articles in many disciplines are published in English. So long as this strong educational push remains, English should continue to prosper globally.

Economically, English is the major language of international trade, largely through the activities of the three largest trading blocks: North America, the European Union, and Japan. It will probably remain the most influential trading lingua franca in the foreseeable future. However, with the large projected increases in Asia's and Latin America's population and economic clout, it is possible that new important regional trading blocks will arise in these and other areas, and regional lingua francas may develop out of them. For example, Mercosur (a common market consisting of Argentina, Brazil, Paraguay, and Uruguay) uses Spanish and Portuguese. A future Asian trading block may well use Mandarin as a common language. As it is always good business to speak the consumer's language when you are trying to sell them something, it may become important to learn these regional lingua francas to do business in the new trading blocks. This may lead to alternative lingua francas joining English on the world stage.[12]

The world is also moving toward a situation where the proportion of the economy taken up by traditional heavy industries that produce tangible goods (like cars and televisions) is being eroded by the "light" service sector, which primarily deals in information transfer (e.g., education, telemarketing). This trend has been so strong that in 1995 nearly 75 percent of the U.S. labor force was employed in service industries. In these, companies are often able to move work across international borders. For example, in England and the United States, many customer service telephone operations are being moved to India, where there is a large pool of qualified workers willing to work for much lower wages than in England or the United States. This is a global phenomenon, where cheaper labor is exploited by businesses shifting operations from country to country. Many of these operations will be conducted in English, and countries that have skilled English speakers will have an advantage in this newly internationalized labor market. To compete, countries will be likely to promote education in English, and so this factor is bullish for the language.[13]

In sum, instead of English becoming the sole world language, there may end up being several that will have different spheres of influence. English will probably continue to be the most influential worldwide, but other languages may grow in stature to serve as lingua francas in various regions, for example, Spanish in South and Central America and perhaps Mandarin in Asia. If we take into account the likely economic and demographic developments in the next few decades, we may end up with English, Chinese, Hindi/Urdu, Spanish, and Arabic as the world's big languages by the year 2050.[14] So English is probably not threatened as a world language, but it may share that honor with several others in the future.[15]

What Will English Look Like in the Future?

We have discussed how English has been changing from the time it first came to England as a group of Germanic dialects to the present day, where new varieties of English are still appearing. From this, one fact has become clear—that living languages (including English) change. Although grammar books and dictionaries may give the impression that English is fixed and that there is a "correct" way of using it, if we look at the real world, we find a language of great flexibility that continues to vary and to evolve. One reason for this is that the human speech apparatus is slightly different from person to person and, therefore, no two people produce sounds that are precisely the same; so it is no wonder that in the course of hundreds of years the sounds of English have changed. In vocabulary, fashion plays its part. Anyone who is familiar with slang is aware of how quickly some words become "unstylish" and new ones replace them.

Grammar has also developed to suit the convenience of English speakers. The numerous noun, verb, and adjective inflections of Old English became less and less important as other means, such as word order, were used to establish meaning in a sentence. Eventually, the only inflectional markers left were those of the plural and possessive for nouns; the comparative and superlative for adjectives; and, for verbs, the past tense, the present and past participles, and the third-person singular of the present tense. This latter inflection is theoretically as redundant as the many others that were dropped and adds nothing to the meaning of a discourse, but it unaccountably persisted and is enshrined in the rules of grammar. In some English dialects, however, it has been lost. These dialects have adopted other grammatical simplifications as well, such as the reduction of all forms of the verb *to be* to *is*. So English grammar is still changing too, albeit at a slow rate. It is important to also remember that grammar always tends to be more flexible in practice than it is in textbooks.

As long as people speak a language, it is "living" and is as subject to change as its speakers are. Wherever there is language variation, there is the possibility of change. If a particular language feature is used one way by one person and another way by another, then the door is open for one of those ways to become more common and the other less common. Over time this leads to permanent change—but only "permanent" until it is subject to more variation and change in the future. David Crystal gives a good description of the constant flux of language, emphasising that this is not something to be evaluated as good or bad, but rather as a natural phenomenon:

> As you read this article, language is changing around you in thousands of tiny different ways. Some sounds are slowly shifting; some words are changing their senses; some grammatical constructions are being used with greater or less frequency; new styles and varieties are constantly being formed and shaped. And everything is happening at different speeds and moving in different directions. The language is in a constant state of multidimensional flux. There

is no predictable direction for the changes that are taking place. They are just that: changes. Not changes for the better; nor changes for the worse; just changes, sometimes going one way, sometimes another.[16]

English has changed from its beginnings until the present in ways that would astonish the speakers of 1,500 years ago, and there is no reason to doubt that it will continue to evolve. Future changes may well be less dramatic than in the past, but there is also the possibility that a cataclysmic event or series of events could cause changes just as profound. Exactly what English will look (and sound) like in the future is anybody's guess. One author, Russell Hoban, has speculated about this and has written a science-fiction story in what he imagines the English of the distant future might be like. One can only wonder whether he predicted correctly, or whether English will be altered in a different direction by factors as yet unforeseeable.

That wer when I clappt my han over his mouf it wer giving me the creaps how he wer going on. He wer stomping in the mud he wer dantsing and shouting and his face all wite with no eyes in the litening flashes. He begun to groan then like some terbel thing wer taking him and got inside him. He startit to fall and I easit him down I knowit he wer having a fit I seen that kynd of thing befor. I stuck the clof part of the hump back figger be twean his teef so he wunt bite his tung. I wer on my knees in the mud and holding him wylst he twissit and groant and that hook nose head all black and smyling nodding in the litening flashes. The dogs all gethert roun and them close to him grovvelt with ther ears laid back.[17]

FURTHER READING

The most-quoted source on the possible future directions of English.

- Graddol, D. (1997). *The future of English.* London: The British Council.

Chapter 5 gives Crystal's evaluation of the possible futures of English.

- Crystal, D. (2003). *English as a global language.* Cambridge: Cambridge University Press.

This volume speculates on the status of language in the future by considering the connections between it and culture and society.

- Tonkin, H., & Reagan, T. (Eds.) (2003). *Language in the 21st century.* Amsterdam: John Benjamins.

ENDNOTES

Chapter 1

1. Estimates are by Otto Jespersen and are taken from Pennycook, A. (2001). English in the world/The world in English. In A. Burns & C. Coffin, (Eds.), *Analyzing English in a global context* (p. 78). London: The Open University.

2. Insert to the *National Geographic* magazine. (1999). Washington, DC: National Geographic Society.

3. Crystal, D. (2003). *English as a global language*. Cambridge: Cambridge University Press, p. 90.

4. Graddol, D. (1997). *The future of English*. London: The British Council, p. 46.

5. Crystal, (2003). *English as a global language*, p. 105.

6. Graddol, (1997). *The future of English*, p. 37.

7. Wilkinson, J. (1995). *Introducing Standard English*. London: Penguin, p. 48.

8. Based on a tally of the newspapers listed on www.theworldpress.com taken on February 17, 2004.

9. Graddol, *The future of English*, p. 9.

10. Crystal, *English as a global language*, p. 93.

11. Graddol, *The future of English*, p. 9.

12. Ibid., p. 61.

13. Crystal, *English as a global language*, pp. 119–120. And Crystal, D. (2001). *Language and the Internet*. Cambridge: Cambridge University Press, pp. 216–218.

14. Crystal, *English as a global language*, p. 119.

15. *Is English taking over?* (2003). *Newsweek* [Issues Today Map].

16. Crystal, *English as a global language*, p. 95.

17. Ibid., p. 87.

18. Wilkinson, *Introducing Standard English*, p. 48.

19. Crystal, *English as a global language*, pp. 99–100.

20. Ibid.

21. *TOEFL test and score data summary, 2002–2003 test year data*. Retrieved from http://www.ets.org/

22. http://www.cambridgeesol.org/research/grades_current.htm

23. Crystal, *English as a global language*, p. 3.

24. Ibid., p. 5.

25. Schmitt, N. (2000). *Vocabulary in language teaching.* Cambridge: Cambridge University Press, p. 2.

26. Claiborne, R. (1983). *Our marvelous native tongue.* New York: Times Books, pp. 9–11.

27. Feigenbaum, L. H. (1958). For a bigger better alphabet. *High Points, 40,* 34–36.

Chapter 2

1. Voices of the world. (August 1999). *National Geographic* insert *196,* no. 2. Washington, DC: National Geographic Society.

2. Savage-Rumbaugh, S., & Lewin, R. (1994). *Kanzi: The ape at the brink of the human mind.* New York: John Wiley & Sons.

3. Tierney, J., Wright, L., & Springen, K. (1988, January 11). The search for Adam and Eve. *Newsweek,* pp. 39–40.

4. Shevoroshkin, V. (1990, May/June). The mother tongue. *The Sciences,* pp. 20–27.

5. Ross, P. E. (1991, April). Hard words. *Scientific American,* p. 78.

6. Shevoroshkin, The mother tongue, pp. 20–27.

7. Fortson, B. W. (2004). *Indo-European language and culture : An introduction.* Malden, MA: Blackwell, Chapter 2. Note that datings for Indo-European migration are impossible to set with any real precision; this figure should be seen as an approximation.

8. Shevoroshkin, The mother tongue, p. 20.

9. The histories of England and English in this and later sections have been based on a number of sources, including those in the Further Reading section. Other books consulted include:

Claiborne, R. (1983). *Our marvelous native tongue.* New York: Times Books.

Roberts, P. (1985). A brief history of English. In V. P. Clark, P. A. Eschholz, & A. F. Rosa (Eds.), *Language* (pp. 600–611). New York: St. Martin's Press.

10. Horobin, S., & Smith, J. (2002). *An introduction to Middle English.* Edinburgh: Edinburgh University Press, p. 33.

11. Hughes, G. (2000). *A history of English words.* New York: Oxford University Press, p. 152.

Chapter 3

1. Schmitt, N., & Celce-Murcia, M. (2002). An overview of applied linguistics. In N. Schmitt (Ed.), *An introduction to applied linguistics.* London: Arnold, p. 11.

2. DeCarrico, J., & Larsen-Freeman, D. (2002). Grammar. In N. Schmitt (Ed.), *An introduction to applied linguistics.* London: Arnold, pp. 19–34.

3. DeCarrico & Larsen-Freeman, Grammar, p. 24.

4. The pie chart appeared previously in Celce-Murcia, M., & Larsen-Freeman, D. (1998). *The grammar book: An ESL/EFL teacher's course* (2nd ed.). Boston: Heinle & Heinle.

5. Biber, D., Johansson, S., Leech, G., Conrad, S., & Finegan, E. (1999). *Longman grammar of spoken and written English*. Harlow: Longman, pp. 328–340.

6. Ibid., pp. 612–616.

7. Marsden, R. (2004). *The Cambridge Old English reader*. Cambridge: Cambridge University Press, pp. 386–388.

8. Pyles, T., & Algeo, J. (1993). *The origins and development of the English language*. Fort Worth, TX: Harcourt Brace Jovanovich, pp. 161, 202; Barber, C. (1993). *The English language*. Cambridge: Cambridge University Press, p. 165.

9. Pyles & Algeo, *The origins and development of the English language*, p. 191.

Milroy, J., & Milroy, L. (1991). *Authority in language: Investigating language prescription and standardization*. London: Routledge, p. 39.

10. Sinclair, J. M. (1972). *A course in spoken English: Grammar*. Oxford: Oxford University Press, Chapter 3.

11. Biber et al., *Longman grammar of spoken and written English*, pp. 105–106.

12. Ibid., p. 625.

13. Celce-Murcia, M., & Larsen-Freeman, D. (1983). *The grammar book: An ESL/EFL teacher's course*. Cambridge, MA: Newbury House, Chapter 4.

14. Gowers, E. (1951). *ABC of plain words*. London: Her Majesty's Stationery Office, p. 129.

15. Biber et al., *Longman grammar of spoken and written English*, p. 493.

16. Ibid., pp. 167–168.

17. Wilkinson, J. (1995). *Introducing Standard English*. London: Penguin, p. 56.

18. Biber et al., *Longman grammar of spoken and written English*, pp. 18–19.

19. Ibid., p. 397.

20. Carter, R., & McCarthy, M. (2005). *Cambridge grammar of spoken and written English*. Cambridge: Cambridge University Press.

Chapter 4

1. Goulden, R., Nation, P., & Read, J. (1990). How large can a receptive vocabulary be? *Applied Linguistics*, *11*(4), 341–363.

2. Adolphs, A., & Schmitt, N. (2002). Lexical coverage of spoken discourse. *Applied Linguistics*, *24* (4), 425–438.

3. Hazenberg, S., & Hulstijn, J. H. (1996). Defining a minimal receptive second-language vocabulary for non-native university students: An empirical investigation. *Applied Linguistics*, *17*(2), 145–163.

4. Crystal, D. (1988). *The English language*. London: Penguin, p. 156.

5. Bird, N. (1987). Words, lemmas, and frequency lists: Old problems and new challenges (Parts 1 & 2). *Al-manakh, 6*, 42–50, as cited in Nation, P. (2001). *Learning vocabulary in another language*. Cambridge: Cambridge University Press, p. 265.

6. Pyles, T., & Algeo, J. (1993). *The origins and development of the English language*. Fort Worth, TX: Harcourt Brace Jovanovich, p. 311.

7. Barber, C. (1993). *The English language*. Cambridge: Cambridge University Press, pp. 145–150.

8. Baugh, A. C., & Cable, T. (1993). *A history of the English language*. London: Routledge, p. 222.

9. Hughes, G. (2000). *A history of English words*. Malden, MA: Blackwell, pp. 14–15.

10. Baugh & Cable, *A history of the English language*, p. 297.

11. Cannon, G. (1987). *Historical change and English word-formation: Recent vocabulary*. New York: Lang, as cited in Pyles & Algeo, *The origins and development of the English language*, p. 310.

12. Adapted from Carter, R., Goddard, A., Reah, D., Sanger, K., & Bowring, M. (1997). *Working with texts*. London: Routledge, p. 113.

13. Coxhead, A. (2000). A new academic word list. *Applied Linguistics, 34*(2), 213–238.

14. Baugh & Cable, *A history of the English language*, p. 63.

15. Bryson, B. (1990). *Mother tongue*. New York: Avon Books, p. 81.

16. Pyles & Algeo, *The origins and development of the English language*, pp. 266–269.

17. Crystal, D. (1995). *The Cambridge encyclopedia of the English language*. Cambridge: Cambridge University Press, p. 128.

18. Bird, Words, lemmas, and frequency lists, pp. 42–50 and Bird, N. (1990). *A first handbook of the roots of English*. Hong Kong: Lapine Education and Languages Services Ltd., as cited in Nation, *Learning vocabulary in another language*, p. 265.

19. Nagy, W. E., & Anderson, R. C. (1984). How many words are there in printed school English? *Reading Research Quarterly, 19*, 304–330.

20. Stauffer, R. G. (1942). A study of prefixes in the Thorndike list to establish a list of prefixes that should be taught in the elementary school. *Journal of Educational Research, 35*(6), 453–458, as cited in Nation, (1990). *Teaching and learning vocabulary*. New York: Newbury House, p. 169.

21. White, T. G., Power, M. A., & White, S. (1989). Morphological analysis: Implications for teaching and understanding vocabulary growth. *Reading Research Quarterly, 24*, 283–304.

22. Wilton, David. (2004). *Word myths: Debunking linguistic urban legends*. New York: Oxford University Press, pp. 29–33.

23. Nation, *Learning vocabulary in another language*, p. 268.

24. Ibid., p. 274.

25. Nation, *Teaching and learning vocabulary*, pp. 168–174.

26. Nation, P. (Ed.). (1994). *New ways in teaching vocabulary*. Alexandria, VA: TESOL.

27. Laufer, B., & Bensoussan, M. (1982). Meaning is in the eye of the beholder. *English Teaching Forum, 20*(2), 10–14; Bensoussan, M., & Laufer, B. (1984). Lexical guessing in context in EFL reading comprehension. *Journal of Research in Reading, 7*, 15–32.

28. Haynes, M. (1993). Patterns and perils of guessing in second language reading. In T. Huckin, M. Haynes, & J. Coady (Eds.), *Second language reading and vocabulary learning* (pp. 46–64). Norwood, NJ: Ablex.

29. Schmitt, N., Schmitt, D., & Clapham, C. (2001). Developing and exploring the behavior of two new versions of the Vocabulary Levels Test. *Language Testing, 18*(1), 55–88.

30. Nation, *Teaching and learning vocabulary*, pp. 261–264.

31. Read, J. (2000). *Assessing vocabulary*. Cambridge: Cambridge University Press, pp. 118–126.

32. Schmitt, N. (2000). *Vocabulary in language teaching*. Cambridge: Cambridge University Press, pp. 192–200.

Chapter 5

1. Barber, C. (1993). *The English language: A historical introduction*. Cambridge: Cambridge University Press, p. 43; Pyles, T., & Algeo, J. (1993). *The origins and development of the English language*. Fort Worth, TX: Harcourt Brace Jovanovich, pp. 35–39.

2. Ibid., p. 36. (Pyles)

3. Ibid.

4. Ibid.

5. Barber, *The English language*, pp. 41–42.

6. Crystal, D. (1995). *The Cambridge encyclopedia of the English language*. Cambridge: Cambridge University Press, p. 327.

7. Jenkins, J. (2003). *World Englishes*. London: Routledge, p. 114.

8. Pyles & Algeo, *The origins and development of the English language*, pp. 57–59, 169–170; Vallins, G. H. (1965). *Spelling* (Rev. ed.). London: Deutsch, pp. 22–25.

9. For more examples, see Pyles & Algeo, *The origins and development of the English language*, pp. 57–59, 169–170.

10. Some examples are taken from Pyles & Algeo, *The origins and development of the English language*, pp. 297–299.

11. Examples from Barber, *The English language: A historical introduction*, p. 211.

12. Crystal, *The Cambridge encyclopedia of the English language*, p. 365.

13. As cited in Knowles, G. (1997). *A cultural history of the English language*. London: Arnold, p. 36.

14. Ibid., p. 35.

15. Ibid., p. 128.

16. Ibid., pp. 148–150.

McArthur, T. (Ed). (1992). *The Oxford companion to the English language*. Oxford: Oxford University Press, pp. 850–852.

Crystal, *The Cambridge encyclopedia of the English language*, p. 365.

17. Mugglestone, L. (1995). *"Talking proper": The rise of accent as social symbol*. Oxford: Clarendon Press, pp. 107–108.

18. Ibid., pp. 113–115.

19. Ibid., pp. 107–108.

Chapter 6

1. Senner, W. M. (1989). Theories and myths on the origins of writing: A historical overview. In W. M. Senner (Ed.), *The origins of writing*. Lincoln: University of Nebraska Press, p. 23.

2. Cross, F. M. (1989). The invention and development of the alphabet. In W. M. Senner (Ed.), *The origins of writing*. Lincoln: University of Nebraska Press.

3. Based on McArthur, T. (Ed). (1992). *The Oxford companion to the English language*. Oxford: Oxford University Press, pp. 188–189.

4. Blake, N. (1996). *A history of English*. London: Macmillan, pp. 172–180.

5. Vallins, G. H. (1965). *Spelling* (Rev. ed., with a chapter on American spelling by Prof. J. W. Clark). London: Deutsch, pp. 125–132.

6. Ibid., pp. 22–25.

7. Baugh, A. C., & Cable, T. (1993). *A history of the English language*. London: Routledge, pp. 357–365.

8. McArthur, *The Oxford companion to the English language*, p. 44.

Chapter 7

1. Nihalani, P., Tongue, R. K., & Hosali, P. (1979). *Indian and British English*. Delhi: Oxford University Press, pp. 103, 160.

2. Trudgill, P., & Chambers, J. K. (1991). Introduction: English dialect grammar. In J. K. Chambers & P. Trudgill (Eds.), *Dialects of English*. London: Longman, p. 2.

3. This approach is discussed in more detail in Biber, D., Johansson, S., Leech, G., Conrad, S., & Finegan, E. (1999). *Longman grammar of spoken and written English*. Harlow: Longman, pp. 18ff.

4. Baugh, A. C., & Cable, T. (1993). *A history of the English language*. London: Routledge, pp. 187–192.

5. Kachru, B. B. (1985). Standards, codification, and sociolinguistic realism: The English language in the outer circle. In R. Quirk & H. G. Widdowson (Eds.), *English in the world*. Cambridge: Cambridge University Press, pp. 11–30.

   Kachru, B. B. (1992). Teaching world Englishes. In B. B. Kachru (Ed.), *The other tongue: English across cultures* (2nd ed., pp. 355–365). Urbana: University of Illinois Press.

6. Graddol, D. (1997). *The future of English*. London: The British Council, p. 10.

7. Crystal, D. (1998). *English as a global language*. New York: Cambridge University Press, p. 130.

8. Benson, M., Benson, E., & Ilson, B. (1986). *Lexicographic description of English*. Amsterdam: John Benjamins.

9. Although this passage is not strictly authentic because it was not recorded from actual speech, it was felt to be a better illustration of the dialect because a greater variety of features could be illustrated in a short space. The source is: Llamas, C., & Stockwell, P. (2002). Sociolinguistics. In N. Schmitt (Ed.), *An introduction to applied linguistics* (pp. 167–169, 296–297). London: Arnold.

10. Crystal, D. (1995). *The Cambridge encyclopedia of the English language*. Cambridge: Cambridge University Press, pp. 94, 325.

11. The discussion on this section is indebted to Celce-Murcia, M., Brinton, D. M., & Goodwin, J. M. (1996). *Teaching pronunciation*. Cambridge: Cambridge University Press, Appendix 1. It also drew from Collins, B., & Mees, I. M. (2003). *Practical phonetics and phonology*. London: Routledge, Section C.

12. Crystal, *The Cambridge encyclopedia of the English language*, p. 308.

13. McArthur, T. (Ed.). (1992). *The Oxford companion to the English language*. Oxford: Oxford University Press, p. 46.

14. Mindt, D., & Weber, C. (1989). Prepositions in American and British English. *World Englishes*, 8, 229–238.

15. Crystal, *The Cambridge encyclopedia of the English language*, p. 311.

16. McArthur, *The Oxford companion to the English language*, p. 44.

17. The description of Indian English in this section is mainly based on the following three texts, from which most of the examples are drawn:

Kachru, B. B. (1983). *The Indianization of English: The English language in India*. Delhi: Oxford University Press.

Crystal, *The Cambridge encyclopedia of the English language*, p. 360.

Trudgill, P., & Hannah, J. (2002). *International English*. London: Arnold.

18. Richards, J., Platt, J., & Weber, H. (1985). *Longman dictionary of applied linguistics*. Harlow: Longman, pp. 275, 283.

19. McArthur, *The Oxford companion to the English language*, pp. 506–507.

20. Ibid., pp. 1044–1045.

21. The texts and translations originally appeared in Sebba, M. (1997). *Contact languages*. London: Macmillan, pp. 20–21. We extracted them from Jenkins, J. (2003). *World Englishes*. London: Routledge, pp. 59–60.

22. Crystal, D. (2001). The future of Englishes. In A. Burns & C. Coffin (Eds.), *Analyzing English in a global context*. London: The Open University, p. 63.

Chapter 8

1. Graddol, D. (1997). *The future of English*. London: The British Council, p. 56.

2. *Text messaging made simple: Chat abbreviations and emoticons (printer friendly)*. (n.d.). Retrieved June 1, 2005, from http://www.see-search.com/wap/textmessaging.htm.

3. Graddol, *The future of English*, pp. 46–47.

4. Ibid., pp. 44–45.

5. Ibid., p. 56.

6. Bruthiaux, P. (2003). Contexts and trends for English as a global language. In H. Tonkin, & T. Reagan (Eds.), *Language in the 21st century*. Amsterdam: John Benjamins, pp. 9–22.

7. Crystal, D. (2003). *English as a global language*. New York: Cambridge University Press, p. 27.

8. Crystal, *English as a global language*, p. 124.

9. Graddol, *The future of English*, pp. 26–27.

10. Statistics from the Global Report on Human Settlements 2001. It is available on the Global Urban Observatory website at: http://www.unhabitat.org/habrdd/statannexes.htm.

11. Graddol, *The future of English*, pp. 44–45.

12. Ibid., pp. 28–29, 52.

13. Ibid,. pp. 34–35, 54.

14. Ibid., pp. 58–59.

15. Bruthiaux, Contexts and trends for English as a global language, pp. 9–22.

16. Crystal, D. (1999, June-July). Swimming with the tide in a sea of language change. *IATEFL Issues, 149,* 2–4.

17. Hoban, R. (1980). *Riddley Walker.* New York: Washington Square Press, p. 95.

Teacher's Notes and Answers to Classroom Exercises

1. Celce-Murcia, M., Brinton, D. M., & Goodwin, J. M. (1996). *Teaching pronunciation.* Cambridge: Cambridge University Press, p. 41.

Teacher's Notes and Answers to the Classroom Exercises

Classroom Activity 1.1: The Importance of English in Today's World (page 13)

1. True
2. False. At least half and perhaps more than two-thirds write in English.
3. True
4. True, based on mid-1990s data
5. False. English has approximately 322 million native speakers, but Chinese has about 885 million.
6. False. There are about 3,000 English newspapers in India.
7. True
8. True
9. True. One estimate is that more than 40 percent of the people using the Internet speak English.
10. False. As of 2005, neither of these countries has legally defined English as its official national language, although there is discussion about this in America.
11. True. Other official languages include French, Russian, Spanish, Chinese, and Arabic.

Comment: English is becoming increasingly important as the language of communication among peoples of different countries. This is happening in a wide spectrum of areas, including diplomacy, entertainment, business, and international transportation, where both aviation and marine traffic is directed in English.

Classroom Activity 1.2: How Does English Compare to Other Languages? (page 14)

1. bigger than average. English has one of the largest vocabularies of any known language.
2. fewer than average. English mainly uses word order and prepositions to indicate grammatical relationships, and so has far fewer inflections than languages like German.
3. more than average. Languages have on average between 25–30 sounds, so English is well above average with more than 40 sounds.
4. about average. English has many spelling irregularities compared to a language like Spanish, where spelling is very closely related to pronunciation. But English is still more transparent than a few other languages, like Scottish Gaelic, where there is a weaker correspondence between spelling and pronunciation.
5. about average. English does not have an official organization that watches over it and controls it, as French has with the *Académie Française*. However, there are numerous dictionaries and grammars available, as well as a huge number of books in print, that have the effect of "freezing" English to some extent. So English is somewhat less free to change than languages without a large written inventory.
6. native speakers: #2 Chinese has approximately 885 million native speakers; English has about 322 million.

   non-native speakers: #1 English is the most learned and used second language in the world today, with at least 400 million speakers.

Comment: In general, English is probably no better or worse than any other language in terms of learning difficulty. Every language has its own difficulties stemming from its particular grammar, spelling, and sound system. What English has that other languages cannot match is its very large and varied vocabulary. This is an advantage when expressing ideas in English but a disadvantage when trying to learn the language. In the end, what makes English special is the number of people who speak it, both as L1 and L2, and this is a result of historical factors, rather than any inherent quality of the language itself.

Classroom Activity 1.3: English Use around the World (page 15)

	Percentage of native English speakers	Percentage of second language speakers
Australia	79%	18%
Bahamas	87%	9%
Canada	63%	22%
Hong Kong	2%	31%
India	<1%	19%
Ireland	97%	3%
Malaysia	2%	31%
New Zealand	96%	4%
Philippines	<1%	48%
South Africa	8%	25%
United Kingdom	97%	3%
United States	77%	9%

(These figures are estimates adapted from Crystal, 2003, pp. 62–65.)

Comment: Not every English-speaking country has 100 percent native speakers. In fact, many, like the United States, have a significant segment of the population who speak English only as a second language or not at all. On the other hand, many countries in which English is not the primary language have large numbers of people who can use it, such as the Philippines. With global travel and communications becoming ever more widespread, the use of English as a second language is likely to continue to grow. Even now, there are probably more people who speak English as a second language than who have it as a mother tongue. Although this exercise may mainly entail guessing by the students, it can act as a springboard for discussion of these issues. The exercise can be simplified by inserting additional numbers so that there are fewer gaps.

Classroom Activity 2.1: The Development of English (page 40)

This activity is probably best used with more advanced students who are able to discuss the differences between the examples. It is designed to stimulate discussion and interest rather than to teach any particular point. There are numerous possible answers to the questions, so it is impossible to give a definitive answer key. However, the following summary lists some of the important attributes of each stage of English with illustrations from the four passages, where relevant. Clearly the observations below on the pronunciation of English cannot be deduced from the written texts.

Old English (c. 450–1100)

1. Old English uses the Latin alphabet, so most letters should be familiar. However, there are four supplementary letters: æ ("ash"), ð ("eth"), þ ("thorn"), and ƿ ("wynn"), the last two taken from the runic alphabet; *w* is substituted for *wynn* in the illustrative passage. Note that the "macron" (bar) used in the passage to show vowels that should be pronounced "long" is a modern convention and was not used by the Anglo-Saxons.

2. Old English has a more complex grammatical system than Modern English. It retains the Germanic system of inflections that involves four major noun **cases** (nominative, accusative, genitive, dative) and three **genders** (masculine, neuter, feminine). This results in variations, which are most clearly seen in the form of the word for "the"—*þām* in line 1 and *se* in line 2; nouns too may vary, as in *wife* and *wif*. The variations and inflections indicate a word's grammatical function in a sentence: *tō þām wife* is a dative phrase (the *woman*, a neuter word in Old English, is the indirect object); *wif* is nominative (the *woman* is the subject); *se wyrtweard* is nominative (the *gardener*, a masculine word, is the subject).

3. The syntax of Old English is often like that of Modern English, although verbs tend to come before their subjects (*cwæþ Iesus*), and objects often come before their verbs (*þū hine lǣdest*). However, the inflection system helps define the relationships between words, allowing for freer word order. The simple present tense often has a future sense (*ic hine nime*).

4. Old English consists almost exclusively of Germanic words, with many still being recognizable today (allowing for spelling changes). Some words without current equivalents may nevertheless be recognizable to students with some experience of Shakespearean English: *cwæþ* is equivalent to *quoth* (which survived into the Early Modern English period alongside *said*). Compounding is used a great deal in creating new words: *wyrt-weard* (*plant guardian*, i.e., gardener).

5. Concerning pronunciation, all letters are sounded, and most consonants and short vowels are pronounced as they are in Modern English. There is a close correlation between sound and spelling. Typical stress is on the initial main syllable of words, which tends to make the inflections at the ends of words less prominent.

Middle English (c. 1100–1500)

1. All the special Old English characters are lost, except þ, which survives, alongside new French-influenced *th*. There is a substitution of some forms, *qu* for *cw* and *wh* for *hw* (*hwi > why*), among others. There is much use of "yogh," ȝ, with a range of phonetic values, including /j/ (*seȝe, weȝ*). Y and *i* are more or less interchangeable (*hym, him*); *u* and *v* are not regularly distinguished (*vp*). There is also much variation in spellings, often reflecting dialectal differences.

2. Middle English sees a leveling off, and eventually loss, of most inflections, though semantically redundant *-e* persists on many nouns; the definite article is invariably *the* (though sometimes spelled *þe*). The pronoun system remains more or less as it was in Old English. For the possessive, *-es* dominates, and for the plural, *-s* or *-es*.

3. Subject-verb-object word order is now the rule, and use of the present participle widens (*wepynge, gessinge*). There is increased use of constructions with auxiliary verbs (*thou hast taken, I schal take him*).

4. The Norman Conquest sparks a great influx of French words (*sire, gardner*), and many Old English words are lost.

5. There is little detectable change in pronunciation since Old English until late in the period, but there is much dialectal variation, as is evident from Middle English spellings.

Early Modern English (c. 1500–1700)

1. Spelling is inconsistent until the end of the period (*him, hym; vnto, unto*). Redundant final *-e* persists in many words (*sayde*). There is much variety in the use of capital letters.

2. Inflections are now largely reduced to plural in *-es* or *-s* and possessive case in *-es*. "Intimate" *thou/thee* forms of the second-person pronoun singular are in use alongside *you*. In verbs, *-eth* still competes with *-s* in third-person singular, but before the end of the 17th century, *-s* is standard.

3. Subject-verb-object order is usual, but verbs before subjects are common, especially earlier in the period. Periphrastic tenses with *do* are available but not universally used (thus, *Why weepest thou?* and *whom dost thou seek?*). Subjunctive mood is much used (*he were, thou have*). Present participle constructions are more and more widely used.

4. The new learning of the Renaissance sparks a huge influx of new words from many languages, particularly Latin, but not all of them last. *Sepulcre* is an early Latin borrowing through French.

5. The Great Vowel Shift is completed by about 1650, bringing with it radical, but systematic, change to the value of long vowels.

Modern English (c. 1700–PRESENT DAY)

1. Spellings from Johnson's *Dictionary* (1755) have been preserved, with a few exceptions. But there are some differences between British and American spellings.

2. The only inflections in the standard language are plural *(e)s* and possessive *'s* on nouns and *s* on third-person singular verbs. *You* is the only regularly used second-person pronoun (though the *thou* form is still encountered, including in some older versions of the Bible). The object-pronoun form *whom* has barely survived into the 21st century (thus, *Who are you seeking?*).

3. During the 19th century, inverted questions such as *What say you?* are still possible, but the periphrasis with *do* became the norm: *Why do you weep?* However, a present participle construction is increasingly widespread: *Who are you seeking?* Use of *to get* in periphrastic (roundabout) expressions of obligation, as in *I have got to do it*, and as a passive marker, as in *He got hurt in the fight*, becomes frequent from the 19th century.

4. A mass of new words from many languages is borrowed, especially Greek and Latin. *Assume* is a Latin borrowing of the 16th century.

5. After the 18th century, the short half-closed vowel *a* /æ/ in words like *last* is opened and lengthened (/aː/) in southern standard English, but not in American and most northern British varieties. Pronunciation of initial *h*, which was unstable early in the period, has become obligatory. Received Pronunciation dominates educated and official discourse in Britain, but it is itself variable, and is now losing its grip.

Classroom Activity 3.1: Irregular Verbs in English (page 75)

1. There are about 200 irregular verbs in English today.

2.

verb	past tense	past participle
bite	bit	bitten
draw	drew	drawn
forgive	forgave	forgiven
hurt	hurt	hurt
lie	lay	lain
ring	rang	rung
shake	shook	shaken
speak	spoke	spoken
spread	spread	spread
tear	tore	torn

3. verb	most common past form
hang	hung
dive	dived
sneak	sneaked
slay	slew

Comment: This exercise focuses on irregular verbs in English. Students will probably already be aware of their existence but may have learned the individual irregular verbs piecemeal. The exercise brings together a range of irregular verb types so that students can see the different variations in one place. It might be useful to point out to the students the three major types as explained in the chapter. At the most basic level, this exercise provides practice with the irregular verbs included in it. Beyond that, the exercise shows that there can be variation within an irregular verb—that is, more than one past form can be correct for certain verbs (i.e., *dived* or *dove*), although one form is normally more frequent than the other. This can be a useful means to illustrate to students that there is not always a single correct form in English; rather, the language contains a certain amount of variation. The British National Corpus, a large database of 100 million words of both British and American English, was consulted to determine the most frequent forms overall. However, the most common forms will depend to some extent on which variety of English one speaks.

You might note that some grammar books might use different terminology for regular/irregular verbs (e.g., weak/strong verbs).

Classroom Activity 3.2: Irregular Plural Nouns in English (page 77)

noun	irregular plural form
woman	women
foot	feet
goose	geese
child	children
ox	oxen
criterion	criteria
phenomenon	phenomena
sheep	sheep
deer	deer
fish	fish (or fishes)
buffalo	buffalo (or buffaloes)

Comment: This is a straightforward exercise designed to get students thinking about irregular plurals in English. The words were selected so that some should be relatively easy, whereas others may be more challenging. For stronger students, this exercise could serve as a springboard into a classroom discussion of irregular plurals. For weaker students who may not know many of the words, it could serve as the basis for a dictionary exercise where students look up the words and their plurals.

Classroom Activity 4.1: Old English Vocabulary in Today's English (page 102)

Exercises 1–3 are designed to be completed one at a time, with students receiving the answers after each task. Exercise 1 could be done aloud in class as a guessing task to stimulate interest. Students will need the answers to Exercise 2 to complete Exercise 3. These exercises could lead to a discussion of a number of different linguistic topics, such as formality, frequency, academic discourse, appropriateness of vocabulary, and persuasive discourse. Students should be reminded that what are described as Old English words are of Old English origin; their actual forms in Old English will nearly always have been a little different (e.g., *angel* occurred as *engel*, *child* as *cild*, *fight* as *feoht*).

1. About 15 percent of Old English's vocabulary has survived in today's English. Most of the rest was lost because of competition from foreign loanwords.

2. <u>The man with the white</u> carnation <u>in his</u> buttonhole, <u>who</u> enjoyed <u>the</u> grand title Executive Director <u>for</u> Human Resources, <u>went up to the young woman and</u> announced arrogantly <u>that the</u> current economic situation <u>was</u> unsustainable <u>and her</u> employment <u>would be</u> terminated <u>with</u> immediate effect.

<u>"Are you saying that my work is to end now, at once? Is that right, and must I</u> <u>leave today?" she asked him fearfully.</u>

"Absolutely correct! Please vacate <u>the</u> office."

<u>When the woman heard this, she wept and said, "How can I live, with two</u> <u>children to feed and a husband who has long been sick</u>?"

3. Old English words make up the most basic and essential words in the language. This includes almost all of the grammatical words, which are the most frequent words in English, and many other words frequently used because of their everyday utility. Thus, the percentage of Old English words in any text is likely to be high. Out of the 100 words in the passage in Exercise 2, only 24 are not of Old English origin. (This includes *buttonhole*, a compound word that is actually half and half: *button* is of Old French origin, not borrowed until the Middle English period, and *hole* is an Old English word. The compound noun itself is not known until the 16th century, and it was first used as verb in the 19th century.)

Note how many of the Old English words are monosyllabic. This is especially obvious when we look at Old English and non–Old English synonyms in pairs: *end/terminate, leave/vacate, said/announced,* and *right/correct.*

Old English words tend to be less formal than others. This means that they are particularly suited to spoken discourse, which is usually less formal than written discourse. Thus, Old English words do not usually provide a formal or academic tone and so would not be so dominant in an academic composition, for example. Note how in the first paragraph of the passage the man is trying to appear very formal and official and how this is partially indicated by the heavy use of non–Old English vocabulary.

Old English words have connections with day-to-day life and can therefore have a powerful appeal when used in rhetorical discourse—for example, in a political speech when the speaker is trying to play on people's emotions.

Classroom Activity 4.2: Where Did Old English Vocabulary Come From? (page 103)

The aim of this exercise is to make the ideas in the hints section real for the learners and give them an interesting look into the origins of English vocabulary.

The original Old English language	Old Norse	Latin
	/sk/	(religion)
child	scab	angel
eat	score	candle
fight	scowl	priest
good	scrap	temple
high	scrape	
house	scrub	(trade)
leaf	skill	cap
man	skin	chest
meat	skirt	silk
wife	sky	
		(education)
		grammar
		master
		paper

Classroom Activity 4.3: Where Did English Vocabulary Come From? (page 104)

I American Indian languages
H Chinese
A Dutch
B French
C Irish and Scots Gaelic
G Hindi
D Italian
E Latin and Greek
F Spanish/Portuguese

Comment: The groups of loanwords were chosen to reflect an aspect of the donor language during the Early Modern English period. Many of them reflect the world exploration that was occurring at this time—for example, words from American Indian languages, Chinese, Hindi, and Spanish/Portuguese. In particular, the Spanish/Portuguese loanwords reflect the Spanish and Portuguese explorers' travels to the tropics and the New World. Loanwords from Dutch indicate the strengths of Holland at that time in seamanship and painting. English received many of her musical terms from Italian. French continued to supply a diverse range of loanwords. But by far the greatest number of loanwords during this period came from the classical languages of Latin and Greek, reflecting the advances in science and the humanities during the Renaissance and the Age of Reason.

Classroom Handout: A List of Useful Latin Prefixes (page 105)

The list is provided as a convenient reference list for your students.

Classroom Activity 5.1: When Did Words Come into English? (page 144)

This exercise is largely a vocabulary exercise that reviews words students already know as well as introducing some lower-frequency words that they are unlikely to know. In providing students with a logical reason for differing pronunciations for the consonant cluster *ch*, the exercise also illustrates the importance of change through time and the tendency of a language to naturalize words that are borrowed, though this may take a long time. It might be interesting to ask whether some speakers may see prestige attached to trying to pronounce French words (as long as they are still recognized as French) in the French way. Another interesting fact, however (as we noted on pp. 119–120), is that Americans tend to retain the French stress patterns on recent French borrowings, whereas British speakers seem keen to anglicize as soon as possible. We do not assume that your students know a phonemic alphabet for this exercise and so use the expedient of word examples (<u>ch</u>air and <u>sh</u>ape) to illustrate the phonemes /tʃ/ and /ʃ/ respectively.

Before 1600:	More recently:
chamber	brochure
champion	chalet
chance	chamois
change	château
charge	chauffeur
chase	chef
check	chevron
choice	chic
match	chiffon
merchant	machine

Chargé d'affaires, chateaubriand, and *chemin de fer* all entered English after 1600 and so take the "<u>sh</u>ape" /ʃ/ pronunciation. Indeed, they remain distinctly "foreign" and, given their limited usefulness, are perhaps unlikely ever to be thoroughly anglicized.

Classroom Activity 5.2: Find the Silent Letter (page 146)

This activity raises students' awareness that there is some rationale behind the silent letters in English. You can supplement this activity by explaining their historical basis, if you think it is worthwhile. It should also be possible to use this exercise as a springboard for pronunciation practice (asking the students to pronounce the words in the activity) or to expand it by asking students to think of other words that have these silent letters.

Word	Silent letter	Silent letter position

1. knee
   knock
   knight
	k	before "n" at the beginning of a word

2. write
   wrong
   wrist
	w	before "r" at the beginning of a word

3. half
   calf
   halves
	l	after "a" and before "f" or "v"

4. talk
   chalk
   walk
	l	after "a" and before "k"

5. calm
   palm
   balm
	l	after "a" and before "m"

6. could
   should
   would
	l	between the vowels and final "d" in modal verbs

7. sign
   impugn
   paradigm
	g	after vowel and before "m" or "n"

8. bomb
   thumb
   lamb
	b	after "m" if "b" is the last letter

9. listen
   soften
   hasten
	t	after "f" or "s" and before "-en"

10. honest
    hour
    heir
	h	"h" at the beginning of some words, particularly these words and *honor* (also *herb* in American English)

Classroom Activity 5.3: Many Spellings for One Sound (page 148)

This set of exercises can be used to raise students' awareness of the need for a phonemic alphabet when describing the pronunciation of English. It can also be used as a dictionary activity focusing on the element of pronunciation. Exercise A was adapted from an idea in Celce-Murcia, Brinton, & Goodwin.[1] Most of the example words in Exercise A are theirs and reflect an American English pronunciation. In fact, *nauseous* is more often pronounced without *sh* in British English. The interjection *pshaw* can also be pronounced with a *p* sound.

A.
1. <u>sh</u>irt
2. o<u>ce</u>an
3. <u>s</u>ugar
4. i<u>ss</u>ue
5. man<u>si</u>on
6. mi<u>ssi</u>on
7. ra<u>ti</u>on
8. suspi<u>ci</u>on
9. nau<u>se</u>ous
10. con<u>sci</u>ous
11. <u>ch</u>ivalry
12. <u>sch</u>napps
13. fu<u>schi</u>a
14. <u>p</u>shaw

B.
1. The phonemic symbol for the sounds in Exercise A is /ʃ/.
2.

/drɪŋkɪŋ/	=	drinking
/gəʊldən/	=	golden
/aɪdentɪfaɪ/	=	identify
/nɒk/	=	knock
/məʤɒrəti/	=	majority
/njuːmərəs/	=	numerous
/ɔːt/	=	ought
/pærəgræf/	=	paragraph
/ʃædəʊ/	=	shadow
/juːniːk/	=	unique

Comment: The exact phonemic transcriptions in your students' dictionaries may be somewhat different from the ones in this exercise but should be close enough for them to successfully work out the answers.

Classroom Activity 6.1: Comparing British and American English (Spelling) (page 169)

As with vocabulary, the differences in spelling are unlikely to cause many problems for native speakers. However, non-native speakers can be confused by spellings they are not familiar with, and so it is probably useful to raise learners' awareness of the spelling differences between British and American English.

British	American
colour	color
flavour	flavor
honour	honor
theatre	theater
centre	center
litre	liter
pretence	pretense
offence	offense
licence	license
normalise	normalize
jeopardise	jeopardize
standardise	standardize
archaeology	archeology
haemorrhage	hemorrhage
anaesthetic	anesthetic

American	British
check (money)	cheque
curb (road)	kerb
donut	doughnut
draft (air)	draught
mold	mould
pajamas	pyjamas
plow	plough
program	programme
skeptical	sceptical
tire	tyre

Classroom Activity 7.1: Comparing British and American English Vocabulary (page 202)

Comment: A list of some of the more common British/American vocabulary differences follows. For a larger sample, see Crystal's *English as a Global Language*. It is important to note that although the differences in vocabulary may be interesting, very few of them would cause serious misunderstandings. There are a few word pairs such as *hoarding* (British) and *billboard* (American) that would be completely novel to a visitor from across the Atlantic Ocean, but most pairs are like *post* (British) and *mail* (American), which can be easily understood in context. The increased use of electronic communications and the wide distribution of English-language movies ensure that people will become increasingly exposed to the vocabulary from alternative varieties of English.

B lift	A elevator
A hood	B bonnet (of a car)
B boot	A trunk (of a car)
A apartment	B flat
A line	B queue (when waiting for something)
B pub	A bar/tavern
A lawyer/attorney	B solicitor/barrister
B tin	A can (of food)
A check	B tick (mark with a ✓ symbol)
B diversion	A detour (on a road)
B nappy	A diaper
B autumn	A fall
B paraffin	A kerosene
A liquor store	B off-license
A potato chips	B crisps
A first floor	B ground floor
B pavement	A sidewalk
B drawing pin	A thumbtack
A checkers	B draughts (game)
A trash	B rubbish
B lorry	A truck
B waistcoat	A vest
B nought	A zero
B petrol	A gasoline
A freeway	B motorway
B chemist	A druggist
A subway	B underground (underground train)

Classroom Activity 7.2: Comparing Different Kinds of English (page 204)

The boxes contain the following types of English:

A. Shakespearean
B. British English
C. Inner Sydney English, a dialect of Australian English
D. A technical report about airport noise that appeared in an academic book on aviation

The passage from Shakespeare (A) contains some unfamiliar lexical forms such as *court of guard* (=guardroom) and *servitors* (=servants). However, the biggest difference is in the grammar. Note that Shakespearean English is more different from the other examples than they are from each other. But nobody would suggest that Shakespearean English is incorrect. It is simply different, and of its time, and suitable for its own context. We should view any other "different" types of English in the same way.

The passage in B is a service encounter that is interactional (serving to enhance social relations) as well as transactional (transferring information or realizing a business function). Note the use of *me* for *my*, and the use of *Have you?* where Americans would use *Did you?* Also notice that the grammar of spoken discourse is somewhat different from written discourse. For example, *And one penny thank you* would probably be rendered in written discourse as something like *Here is your change of one penny. Thank you for your business.*

One of the notable features of Inner Sydney English (C) is the use of *was* with plural nouns (*we was*). It is also interesting to note that the story is told as a string of details, often connected with *and* or *an*. It is often difficult to decide how to punctuate spoken discourse like this when it is transcribed into a written format, as sentences like *An he took us down the ranger's station an they just sat there, an then he called the coppers* would be considered run-on sentences in written discourse but are quite normal in spoken discourse. Inner Sydney English is non-standard, but use of this dialect serves as a recognizable identity feature of a certain underprivileged social group in the area.

The technical report (D) is an example of academic discourse. Academic discourse typically has a much denser information load, more complex syntax, and more low-frequency vocabulary than spoken discourse or informal written discourse. This report has been written by a Dutch ESL speaker, although edited to some unknown extent by the British editors of the book it resides in.

The students may conclude that the English in passage C is the least "correct," and it certainly is non-standard. However, it serves as a perfectly functional means of communication between speakers who use it and is also comprehensible outside the group. Many speakers are probably proud of it as a symbol of their group identity. The Shakespearean passage is intended to be spoken, yet it contains archaic grammatical and lexical features that make it more dissimilar to most modern spoken discourse than even non-standard Inner Sydney English. Yet the English in Shakespeare might be considered by some people to be more "correct" simply because it is Shakespeare. Students may consider the discourse in passage B as somehow less "correct" than the academic passage in D, but this would probably stem from judging the spoken passage according to rules of written grammar. In fact, spoken discourse operates according to its own grammatical conventions and cannot be judged according to the rules for written English. The academic passage in D is a good example of written Standard English, as it has undoubtedly been scrutinized by numerous people (the author and the book's editors and copyeditors in the publishing house) for conformity to the standard.

This analysis suggests that all varieties and dialects of English are equally good and correct for their own speakers. Any value judgment about varieties and dialects must focus on utility rather than correctness. Using a widely spoken standard variety of English has the benefit of allowing one to be comprehensible to a greater range of people, but such a variety is not inherently more correct than any other variety. In fact, a non-standard dialect may be better for speaking to people in the local region, which may make it more useful than a standard variety if one does not travel far from home.

INDEX